W9-ADI-723

Voicing America

Voicing

LANGUAGE, LITERARY FORM, AND

THE UNIVERSITY OF CHICAGO PRESS

Christopher Looby

America

THE ORIGINS OF THE UNITED STATES

CHICAGO & LONDON

Christopher Looby is associate professor of English at the University of Chicago.

The University of Chicago Press, Chicago 60637
The University of Chicago Press, Ltd., London
© 1996 by The University of Chicago
All rights reserved. Published 1996
Printed in the United States of America
05 04 03 02 01 00 99 98 97 96   1 2 3 4 5
ISBN: 0-226-49282-6 (cloth)

Library of Congress Cataloging-in-Publication Data

Looby, Christopher.
    Voicing America : language, literary form, and the origins of the
United States / Christopher Looby.
        p.   cm.
    "Began as a dissertation in the Department of English and
Comparative Literature at Columbia University"—P. vii.
    Includes bibliographical references and index.
    1. American literature—1783–1850—History and criticism.
2. National characteristics, American, in literature.   3. United
States—Intellectual life—1783–1865.   4. English language—United
States.   5. Literary form.   6. Americanisms.   I. Title.
PS193.L66   1996
810.9′001—dc20   95-29993
                                                                  CIP

♾ The paper used in this publication meets the minimum requirements
of the American National Standard for Information Sciences–
Permanence of Paper for Printed Library Materials, ANSI Z39.48–
1984.

For my parents

CONTENTS

Acknowledgments   ix
Introduction   1

1   Logocracy in America   13
    I. *Originary Utterance*   16
    II. *Semantic Transvaluation*   28
    III. *Neology*   45
    IV. *History and Language*   54
    V. *Letters*   67
    VI. *Words*   78
    VII. *Orator Mums*   86
    Appendix to Chapter 1   96

2   "The Affairs of the Revolution Occasion'd the
    Interruption": Self, Language, and Nation in
    Franklin's *Autobiography*   99
    I. *Authorship and Revolution*   99
    II. *Fathers and Sons*   102
    III. *The Subject of Language*   112
    IV. *Verbal Imposture*   118
    V. *Revolution at a Distance*   124
    VI. *Textual Self-Difference*   131
    VII. *Conversation and Conciliation*   138

3   "The Very Act of Utterance": Law, Language, and
    Legitimation in Brown's *Wieland*   145
    I. *The Novel in the 1790s*   145
    II. *Ruptured Genealogy*   149

III. *Saxon Constitution* 154
IV. *Ciceronian Elocution* 158
V. *The Politics of Ventriloquism* 165
VI. *Post-Revolutionary Nostalgia* 174
VII. *Law and Liberalism* 180
VIII. *Legal Epistemology* 188
IX. *Counter-Revolution* 193

4 "Tongues of People Altercating with One Another":
Language, Text, and Society in Brackenridge's
Modern Chivalry 203
I. *The Polyglot World* 203
II. *Magnum Opus* 206
III. *Fixing the Language* 216
IV. *Revolutionary Rhetorical Hybridity* 224
V. *Language and Events* 229
VI. *Chronotopic Equation* 240
VII. *Ethnic Idioms* 249
VIII. *Phonology and Politics* 256

5 Coda: The Voice of Patrick Henry 266

Index 279

ACKNOWLEDGMENTS

VOICING AMERICA began as a dissertation in the Department of English and Comparative Literature at Columbia University. My first thanks must assuredly go to my director there, Sacvan Bercovitch, the example of whose work was always a challenging one, and the presence of whose acute mind and inquiring imagination was of inestimable influence. Other readers of the dissertation — Ann Douglas, Jonathan Arac, Eric Foner, and Robert Austerlitz — gave me useful criticism and necessary encouragement. Priscilla Wald made graduate school a lively learning experience, and she continues to be a valuable friend and remarkable intellectual stimulus. My colleagues on the editorial staff at the Library of America from 1981 to 1987 — especially Hannah M. Bercovitch, Paul Royster, and Max Rudin — made my time there wonderfully interesting.

Fellowship support during graduate school from Columbia University, the Andrew W. Mellon Foundation (via the Philadelphia Center for Early American Studies), and the Mrs. Giles Whiting Foundation was generously provided and much appreciated. At the Philadelphia Center, the then-director Richard Beeman and the other fellows resident with me — Michael Meranze, Betsy Fisher, and Ric Northrup — were gracious and stimulating colleagues. An early version of chapter 2 was presented to the seminar at the Philadelphia Center, and many of those present gave me helpful responses.

Since joining the English Department at the University of Chicago, I have been provoked and reeducated in incalculable ways. I was immensely fortunate to have Robert Ferguson as a colleague for a short time, and I am very glad to benefit from his advice and kindness still. Janice Knight, Loren Kruger, Laura Rigal, Lawrence Rothfield, Lisa Ruddick, Joshua Scodel, and Stuart Sherman have been wonderful new friends and compatriots. I have benefited from my involvement with the American Studies Workshop, to which I presented a version of chapter 2, and wish to thank the graduate students who participate in it and Bill Brown, who has shared supervision of it with me.

The Huntington Library and the W. M. Keck Foundation provided a timely summer fellowship in 1990, and the George A. and Eliza Gardner Howard Foundation Fellowship in 1991–92 enabled considerable progress on this study. The English Department and the Humanities Division of the University of Chicago kindly gave me a year of research leave to take advantage of the Howard Foundation fellowship. Librarians at the Newberry Library, Huntington Library, University of Pennsylvania, American Philosophical Society, Library Company of Philadelphia, Historical Society of Pennsylvania, Columbia University, and the University of Chicago have always been remarkably helpful, and deserve profuse thanks. Several research assistants—LeeAnne Richardson, David Coe, and especially Brad Evans—have given me important aid. Earlier versions of chapter 2 and a section of chapter 1 were published in *American Quarterly* 38 (1986): 72–96, and *Arizona Quarterly* 46, no. 2 (1990): 1–12, respectively, and the editors and anonymous readers for those journals provided acute commentary; I thank them for permission to reuse this material, which has been revised.

My interest in American literature and culture, and in their relationships to American history, were first aroused by Richard Ruland at Washington University; he and Daniel Shea and Rowland Berthoff sustained my interest, gave me crucial encouragement, and probably determined my future in ways I can't begin to account for. Steven Zwicker and Gerald Izenberg, who codirected the Literature and History Program at Washington, admitted me to it and thus resolved me to go to graduate school.

In its final stages *Voicing America* was read by several experts in the field: Mitchell Breitwieser, Thomas Gustafson, and Michael P. Kramer. I have benefited from their own scholarship in the past, as I learned from their responses to this work, and I am glad to be working on matters in which we share an interest and that make us, therefore, colleagues.

I owe a long-standing debt of a more personal sort to my dear friends Lauren Lambert, Scott Stefan, and Philip Rosenzweig, without whom life in New York would not have been as delightful and unforgettable as it was. My parents, Thomas and Dorothy Looby, and my brothers Peter, Daniel, Thomas, and John, warmly supported and unfailingly mocked my intellectual pursuits. I am especially grateful for the mockery, and hope this book means their faith in me was not utterly misplaced. Finally I thank, inadequately but truly, Joseph Dimuro for his love and companionship.

INTRODUCTION

NATIONS ARE NOT BORN, but made. And they are made, ineluctably, in language. These are perhaps the most basic assumptions of the present study, which traces in some detail various ways in which writers in the early period of the national existence of the United States thought about the self-creation of the new nation as a process enacted in language. Various theorists of late have accustomed us to considering the nation as an imaginary entity, a phenomenon of collective consciousness. The fictive status of the nation is particularly evident at the time of a new nation's founding: Cornelius Castoriadis in *The Imaginary Institution of Society* urges us to "recall the common meaning of the term 'imaginary' . . . we speak of the 'imaginary' when we want to talk about something 'invented'—whether this refers to a 'sheer' invention ('a story entirely dreamed up'), or a slippage, a shift of meaning in which available symbols are invested with other significations than their 'normal' or canonical significations."[1] The first chapter, "Logocracy in America," considers successively, on the basis of a

1. Cornelius Castoriadis, *The Imaginary Institution of Society*, trans. Kathleen Blamey (1975; Cambridge, Massachusetts: The MIT Press, 1987), p. 127. Castoriadis's insistence here on the "common meaning" of the term *imaginary* follows his careful disavowal earlier of "that which is presented as 'imaginary' by certain currents in psychoanalysis" (p. 3), by which he appears to mean the Lacanian concept. This is in keeping with his general disavowal of "theory . . . in the inherited sense of the term 'theory,'" since in the area of society and history "the idea of pure theory is an incoherent fiction" (p. 3). Because he rejects the notion that there is any "point of view outside of history and society, or 'logically prior' to them, where one could be placed in order to construct the theory of them," he prefers to call his work an "elucidation," a reflection *from within* history and society upon one's place in history and society. "What I term elucidation is the labour by means of which individuals attempt to think about what they do and to know what they think" (p.

variety of textual sources, several ways in which early national writers conceived of this process of national-creation-through-signification. The figuration of a nation "spoke[n] into existence" in (for instance) an anonymous newspaper account of a Fourth of July celebration and in an important early Supreme Court decision; polemics in Philadelphia newspapers at the time of the decisive agitation for independence in which political issues devolved with uncanny regularity into debates about abuses and deformations of words; Jefferson's and others' arguments about the efficacy of neology in effecting revolutionary political and social change — arguments that were renewed when semantic revolution was foregrounded in France in the 1780s and 1790s; Franklin's understanding of the political connection between Great Britain and its American colonies as a linguistic connection, and of political independence as therefore essentially and necessarily a break in communication; Washington Irving's creation in *Salmagundi* of an oriental persona who pronounces the United States a "LOGOCRACY or *government of words*," and his dramatization in *The History of New York* of the process of retrodiction by which the historical past is constituted: these are among the contemporary analyses of the linguisticality of the nation that I attempt to elucidate. By no means does this inventory of topics exhaust the general question of the institution of the nation through language, but it does, I trust, describe some of the crucial ways in which early national writers made discursively available in the public sphere the relatively unique situation of a new nation that imagined its inception as an effect of linguistic action.

Although the word *nation*, as has often been recognized, attempts to install the nation within nature as an organic phenomenon (the word *nation* is derived from the same root as *nature* and *nativity*), it is in fact a human contrivance, an artifact of history. We may wish to say that this is inherently true of all nations, even of those nations that take their existence to be rooted in blood, kinship, or a remote past that can be construed as presocial. Never-

---

3). In what follows, my general aim is likewise to elucidate the reflections of writers like Franklin, Brockden Brown, and Brackenridge upon the moment of national imagination, the creation of the United States in a collective historical act of representing/saying.

theless, modern nations that recognize their own historicity are by dint of that fact different in immensely consequential ways from premodern nations that disclaim the artifice of their existence. One central assumption of the present study is that the United States, as "the first new nation"[2] — that is, the first modern nation deliberately fabricated *de novo,* founded in a self-conscious performative act of new political creation — has therefore been the site of important acts of recognition of the artificiality and historical contingency of the nation. The Declaration of Independence is clearly the paradigm of such self-recognizing acts of nation-making, the autoreferential rhetorical act that claims to be effectively founding the nation.[3] But because performative nation-institution is essentially a linguistic act, we can find in the early period of the United States a number of other documents, among them some notable literary texts, in which, in various ways, the linguisticality of the nation is directly observed, searchingly explored, and trenchantly critiqued.

The present study looks at several of the most interesting and arguably most indicative texts of the early national period, and describes the multiplicity of ways in which they expose the intimate association between the revolutionary founding of the United States and acts of voice. The title, *Voicing America,* is meant to register the saliency, in many of the texts of the period, of vocal utterance as a deeply politically invested phenomenon of the social world. Despite the recent demonstrations by a number of scholars of the ideological importance of print culture in the early national years, demonstrations which have attended to the crucial ways in which print embodied for citizens the ideal of a political public sphere characterized by general democratic rationality,[4] there is a distinct countercurrent in the literature of the period that valorizes the grain of the voice in addition to, or instead of, the silence of print. Precisely because the new nation's self-image was characterized by its difference from a traditional (quasi-natural) conception

---

2. Seymour Martin Lipset, *The First New Nation: The United States in Historical and Comparative Perspective* (1963; New York: Norton, 1979).

3. Jacques Derrida, "Declarations of Independence," *New Political Science* 15 (Summer 1986): 7–15.

4. Larzer Ziff, *Writing in the New Nation: Prose, Print, and Politics in the Early United States* (New Haven: Yale Univ. Press, 1991); Michael Warner, *The Letters of*

of the nation, indeed by the conscious recognition of its historical contingency that was produced by the abrupt performativity of its inception, vocal utterance has served, in telling instances, as a privileged figure for the making of the United States.[5] This figuration has occasionally taken the odd form of an improbable claim that the United States was actually "spoken into being." In the first chapter I cite several instances of this figure of speech from the literature of the early national period, and I draw out some of the densely impacted implications of this peculiar figuration. For the moment let me just say that I take this strange trope to register in a particularly condensed form the more widespread American sense of nation fabrication as an intentional act of linguistic creation, the belief that the nation was made out of words. The question of whether such a linguistically grounded nation is best figured as *written* or *spoken* is not, for many writers of the period, a foregone conclusion but, on the contrary, a live issue of some consequence. To anticipate a bit: since the new United States, by all accounts, manifestly lacked the kind of legitimacy and stability that might be expected of a nation that was grounded in blood loyalty or immemorial facticity — since its legitimacy was explicitly grounded in an appeal to rational interest, not visceral passion — *voice* embodied a certain legitimating charisma that print could not. Linguists speak of those speech sounds in which the vocal chords are clenched and the larynx is thereby made to vibrate as *voiced* phonemes, whereas those speech sounds that do not involve such vibration are called *breathed* or *unvoiced*. Thus the same position of the tongue, lips, and teeth will produce quite different sounds depending on the open or closed position of the glottis:

---

the Republic: Publication and the Public Sphere in Eighteenth-Century America (Cambridge, Massachusetts: Harvard Univ. Press, 1990).

5. Jay Fliegelman's recent book, *Declaring Independence: Jefferson, Natural Language, and the Culture of Performance* (Stanford: Stanford Univ. Press, 1993), came to me late in the formation of the present study, but happily confirms many of my arguments. In particular, his dissatisfaction with the print-culture thesis (see pp. 128–29), and his emphasis on the ideological importance of vocal effects — for example, the Declaration of Independence as a document made to be "heard as performance" rather than "read silently" (p. 24), and the fetishization of Patrick Henry's voice (pp. 94–107) — provide such confirmation, even though Fliegelman's general terms (the context of theories of natural language and eloquence) are somewhat different from mine.

/f/ is unvoiced, /v/ is voiced, the latter entailing a resonant buzzing in the larynx that is missing in the former. It is perhaps only a critical conceit, but the title *Voicing America* might be taken to register not this vocal difference specifically, but rather the difference between the abstract, alienated, rational polis of print culture and the more passionately attached, quasi-somatically experienced nation for which many Americans longed. In chapter 3 in particular, which deals chiefly with the politics of voice in Charles Brockden Brown's *Wieland,* I look at the way the rational-legal foundation of the United States could seem dangerously inadequate by virtue of its neglect of the visceral need of citizens for more psychically compelling modes of attachment to their nation. The fetishization of voice in that novel, and in other places as well (for instance, the patriotic celebration of the sublime voice of Patrick Henry, with which this study concludes), obscurely registers this sense of the weakness and inadequacy of a nation embodied in print.

Because the postrevolutionary period of American history is one overwhelmingly marked by dire political contention and exigent popular disunity, as well as by a powerful countervailing aspiration to national solidarity—that is, by the unresolved *problem* of national unity—I have taken care not to endorse this notion of America-as-voiced as a totalizing account of the historical period or of its literature. Such critical totalization is what is potentially misleading about the print-culture thesis and any number of other compelling accounts of the literature of the new nation, accounts that attempt to organize our understanding of an unruly and unresolved political experiment around a single concept. No doubt *Voicing America* risks such critical deformation also, merely by raising to prominence the singular figure of a nation "spoken into being." But I would like to state unambiguously that the figure of the voiced nation, as it appears in the literature under consideration here, itself represents both an aspiration to intentional unity and a recognition of the fragility, temporality, and intrinsic dissemination of the imagined nation. To borrow (and modify) an idea from Benedict Anderson's influential study of nationalism, *Imagined Communities,* it appears that "there is a special kind of contemporaneous community which language alone suggests," that of a coherent nation of speakers of the same language, simultaneous participants in the same fundamental cultural system of communication. Anderson particularly specifies poetry and songs, especially national anthems, as embodiments of this "experience of simultaneity" — "the image: unisonance." Anderson emphasizes "the primordialness of languages," which "[loom] up imperceptibly out of a horizonless past" and therefore "appear rooted beyond almost anything in contemporary societies," and thus "connect us affectively to the dead."[6] His earlier implication (mistaken, in my view) that language was not an issue in the American Revolution[7] may be connected to his stringent emphasis on the affective importance of the primordiality of language. Language *was* important for revolutionary Americans, although not because it figured for them in a collective fantasy of an immemorial national past. Americans did (and still do) imagine the nation as "unisonance" — the "voice of the people," the "general voice," the "popular voice," and other variations on the phrase were bywords of the political culture of the time — but they also imagined the nation frequently as *dissonance,* and sometimes even as muteness, as ventriloquism, or as stammering. The image of the nation as an effect of vocal utterance was in the early United States more often a measure of a fearful sense of its foundationless instability and fragile temporality than of its primordial rootedness.

These matters are explored at length in the first chapter especially, but they are the issues that thread through the succeeding chapters as well. Because I want to foreground the disunity of the period, and the literature's formal mirroring of that disunity, my practice throughout has been to relate textual issues of literary and linguistic form to the extratextual historical ruptures and political fractures of the period. There have been many instructive theoretical explorations of nationality and nationalism in recent years, and while I have drawn on them occasionally and cite them sporadically, my critical purpose here is not primarily a theoretical one. It is, instead, one of practical criticism. This practical emphasis is

---

6. Benedict Anderson, *Imagined Communities: Reflections on the Origin and Spread of Nationalism* (London: Verso, 1983), p. 132.
7. Ibid., p. 66. Anderson generalizes that "Spanish and English were never issues in the revolutionary Americas."

dictated by the need, as I see it, for a more strenuous and close-grained interpretation of the literature of the period. As Mitchell Breitwieser has recently observed, eighteenth-century American writing has more often than not been treated as "by-the-ton orals reading" and surrendered therefore to historians and antiquarians. In recent years, however, it has fitfully "emerged as a compelling object of [literary] inquiry" and received renewed scrutiny in English departments. Breitwieser credits this shift in part to "the shift [in academic literary studies] from a text-explication-based criticism . . . to a sociology-history-based criticism."[8] This is probably accurate as an account of recent history in the academic discipline of literature, but I would not like it to stand as an imperative. What interests me about the period has been the legible relationships *between* textual forms and the sociohistorical contexts in which they appear. The literary forms in question here, it will be clear, are not forms of perfection offered for aesthetic appreciation or celebration: the forms I have in mind are chiefly those frayings, fracturings, and inelegancies of the text that betray the performative act of writing—for example, the ill-sorted fragments that make up Franklin's account of his life, even the physical form of his autograph manuscript; or the conglomerated pieces that make up Brackenridge's cumbersome, jerry-built novel. As a result of this interest in the relation of textual form to historical circumstance, my practice in the present study is largely one of persistent and detailed explication of several literary texts—most prominently, in chapters 2–4, Benjamin Franklin's *Autobiography,* Charles Brockden Brown's novel *Wieland,* and Hugh Henry Brackenridge's hybrid satirical novel/polemic *Modern Chivalry.* The order of these chapters roughly follows the chronology of the composition and publication of the texts they interpret (although, since Franklin's and Brackenridge's books were written intermittently over rather long spans of years and, in the latter case, published serially, there is some temporal overlap, and the chronology is consequently somewhat murky). But the sequence of chapters also traces a formal transition, from a text (Franklin's) that is at

---

8. Mitchell Breitwieser, "Commentary: Afterthoughts," *American Literary History* 5 (1993): 589. This commentary concludes a special issue on "Eighteenth-Century American Cultural Studies."

least predominantly organized by the formal device of a single autobiographical voice, to a text (Brackenridge's) that promises such
formal unification but then (in my account) dramatically undoes
such a program by its disintegration into narrative and stylistic
chaos and by its devolutionary vision of America as, in Brackenridge's words, "tongues of people altercating with one another."
To recall Anderson's term, this study begins with unisonance but
proceeds to dissonance. The final chapter describes a belated and
vain attempt to recuperate a sublime moment of voiced revolutionary solidarity, William Wirt's textual reconstruction of Patrick
Henry's celebrated "Liberty or Death" speech.

Describing the interaction of literary forms with historical problems has required something like what Sacvan Bercovitch has recently called "cultural close reading,"[9] a critical method that derives its ongoing account of the imbrication of text and context
from attentive explication and patient local critique of the literary
work's own inscription of its cultural embeddedness. Another way
of putting this is to say that rather than assume a prior account of
the sociohistorical moment of national inception (or, for that matter, a prior account of the theoretical problem of nationality) and
then read the text according to the requirements of that account,
I have chosen instead to exfoliate the historicizing and theorizing
moments *within* Franklin's, Brown's, and Brackenridge's own texts
and subject them to examination, comparison, and elaboration.
(If there is a presiding theorist in the present study it is probably
Mustapha Rub-a-Dub Keli Khan, the oriental visitor to America
in Washington Irving's *Salmagundi*, who claims — as I said above,
and as I detail in the first chapter — that the United States is a
"LOGOCRACY, or *government of words*.") This is not meant simply to resanctify "the text itself" in the manner of an older literary
criticism. It is meant, on the contrary, to avoid the symmetrical
error of privileging "the context itself." The immediately pertinent
context for my purposes here is the public world of political writing and speaking; these texts themselves *belonged* to that world,
were interventions in that world, and contributed to the production of that world. They are instances of what Anthony Giddens

9. Sacvan Bercovitch, "Games of Chess: A Model for Cultural Studies," unpub.

has called the reflexive self-monitoring of social actors, the on-going process of a society's critical reflection on its own development— "reflection[s] on social processes (theories, and observations about them) continually enter into, become disentangled with and re-enter the universe of events that they describe."[10] The writings I explore in *Voicing America* are, to be sure, among those that made discursively available to early national Americans the knowledge that the social and political world they lived in was linguistically constituted and historically malleable, and therefore effectively open to purposive verbal action. As *literary* texts that persistently called attention to their own formal linguistic artifice, they raised to an unusually high pitch of self-reflexivity this knowledgeability about the conditions of historical agency and verbal performativity in the United States.

These three writers— Franklin, Brown, and Brackenridge— deserve particular attention for a number of reasons, most especially because they brought this collective historical moment of linguistic self-scrutiny to a high level of self-consciousness. My approaches in the chapters in which they figure vary according to the demands of the material: most prominently, a kind of historicized psychoanalysis in the case of Franklin, a philosophical sociology for Brown, and a more or less Bakhtinian sociology of language for Brackenridge. I have not attempted to be theoretically programmatic, however, allowing myself instead an honest eclecticism that is conducive, I hope, to a nontendentious close reading. This is not the place (nor do I have any taste) for an elaborate discussion of the importance (and difficulty) of integrating theoretically or linguistically oriented readings with critical practices of historicization, but such an integration is what I want to achieve, and the readings that follow will either practically establish this possibility or not. I should also acknowledge that my three main authors are all Pennsylvanians (at one time or another, all Philadelphians). Far from limiting the application of generalizations drawn from reading their texts, however, their geographical locatedness installs them at the heart of the nation's political formation,

---

10. Anthony Giddens, *The Constitution of Society: Outline of the Theory of Structuration* (Berkeley: Univ. of California Press, 1984), p. xxxiii.

as well as at the heart of demographic and economic trends that would soon characterize other areas of the nation. Philadelphia was where ethnic diversification and economic modernization first registered as crucial problems for the nation-in-formation, and although this study does not attempt thoroughly to map relationships between economic and material processes and literary texts, it does occasionally (and, in chapter 4, in somewhat more detail than elsewhere) approach these questions.

The study of early national American literature and culture has flourished during the last decade or so with the publication of a considerable number of books that converge with my own in some ways. Where it has seemed urgent, I have engaged some of these works in specific ways, but I have kept my arguments with (and acknowledgments of) other critics to a minimum. It is therefore worth recording their collective importance to my project here: Mitchell Robert Breitwieser, *Cotton Mather and Benjamin Franklin: The Price of Representative Personality* (Cambridge: Cambridge Univ. Press, 1984); Kenneth Cmiel, *Democratic Eloquence: The Fight over Popular Speech in Nineteenth-Century America* (New York: William Morrow & Co., 1990); Cathy N. Davidson, *Revolution and the Word: The Rise of the Novel in America* (New York: Oxford Univ. Press, 1986); Emory Elliott, *Revolutionary Writers: Literature and Authority in the New Republic, 1725–1810* (New York: Oxford Univ. Press, 1982); Robert A. Ferguson, *Law and Letters in American Culture* (Cambridge, Massachusetts: Harvard Univ. Press, 1984); idem, *The American Enlightenment, 1750–1820*, in Sacvan Bercovitch, ed., *The Cambridge History of American Literature, Vol. 1: 1590–1820* (Cambridge: Cambridge Univ. Press, 1994), pp. 345–537; Jay Fliegelman, *Prodigals and Pilgrims: The American Revolution Against Patriarchal Authority 1750–1800* (Cambridge: Cambridge Univ. Press, 1982); idem, *Declaring Independence: Jefferson, Natural Language, and the Culture of Performance* (Stanford, California: Stanford Univ. Press, 1993); Albert Furtwangler, *American Silhouettes: Rhetorical Identities of the Founders* (New Haven: Yale Univ. Press, 1987); Michael T. Gilmore, *The Literature of the Revolutionary and Early National Periods*, in Bercovitch, ed., *The Cambridge History of American Literature, Vol. 1: 1590–1820*, pp. 539–693; Thomas Gustafson, *Representative*

Words: Politics, Literature, and the American Language, 1776–1864 (Cambridge: Cambridge Univ. Press, 1992); Cynthia S. Jordan, *Second Stories: The Politics of Language, Form, and Gender in Early American Fictions* (Chapel Hill: Univ. of North Carolina Press, 1989); Michael P. Kramer, *Imagining Language in America: From the Revolution to the Civil War* (Princeton: Princeton Univ. Press, 1992); Mark R. Patterson, *Authority, Autonomy, and Representation in American Literature, 1776–1865* (Princeton: Princeton Univ. Press, 1988); David Simpson, *The Politics of American English, 1776–1850* (New York: Oxford Univ. Press, 1986); Michael Warner, *The Letters of the Republic: Publication and the Public Sphere in Eighteenth-Century America* (Cambridge, Massachusetts: Harvard Univ. Press, 1990); Larzer Ziff, *Writing in the New Nation: Prose, Print, and Politics in the Early United States* (New Haven: Yale Univ. Press, 1991). Two relevant works that came to my attention too late to be taken into account are Terence Martin, *Parables of Possibility: The American Need for Beginnings* (New York: Columbia Univ. Press, 1995), and Alessandro Portelli, *The Text and the Voice: Writing, Speaking, and Democracy in American Literature* (New York: Columbia Univ. Press, 1994).

CHAPTER ONE

Logocracy in America

*All life therefore comes back to the question of our speech, the
medium through which we communicate with each other;
for all life comes back to the question of our relations with
each other. These relations are made possible, are registered,
are verily constituted, by our speech.*

Henry James

IN A TALK HE GAVE at Bryn Mawr College in 1905, called "The
Question of Our Speech," Henry James remarked that the English
language, when transported to America, had been "disjoined from
all the associations, the other presences, that had attended her"
previously.[1] He meant, of course, all the other institutions that
contribute to forming a nationality of the sort that he, and Hawthorne and other American writers before him, had despaired of
ever finding in their country, where there were, in the words of
his famous catalogue of absences, "No sovereign, no court, no
personal loyalty, no aristocracy, no church, no clergy, no army,"
and so on.[2] In Europe, that is to say, the language system had been
one cultural system among many, part of an ensemble of social
institutions and intricately associated with them. Abstracted from
that ensemble, estranged from all those other attending presences,
what James found was that America was left with just its "collec-

---

1. Henry James, "The Question of Our Speech," in *The Question of Our Speech,
The Lesson of Balzac: Two Lectures* (Boston: Houghton Mifflin, 1905), p. 39.
2. Henry James, *Nathaniel Hawthorne*, in *Literary Criticism: Essays on Literature,
American Writers, English Writers* (New York: The Library of America, 1984), p.
351.

tive vocal presence," and while his hope for the eventual "im-
parting of a coherent culture" was invested in the "national use
of vocal sound," the "*vox Americana*," he worried that in its "unfriended" state it might prove an inadequate foundation for social
solidarity.[3] Other nations experienced their coherence as a matter
of racial and ethnic similarity, religious orthodoxy, population
concentration, geographical definition, massive and dense structures of inherited customary practices, and highly articulated historical self-representations. In America, by contrast, racial and
ethnic diversity, religious heterogeneity, population dispersal,
geographical unboundedness, practical innovation, and exile from
historical precedent all contributed to problematize (if not demol-
ish) traditional notions of nationality. Language, and languages,
remained to negotiate the differences and establish a minimum of
social connection.

Whether "unfriended" language has proved an adequate vehicle
of national consensus or not, it is nevertheless perfectly true that,
as James noted, it has been made to carry a larger burden of social
affect in America than in other nations. As James Boon has
written,

> Ours was the first national identity to project itself as
> a mechanical solidarity of citizens speaking the same
> language and required to prove it if they were born
> outside our sacred territory. America's partial religious
> heterodoxy should be considered together with this
> peculiar linguistic orthodoxy, perhaps even dogma-
> tism. Indeed, recent demands concerning the rights of
> non–American English speakers have registered with
> the impact of heresy in other cultures and times.[4]

This condition of suspension, as it were, in language, was necessarily brought to consciousness at the time of the American Revolution, when the issue of national self-constitution was widely ad-

---

3. James, "The Question of Our Speech," pp. 33, 6, 25, 33, 39.
4. James A. Boon, *Other Tribes, Other Scribes: Symbolic Anthropology in the Comparative Study of Cultures, Histories, Religions, and Texts* (Cambridge: Cambridge
Univ. Press, 1982), p. 73.

dressed. It had been the case, prior to the Revolution, that English customs and traditions enjoyed a definite privilege in America, even if those cultural inheritances had been in some measure appropriated voluntarily rather than instituted organically. But when the Revolution severed the tenuous imperial-colonial historical connection, cultural borrowing thereafter needed to be always justified *discursively* rather than accepted automatically. That is, social norms and values as a rule could no longer be treated as simply and indisputably given, and tacitly consented to, but instead had to be thematized in speech, legitimated with words, and explicitly accorded consent.

We find, therefore, that in the literature of the Revolutionary and post-Revolutionary period, issues of speech, language, discourse, and reason are remarkably prominent, and the discursive foundation of national legitimacy is repeatedly thematized, in ways both obvious and indirect. The basic question of an American national language or linguistic standard has been frequently addressed in recent scholarship, and while it is a matter of some importance in connection to the present study, it will not be elaborated in any detail here.[5] Antonio Gramsci, writing in 1918 about the history of language standardization in Italy and the desirability

5. See Julie Tetel Andresen, *Linguistics in America 1769–1924: A Critical History* (London and New York: Routledge, 1990), ch. 1; Dennis E. Baron, *Grammar and Good Taste: Reforming the American Language* (New Haven: Yale Univ. Press, 1982); V. P. Bynack, "Noah Webster's Linguistic Thought and the Idea of an American National Culture," *Journal of the History of Ideas* 45 (1984): 99–114; Shirley Brice Heath, "A National Language Academy? Debate in the New Nation," *Linguistics: An International Review* 189 (1977): 9–43; Allen Walker Read, "American Projects for an Academy to Regulate Speech," *Publications of the Modern Language Association of America* 51 (1936): 1141–79; Richard M. Rollins, "Words as Social Control: Noah Webster and the Creation of the *American Dictionary*," *American Quarterly* 28 (1976): 415–30; David Simpson, *The Politics of American English, 1776–1850* (New York: Oxford Univ. Press, 1986); Brian Weinstein, "Noah Webster and the Diffusion of Linguistic Innovations for Political Purposes," *International Journal of the Sociology of Language* 38 (1982): 85–108. On nationality and language planning in general, see Joshua Fishman, "Language Modernization and Planning in Comparison with Other Types of National Modernization and Planning," *Language in Society* 2 (1973): 23–43. Two more broad-ranging studies of what might be called the linguistic imaginary in American society are Thomas Gustafson, *Representative Words: Politics, Literature, and the American Language, 1776–1865* (Cambridge: Cambridge Univ. Press, 1992) and Michael P. Kramer, *Imagining Language in America: From the Revolution to the Civil War* (Princeton: Princeton Univ. Press, 1992).

of an artificial uniform language like Esperanto, made the crucial point that partisans of such language-planning efforts "would like artificially to create *consequences* which as yet lack the necessary *conditions*": since "the history of the fortunes and diffusion of a given language depends strictly on the complex social activity of the people who speak it," therefore only when "the shared life of the nation" had achieved the requisite uniformity would linguistic uniformity follow.[6] This principle holds true for American efforts to legislate linguistic uniformity, too. My concern, however, will not be with such utopian programs of linguistic reform, but rather with those problematic conditions (to which those utopian efforts addressed themselves) that made the United States peculiarly dependent upon language, and that made language peculiarly unstable in the United States. The most interesting writers of Revolutionary and post-Revolutionary America were those who subjected themselves to those conditions, and explored that instability.

I. Originary Utterance
It is in words and language that things first come into being and are.

Martin Heidegger

A writer in the *Pennsylvania Packet* of July 8, 1790, vividly described a pleasure ground in Philadelphia called Gray's Gardens, where he had observed "thousands of freemen celebrating the anniversary of that day, on which their rulers spoke them into existence as a nation."[7] The figure of speech is noteworthy: it represented the origin of the United States as an act of speech. The origin myths of many cultures take the form of positing, at the

6. Antonio Gramsci, *Selections from Cultural Writings,* ed. David Forgacs and Geoffrey Nowell-Smith, trans. William Boelhower (Cambridge, Massachusetts: Harvard Univ. Press, 1985): 27, 28.
7. Anon., "Gray's Gardens," *The Pennsylvania Packet,* July 8, 1790, p. 3. Samuel Vaughan designed the romantic garden along the Schuylkill River at Gray's Ferry about 1786. This favorite resort, a short distance from Philadelphia, had acquired patriotic associations with the politics of independence: site of a pontoon bridge built by the British during the occupation of Philadelphia in 1777 which was operated under franchise by George Gray after the war, it was the site of a ceremonial reception of George Washington on his way to New York for his inauguration in 1789. Charles Willson Peale, who decorated the bridge with flags, foliage, and

beginning of everything, a creative enunciation. As Émile Benveniste has written,

> Man has always felt—and poets have often celebrated—the creative power of language, which establishes an imaginary reality, animates inert things, reveals what does not yet exist, and recalls to the present what has disappeared. This is why so many mythologies, having had to explain that at the dawn of time something could be born of nothing, have set up as the creative principle of the world that immaterial and supreme essence, the Word.[8]

"In the beginning was the Word" (St. John 1:1); "By the word of the Lord were the heavens made; and all the host of them by the breath of his mouth" (Psalms 33:6). The case with the United States was somewhat different, since it was not the beginning of the world that was being explained but the origin of a new political entity. Thomas Paine in *Common Sense* represented political independence as a chance "to begin the world over again."[9] And Thomas Jefferson gave a linguistic turn to this conception of an absolute beginning when in 1824 he retrospectively claimed that "our Revolution . . . presented us an album on which we were free to write what we pleased."[10] This writerly figure may have been adapted from Paine's claim, in *The Rights of Man,* that "the case and circumstances of America present themselves as in the beginning of the world," that is, when there simply was no history of established authority to limit those who set about constituting the new nation. As a consequence, according to Paine, "our inquiry into the origin of government is shortened, by referring

---

laurel arches, also devised a mechanism to drop a laurel wreath onto the President-elect's head as he passed beneath the first arch. Two drawings by Peale of Gray's Ferry were engraved and published; they are reproduced in *The Selected Papers of Charles Willson Peale and His Family,* ed. Lillian B. Miller (New Haven and London: Yale Univ. Press, 1983–), vol. 1, pp. 485, 560.

   8. Émile Benveniste, *Problems in General Linguistics,* trans. Mary Elizabeth Meek (Coral Gables, Florida: Univ. of Miami Press, 1971), p. 23.

   9. Thomas Paine, *The Complete Writings of Thomas Paine,* 2 vols., ed. Philip S. Foner (New York: The Citadel Press, 1945), vol. 1, p. 45.

   10. Thomas Jefferson, *Writings* (New York: The Library of America, 1984), p. 1491.

to the facts that have arisen in our own day." Before the eyes of Americans was the "real volume, not of history, but of facts . . . unmutilated by contrivance, or the errors of tradition."[11]

In 1793 James Wilson claimed that the people "spoke [the United States] into existence,"[12] and in 1842, in a review of Longfellow's poetry in *The Southern Quarterly Review*, the anonymous writer, claiming that in the past poetry had "dwelt apart in books," isolated from the ordinary world, insisted that it was different in America: "But, when Republican America was spoken into existence, poetry descended into the hearts of men, and became a part of the life and breath of all. . . . A new era, in that hour, dawned upon the intellectual, as well as the moral, world."[13] Here again was the conceit of a spoken origin of the United States in conjunction with the theme of an utterly new time. The strange figure, attributing to spoken words a magical power of political creation, seems out of place in a culture that credited itself with rational foundations. Jefferson, in a letter to John Adams in 1823, finally gave his thoughts on a question Adams had been raising persistently in their correspondence at least since 1812, that of the metaphysical origin of the world. Commenting on the first verse of the Gospel of St. John, Jefferson argued for translating *logos* as 'reason' rather than 'word.'

> One of its legitimate meanings indeed is 'a word.' But, in that sense, it makes an unmeaning jargon: while the other meaning 'reason', equally legitimate, explains rationally the eternal preexistence of God, and his creation of the world. Knowing how incomprehensible it was that 'a word,' the mere action or articulation of the voice and organs of speech could create a world, they ["modern Christians"] undertake to make of this articulation a second preexisting being, and ascribe to him, and not to God, the creation of the universe.[14]

---

11. Paine, *Complete Writings,* vol. 1, p. 376.

12. Quoted in William F. Harris, II, "Bonding Word and Polity: The Logic of American Constitutionalism," *American Political Science Review* 76 (1982): 35.

13. Anon., "American Poetry," *The Southern Quarterly Review* 1, 2 (April, 1842): 495.

14. Lester J. Cappon, ed., *The Adams-Jefferson Letters: The Complete Correspondence Between Thomas Jefferson and Abigail and John Adams,* 2 vols. (Chapel Hill:

This skepticism was in keeping with Jefferson's usual antimeta-physical attitude. But that the creation of the American nation should have been figured by others, despite the implausibility Jefferson noted, as just such a product of an articulation of the voice, was a measure of how mysterious, unlikely, and incomprehensible that political fabrication must have seemed. Nevertheless, the three quotations above in which versions of this figuration appear all pronounced it casually, as if it were proverbial.

James Wilson's use of the phrase deserves examination, since he employs it in the most intimate conjunction with actual practical exigencies of national creation. As one of the first Justices of the United States Supreme Court, he issued an opinion in the case of *Chisholm v. Georgia* in 1793, a case in which it needed to be decided whether a private citizen of another state could sue the state of Georgia in the federal court. Georgia held that the United States Supreme Court had no jurisdiction over the case, that it would infringe upon the sovereignty of an individual state to have a federal court exercise such authority. The case was an early test of the legitimacy and extent of the newly instituted federal constitutional power. As Wilson said in his opinion, "This is a case of uncommon magnitude."[15]

> The question to be determined is, whether this state, so respectable, and whose claims soar so high, is amenable to the jurisdiction of the supreme court of the United States? This question, important in itself, will depend on others, more important still; and may, perhaps, be ultimately resolved into one, no less *radical* than this — "do the People of the United States form a Nation?" (p. 453)

Wilson acknowledges that in the Constitution "the term *sovereign* is totally unknown," but this absence is eloquent, since "in an instrument well drawn, as in a poem well composed, silence is some-

Univ. of North Carolina Press, 1959), vol. 2, pp. 593–94. For an earlier instance of Adams's putting the question to Jefferson, see vol. 2, p. 309.

15. *Chisholm v. Georgia,* (Supreme Court of the United States, 1793), A. J. Dallas, *Reports of Cases Ruled and Adjudged in the Several Courts of the United States and of Pennsylvania,* ed. Frederick C. Brightly (New York: The Banks Law Publishing Co., 1907), p. 453. Subsequent references will be given parenthetically.

times most expressive" (p. 454). In fact, Wilson goes on to say, the framers of the Constitution "might have announced themselves *sovereign* people of the United States, but . . . they avoided the ostentatious declaration" since it would have been supererogatory: their performance of a sovereign speech act announced their claim implicitly. Sovereignty inheres in the natural persons who initially form a government that will then command their obedience; "laws derived from the pure source of equality and justice must be founded on the *consent* of those whose obedience they require. The sovereign, when traced to his source, must be found in the man" (p. 458).

A state, according to Wilson, is "an artificial person" to be treated under law as such, able to incur debts, enter into contracts, and so forth (p. 455). But this "feigned and artificial person," to which everything else is subordinate, is in turn "subordinate to the People" who created it, since "we should never forget, that, in truth and nature, those who think and speak and act, are men" (pp. 455, 454, 455). Because the "pure source" of sovereignty is the natural man who thinks and speaks and acts, it is a "perversion," "unnatural and inverted," and productive of "confusion and perplexity," to refer to the United States as a sovereign being (pp. 454, 462).

> Sentiments and expressions of this inaccurate kind prevail in our common, even in our convivial, language. Is a toast asked? "The United States," instead of the "People of the United States," is the toast given. This is not politically correct. The toast is meant to present to view the first great object in the Union: it presents only the second: it presents only the artificial person, instead of the natural persons, who spoke it into existence. (p. 462)

The logic of Wilson's argument locates the origin of legitimate authority in the voice of the people — not in a written representation of that voice, and not in the textual artifact (the Constitution) that might be taken to embody the political will of the artificial person formed by the "complete body of free persons united together for their common benefit" (the State), but in the individual, originary, natural voices of separate persons who together spoke the nation into existence. It is as if Wilson, to support his claim "that the people of the United States intended to form themselves into a nation, for national purposes," needs to discern in the "texture of the constitution" an aboriginal *vocal* origin of that textual artifact, a pretextual aural effect as the pure ground of that document's sovereign authority. In the expressive silence of the document's lack of explicit reference to sovereignty, Wilson hallucinates the creative utterance proceeding from the natural voices of embodied persons.

Benjamin Rush, in an essay written some time after the Revolution and published in 1798, contended that "we do not extol it too highly when we attribute as much to the power of eloquence as to the sword, in bringing about the American revolution."[16] His use of the first person plural and his negative formulation implied as well that this was something of a commonplace, perhaps challenged as hyperbolic by some, but wrongly so. "It [eloquence] is the first accomplishment in a republic, and often sets the whole machine of government in motion."[17] Jefferson's figuration of the founding as an act of writing on the blank page of the future was nearly the same thing. Nearly, because Jefferson alluded implicitly both to the very material fact of his own writing of the Declaration of Independence, and also to the written Constitution that followed, and thus referred at least implicitly to actual worldly events and actions. And even though he described the founding in this way — as an unconstrained act of writing — Jefferson also famously insisted at about the same time (1825) that the writing of the Declaration involved not origination but merely repetition, recombination, and synopsis: its object was

16. Benjamin Rush, *Essays, Literary, Moral, and Philosophical* (Philadelphia: Thomas and Samuel F. Bradford, 1798), p. 16. Cf. Hugh Henry Brackenridge in 1786: "The eloquence of our writers and orators at the beginning of this contest was universally felt; it roused like the storm of desert; it hurried to resistance like the sound of a trumpet. Britain fell back with astonishment not more at the power of our oratory in the senate than at the gleam of our bayonets in the field." "Observations on the Country at the Head of the Ohio River," *A Hugh Henry Brackenridge Reader, 1770–1815*, ed. Daniel Marder (Pittsburgh, Pennsylvania: Univ. of Pittsburgh Press, 1970), p. 117. Orig. pub. in *Pittsburgh Gazette,* Aug. 26 and Sept. 2, 1786.

17. Rush, *Essays,* p. 16.

not to find out new principles, or new arguments, never before thought of, not merely to say things which had never been said before; but to place before mankind the common sense of the subject. . . . Neither aiming at originality of principle or sentiment, nor yet copied from any particular and previous writing, it was intended to be an expression of the American mind. . . . All its authority rests then on the harmonizing sentiments of the day, whether expressed in conversation, in letters, printed essays, or in the elementary books of public right, as Aristotle, Cicero, Locke, Sidney, &c.[18]

The rhetoric of "neither . . . nor" and the antinomy of intention and passive reception and transmission perfectly described the dilemma of the revolutionary innovator who attributed all his motion, as it were, to forces acting upon him out of the past, and yet was in some measure deviating from that past, resisting its entailments. As Jefferson wrote, again to Adams, with respect to a controversy that arose when William Wirt in his biography gave Patrick Henry the credit for "the commencement of motion in the revolutionary ball," it would have been "as difficult to say at what moment the revolution began, and what incident set it in motion, as to fix the moment that the embryo becomes an animal, or the act which gives him a beginning."[19] Revolutionary inception was intrinsically undecidable, and, as I will be arguing, that is why it was so aptly figured as a linguistic phenomenon.

The figure, or conceit, as I have been calling it, of the United States being "spoken into existence," and the related, somewhat less extravagant figure of its being written into being on the blank page of the future, verged on the magical, and did so, I want to suggest, precisely because of the inscrutability of revolutionary time and causality. This inscrutability involved the problem of what Jacques Derrida has called the "fabulous event" of the per-

18. Jefferson, *Writings*, p. 1501.
19. Cappon, ed., *Adams-Jefferson Letters*, vol. 2, pp. 523, 524. See chapter 5 for a discussion of Wirt's reconstruction of the linguistic moment of Patrick Henry's revolutionary incitement.

formative effect of the Declaration of Independence.[20] What was "fabulous" about it (in the literal sense of fictive and incredible) was its retroactive structure:

> One cannot decide — and that's the interesting thing, the force and the coup of force of such a declarative act — whether independence is stated or produced by this utterance. . . . Is it that the good people have already freed themselves in fact and are only stating the fact of this emancipation in [*par*] the Declaration? Or is it rather that they free themselves at the instant of and by [*par*] the signature of this Declaration?[21]

The Declaration was simultaneously, on this analysis, constative and performative, at once *referring* to the nation-state (as if it already existed) and *instituting* it (since it did not yet exist), creating by the Declaration the independent political entity that was the only legitimate author of that Declaration: this "fabulous retroactivity" authorized the signers — after the fact, as it were — to (have) sign(ed).[22] To borrow a phrase from a recent study of the French Revolution, the revolutionary moment is a "mythic present," a time in which the state must at once have been already constituted and yet to be, a contradictory fold in time whereby political legitimacy and illegitimacy coincide.[23] This necessary fiction found expression in numerous texts of the revolutionary and early national period — in Jefferson's *Autobiography* (1821), for instance, he claimed "that our emigration from England to this country gave her no more rights over us, than the emigrations of the Danes and Saxons gave to the present authorities of the mother country over England," that is, that the not-yet-independent nation had in truth been always-already-independent;[24] or in Franklin's convenient retrospective realiza-

20. Jacques Derrida, "Declarations of Independence," *New Political Science* 15 (1986): 10.

21. Ibid., p. 9.

22. Ibid., p. 10.

23. Lynn Hunt, *Politics, Culture, and Class in the French Revolution* (Berkeley: Univ. of California Press, 1984), p. 27.

24. Jefferson, *Writings*, p. 9.

tion that the American colonies, which had obeyed Parliamentary law for decades, had in fact never been subject to Parliamentary authority but only to the King.[25] The requisite speciousness of these claims is what made the Revolution thinkable, and they are the kinds of claims that depended precisely upon the powerful conjunction of performative and constative verbal forms. This illicit rhetorical self-engendering was nicely figured by Benjamin Rush:

> America, with respect to the nations of Europe, is like the new planet, with respect to those, whose revolutions have long been described in the solar system. She is placed at too great a distance from most of them, to be within the influence of a reciprocal exchange of the rays of knowledge. Like a certain animal, described by the naturalists, she must impregnate herself.[26]

So happy was Rush to have the United States left to its own devices, separated from all historical precedents, that he chided those who persisted in imagining that European examples had any relevance for America: "We suffer so much from traditional error of various kinds, in education, morals and government, that I have been led to wish, that it were possible for us to have schools established in the United States, for teaching *the art of forgetting*."[27]

Such brilliant speciousness was both admired and detested by John Adams. In one of his complaints about the way the history of the Revolution was then being written, he objected (in an 1805 letter to Rush) to what he saw as the characteristic distortions of his own role. He would prove bold enough in 1809 to claim that independence would never have been achieved without his agency.[28] To Rush he griped that only those historical agents who had an instinct for dramatic performance would be remembered,

---

25. Benjamin Franklin, *Writings* (New York: The Library of America, 1987), pp. 572, 616, 713.
26. Rush, *Essays,* pp. 35–36.
27. Rush, *Essays,* p. 71.
28. John A. Schutz and Douglas Adair, eds., *The Spur of Fame: Dialogues of John Adams and Benjamin Rush, 1805–1813* (San Marino, California: The Huntington Library, 1966), p. 139.

while his own less picturesque contributions would be forgotten. Despite his resentment, however, Adams recognized that such dramatic strokes—he called them "coups de théâtre"—were effectual, and perhaps necessary, devices for achieving revolutionary change. To Rush he wrote,

> The scenery has often if not commonly in all the business of human life, at least of public life, more effect than the characters of the dramatis personae or the ingenuity of the plot. Recollect within your own times. What but the scenery did this? or that? or the other? Was there ever a *coup de théâtre* that had so great an effect as Jefferson's penmanship of the Declaration of Independence?[29]

And again, in 1811, "The Declaration of Independence I always considered as a theatrical show. Jefferson ran away with all the stage effect of that . . . and all the glory of it."[30] At once wishing to derogate Jefferson's authorship as mere "penmanship," "scenery," or "stage effect," yet acknowledging the historical efficacy of such theatricality, performativity or, as I would prefer to call it, rhetoricity, Adams came close to identifying the performative force—the Derridean *coup*—of rhetorical action in the service of revolutionary change.[31]

Adams even considered writing "a book on 'The Scenery of the Business.'"[32] Such a work, had it been written, might have alerted subsequent generations to the essential rhetoricity of American revolutionary innovation, much as Marx's *Eighteenth Brumaire* would describe the necessary use of ideological and linguistic costumery in the imagining of new historical possibilities and the creating of new social forms in France in 1848.[33] What Adams, Wilson, and the others (and, later, Derrida) were trying to do with

29. Ibid., pp. 42–43.
30. Ibid., p. 182.
31. Jay Fliegelman's *Declaring Independence: Jefferson, Natural Language, and the Culture of Performance* (Stanford: Stanford Univ. Press, 1993), explores the place of performativity in a broad array of cultural phenomena in revolutionary America.
32. John A. Schutz and Douglas Adair, eds., *The Spur of Fame*, p. 43.
33. Karl Marx, *The Eighteenth Brumaire of Louis Bonaparte* (New York: International Publishers, 1963), pp. 15ff.

their unlikely metaphors representing the new nation as an effect of language was to describe the problem of accounting for the new nation's imaginary relation to its changed political status and its understanding of how that change had been achieved. These tropes at once express a fact about that status and suggest an illusion about it. They represent the troubled, undecidable relation of Americans to the past they sought to detach themselves from even as they were its products, and they condense in a phrase the nation's desire for unconditioned self-fabrication even as they inadvertently concede the nation's utter determination by the chains of circumstance.

What the figure of a nation "spoken into existence" did, in short, was to create an analogy between, on the one hand, the relation of a social group to its past, and, on the other hand, the relation of an individual speaker or a linguistic community to the inherited language system that makes its utterances possible. Each of these relations is, crucially, one of both freedom and necessity, agency and determination, limitation and enablement. Thus the figure of speech—"spoken into existence"—while it traded upon the illusion that spoken language was the medium of unconstrained willful subjectivity, an instrument wholly subservient to the intentional expressive control of the speaker, nevertheless also implicitly conceded that subjectivity, agency, and intentionality were in some measure the controlled effects of a prior impersonal linguistic system. This paradox is well defined by Benveniste:

> Language permits the indefinite production of messages in unlimited varieties. That unique property belongs to the structure of language, which is composed of signs, of unities of meaning, numerous but always of finite number, which enter into combinations regulated by a code and which permit a number of enunciations that exceeds all calculation, and necessarily exceeds more and more, since the number of signs will always grow and the possibilities for the use and combination of these signs will grow in consequence.[34]

34. Benveniste, *Problèmes de Linguistique Générale, II* (Paris: Gallimard, 1974), p. 97 (my translation).

The figure was therefore an apt one to represent the situation of historical actors whose defiance of historical determination was nevertheless necessarily in some measure historically conditioned: the future was open, its possibilities were infinite, but at the same time governed by conditions and probabilities. Exorbitant revolutionary desire was constrained to operate upon the given world.

The historical world into which, as subjects, we are thrown, is always already represented in the speech of the community. Merleau-Ponty's description is concise: "We live in a world where speech is an *institution*. . . . The linguistic and intersubjective world no longer surprises us, we no longer distinguish it from the world itself, and it is within a world already spoken and speaking that we think."[35] And when we think to change that world, our innovations must operate upon the ready-made linguistic and intersubjective structure which is the form in which we encounter the world the past has prepared for us.

The writer in 1790 in the *Pennsylvania Packet* wanted, then, to claim that on July 4, 1776, the United States was created *de novo,* out of thin air, freely and perfectly: an effect without any cause except the will of the people as expressed by the speech of its rulers.[36] The writer also wanted to give to that moment of inception the glamour of perfect intentional unity: the immediate local context of this instance of the figure was a warning, with reference to the unsettled circumstances of the 1790s, against the possible violent disintegration of the nation. "Should the cords of union be loosened or broken, we shall fall an easy prey to some foreign invader, or we shall see American rising up in arms against American," he wrote, and urged his readers to "adhere to UNION."[37] His model of national political unity was an individual human subject, represented by a self-proximate voice, identical to itself and embodying an undivided intentionality.

The figure of an original voice creating the United States has

35. Maurice Merleau-Ponty, *Phenomenology of Perception,* trans. Colin Smith (London: Routledge & Kegan Paul, 1962), p. 184.
36. His ascription of this speaking-into-existence to unnamed "rulers" introduced an ambiguity into the model. Others who used this figure did not attribute the utterance to leaders but either left it unattributed, as in the case of the reviewer in the *Southern Quarterly Review* in 1842 (see n. 13 above), or attributed it to the people in general, as in the case of James Wilson in 1793.
37. Anon., "Gray's Gardens," p. 3.

recently been adopted by some scholars in treating the founding era. William F. Harris II claims that "the Constitution of the United States did not describe a political constitution that already existed; it generated a republic . . . the words narrate the polity into existence."[38] And Anne Norton, in *Alternative Americas*, which has the explicit goal of problematizing the monolithic, twentieth-century scholarly representation of the founding of American political culture by describing the several discrepant (regional, gender-specific, and so forth) contemporaneous versions of American nationality, nevertheless resorts to the figure of speech — "Americans have spoken themselves into being," "the conception of America as the creation of speech," "the authoritative act in which the people speak themselves into being" — that inadvertently restores a monologic utterance to its privileged place as the putative origin of the nation.[39] Norton qualifies this privilege by describing this originary utterance as "many-voiced," but she does not thoroughly insist upon the principle of the ineluctably dialogic nature of any utterance (despite seeming to invoke Bakhtin/ Vološinov). Such an insistence would be one way to undermine the powerfully persistent prejudice that moves us to understand voice as a unitary phenomenon, even when that voice is represented as a chorus.[40] The chapters to follow, will show that writers like Franklin, Brockden Brown, and Brackenridge were closely engaged with precisely this question and provided powerful imaginative accounts of the linguistic dimension of revolutionary politics.

II. Semantic Transvaluation

The social order is defined by a code of correct denominations wherein all disagreement, all difference immediately appears as a sign of disharmony. . . . Anxiety about language always accompanies the alienation of man, rupture with the world, and it demands a return to order or the establishment of a new order.

Georges Gusdorf

38. Harris, "Bonding Word and Polity," p. 34.
39. Anne Norton, *Alternative Americas: A Reading of Antebellum Political Culture* (Chicago: Univ. of Chicago Press, 1986), pp. 2, 20.
40. Norton, *Alternative Americas,* p. 2. Norton returns to this trope in her more recent *Republic of Signs: Liberal Theory and American Popular Culture* (Chicago:

Again in the *Pennsylvania Packet* in 1790 (this time on November
8), the question of language was addressed, with an implicit reference to the Revolution and its aftermath. An ancient topos, one
that at that time had been revived frequently in recent years, was
used to characterize the conceptual transformations to which
American minds were being subjected:

> The abuse of TERMS is an evil that has produced
> much mischief among mankind: — *Murder,* by being
> called *war,* is advocated by many who would revolt
> from doing a personal injury — *Intrigue* and *finesse* in
> politics are denominated *address* — *Over-reaching* in
> trade is the art of making a *bargain* — *Flattery* is but
> *complaisance* — and universal *deception,* is a complete
> *knowledge of the world.*[41]

The terms to which this writer directed attention were not chosen
at random. The simple fact of semantic dislocation was noted, but
the specific words selected to illustrate the process were themselves words that had to do with the structure of intersubjective
communication and understanding that was disrupted by semantic dislocation *per se.* "Universal *deception*" was claimed to be the
state of things, and this state was implied to be the consequence
of the kinds of abusive, mischievous linguistic trickery of which
these substitutions were exemplary. The theme of "abuse of
words," and its reference to times of revolutionary social and political upheaval, had its famous *locus classicus* in Thucydides' account
of the civil war in Corcyra:

> To fit in with the change of events, words, too, had to
> change their usual meanings. What used to be de-
> scribed as a thoughtless act of aggression was now re-
> garded as the courage one would expect to find in a
> party member; to think of the future and wait was
> merely another way of saying one was a coward; any

Univ. of Chicago Press, 1993), pp. 9 ("The Declaration spoke the nation into
being") and 33 ("America is a nation founded by the word").
41. "Philadelphia, *Nov.* 8: *Extract of a letter from a gentleman at Trinidad, to his
friend in this city, dated Sept.* 30, 1790," *Pennsylania Packet,* Nov. 8, 1790, p. 3.

idea of moderation was just an attempt to disguise
one's unmanly character; ability to understand a question from all sides meant that one was totally unfitted
for action.[42]

As James Boyd White has written, the force of this description
was owing to Thucydides' prior narrative establishment of the discursively constituted character of the city-states of Greece. The
"complex rhetorical universe" of those states, into which the historian drew his reader, with all the "conventions of argument and
action, by which they maintain and regulate their relations with
each other," was vulnerable to the threat posed by any misuse of
language.[43] While White and some other scholars who have addressed the question of the interdependency of social order and
linguistic practice have tended to assume pejoratively that deviation from customary usage is necessarily "abuse," the point is still
well taken that semantic innovation presents a challenge to the
received order of a society.

Traditionally such innovation has been represented as "abuse"
by conservatives, and therefore decried, but it may also be given a
positive valuation, and it may, in fact, be a necessary device for
effecting historical change. John Adams rightly claimed that the
American Revolution had taken place in the consciousness of the
American people:

> As to the history of the Revolution, my Ideas may be
> peculiar, perhaps singular. What do We Mean by the
> Revolution? The War? That was no part of the Revolu-
> tion. It was only an Effect and Consequence of it. The
> Revolution was in the Minds of the People, and this

42. Thucydides, *The Peloponnesian War,* trans. Rex Warner (Harmondsworth:
Penguin, 1954), p. 242. Thomas Gustafson grounds his intricate account of politics and language in the American republic in an analysis of what he calls "the
Thucydidean moment, a moment when, as occurs in Corcyra in Thucydides' account of the Peloponnesian War, the social contract—the bond of faith, affection,
and compromise sustaining harmony between man and man—is broken by political strife and linguistic duplicity." See Gustafson, *Representative Words,* pp. 71ff.
43. James Boyd White, *When Words Lose Their Meaning: Constitutions and Re-
constitutions of Language, Character, and Community* (Chicago: Univ. of Chicago
Press, 1984), p. 59.

was effected, from 1760 to 1775, in the course of fif-
teen Years before a drop of blood was drawn at Lex-
ington.[44]

That is to say that a revolution is only made by people who have
been persuaded that it is possible to make a revolution, and con-
vinced also that they ought to make a revolution. The proleptic
representation of that possibility and the rhetorical performance
of that persuasion are essentially linguistic acts, and their necessary
priority to the material violence of war is worth recalling. That
is all that was being claimed when Benjamin Rush, for instance,
attributed "as much to the power of eloquence as to the sword, in
bringing about the American revolution."[45] Rush also insisted that
the violent struggle of 1776–1783 did not end the Revolution,
but only began it:

> The termination of the war by the peace in 1783 did
> not terminate the American revolution. The minds of
> the citizens of the United States were wholly unpre-
> pared for their new situation. The excess of the passion
> for liberty, inflamed by the successful issue of the war,
> produced, in many people, opinions and conduct,
> which could not be removed by reason nor restrained
> by government.[46]

This "excess of the passion for liberty" deserved to be ranked as
"a form of insanity," Rush held, which he would "take the liberty
of distinguishing by the name of *anarchia*."[47] Thus the war itself
was not only the effect of a prior revolution of consciousness, a
linguistic revolution; it was also a relay station, as it were, for the
impulse of a continuing mental and linguistic revolution.

John Adams quoted the famous passage from Thucydides' *Peloponnesian War* in his *Defence of the Constitutions of Government of the*

44. Cappon, ed., *Adams-Jefferson Letters*, vol. 2, p. 455.
45. Rush, *Essays*, p. 16.
46. Rush, "An Account of the Influence of the Military and Political Events of
the American Revolution Upon the Human Body," in *Medical Inquiries and Observations*, 3d ed., rev. and enl., 4 vols. (Philadelphia: Published by Johnson and Warner . . ., 1809), vol. 1, p. 243.
47. Ibid., p. 243.

United States of America in 1787.⁴⁸ There he claimed that such linguistic instability was an indication of a lack of "checks and balances" in the structure of the state, which if present would impart "equilibrium" to it and forestall the "factions and confusions" that plagued the Greek cities.⁴⁹ But he imagined as well that the establishment of *linguistic* equilibrium would, conversely, have a *political* effect. Writing from Amsterdam in 1780 to the President of Congress, he proposed that among the means of promoting the Revolution one useful device would be the establishment of an "American Academy for refining, improving, and ascertaining the English language." "It is not to be disputed," he wrote, "that the form of government has an influence upon language, and language, in its turn, influences not only the form of government, but the temper, the sentiments, and manners of the people."⁵⁰ In this letter Adams recognized that because the constitutions of the states were "so democratical," leadership under them would necessarily be exercised primarily by means of "eloquence," and he argued that if the polity therefore depended upon language, "it will have a happy effect upon the union of the States to have a public standard for all persons in every part of the continent to appeal to, both for the signification and pronunciation of the language."⁵¹ This was to be, it seems, an Adams family hobby horse, for John Quincy Adams would subsequently urge that Americans "yield the guidance of a nation to the dominion of the voice."⁵²

It was an eighteenth-century commonplace that language was the medium, as it were, of political connection: often this claim was made on the authority of Locke's dictum that language was "the great instrument and common tie of society."⁵³ The indefati-

48. John Adams, *The Works of John Adams,* ed. Charles Francis Adams, 10 vols. (Boston: Little, Brown and Company, 1850–56), vol. 4, pp. 285–86.

49. Ibid., p. 285.

50. Francis Wharton, ed., *The Revolutionary Diplomatic Correspondence of the United States,* 6 vols. (Washington, D.C.: Government Printing Office, 1889), vol. 4, pp. 45–46.

51. Ibid., p. 46.

52. Quoted in Lewis P. Simpson, ed., *The Federalist Literary Mind: Selections from the Monthly Anthology and Boston Review, 1803–1811, Including Documents Relating to the Boston Athenaeum* (Baton Rouge, Louisiana: Louisiana State Univ. Press, 1962), p. 171.

53. John Locke, *An Essay Concerning Human Understanding,* ed. Alexander Campbell Fraser, 2 vols. (New York: Dover Publications, 1959), vol. 2, p. 3.

gible spokesman for this principle in postrevolutionary America was, of course, Noah Webster, whose dictionaries, spellers, and polemics all were designed to promote linguistic standardization. "Our political harmony is . . . concerned in a uniformity of language," he wrote in 1789.[54] This desirable uniformity was to be legislated, he averred, by means of a reformation of orthography. Webster realized the use that could be made of the American habit of "spelling-pronunciation," as it is called. An effect of provincial self-consciousness, Americans had tended during their colonial history toward hyper-correctness in speech, and had therefore often rectified their pronunciation by reference to a "phonetic" standard derived from the frequently irregular spelling of English. Franklin had, in his earlier design of a phonetic alphabet, made use of the same American habit,[55] and Webster now adapted the method. Correctness in spelling would contribute to "annihilate differences in speaking and preserve the purity of the American tongue. A sameness of pronunciation is of considerable consequence in a political view."[56]

More consequential than spelling or pronunciation for political change or stability, however, were the related questions of usage and definition. For while uniformity of pronunciation might, by establishing sameness in the oral/aural domain of human interaction, contribute to "political harmony," the consensus it formed would be at best a surface phenomenon. Necessary, perhaps, for the affectual charge it would carry — "it would remove prejudice, and conciliate mutual affection and respect," according to Webster[57] — it would not prevent the speakers from meaning entirely different things when they pronounced the same word identically. A conceptual discrepancy might survive beneath the phonic conformity. This was the question addressed by Adams and others in the postrevolutionary period, but it was a much-discussed issue even as the Revolution was pending.

A remarkable broadside, published in Philadelphia on Septem-

54. Noah Webster, *Dissertations on the English Language* (Boston: Isaiah Thomas and Company, 1789), p. 20.
55. Christopher Looby, "Phonetics and Politics: Franklin's Alphabet as a Political Design," *Eighteenth-Century Studies* 18 (1984): 6–8 and passim.
56. Webster, *Dissertations*, p. 19.
57. Ibid., p. 397.

ber 1, 1774, and signed by someone calling himself "A Tradesman," began with this statement:

> "We have long since lost the right Names of Things
> from amongst us: the giving of what belongs to other
> People is called Generosity; and the Courage to ven-
> ture upon Wickedness is named Fortitude;" is an Ob-
> servation, if I mistake not, of a noble Roman: how far
> it is applicable to the present Time may not be amiss
> for such among the People, who really mean uprightly,
> to consider.[58]

This writer—who had earlier made this same argument in a letter
to the *Pennsylvania Journal* of August 17, 1774—was also using
the topos of "abuse of words" to delegitimate the movement for
independence. The self-denominated Tradesman was angry with
those "hot brained Impostors" and "riotous Spirits" who deceptively stigmatized all moderates as "Enemies to their Country."

In the beginning of the struggle for American independence,
before it came to know itself as such, the appeal was ordinarily for
a restoration of "English liberties." Liberty was always qualified
as "English," and usually specified as a set of historically given,
constitutionally secured civil freedoms. Once independence was
declared, the national adjective was forthwith abandoned, and the
semantic field of "liberty" was immediately enlarged and general-
ized. The word acquired a new charge, and a new indefiniteness.
It was just that kind of semantic explosion to which the Tradesman
objected: the "alone Measure to be relied on" in seeking political
redress was an appeal to their "Rights as free Men," as those rights
were defined in the authorized dictionary of British political history. From this point of view, a radical appeal to abstract and in-
definite rights and liberty would necessarily require an abuse of
words and an exploitation of the charm of language; for example,
"NON-IMPORTATION is the Word of the Day; you must sub-

---

58. Anon., broadside, "We have long since lost the right names of Things from
amongst us" (Philadelphia, 1774). This broadside, in the collection of the Historical Society of Pennsylvania, is Evans 13545. It appears in full in the appendix to
this chapter.

mit to it, fellow Subjects, the great Patriots tell you so; those very Patriots who tickle your Ears with the *Words* 'SALVATION OF AMERICA.'" When the Tradesman's letter appeared in the *Pennsylvania Journal,* a writer calling himself "Sidney" replied to it: "ALL vices have travelling names. Submission to the British Parliament, for a while, assumed the name of Moderation. After being detected and exposed under the garb of that necessary virtue, it has assumed the name of PETITION and REMONSTRANCE."[59] This turned the charge of "abuse of words" directly around: it was the secret loyalist who was alleged to be using words deceptively, cloaking his "vices" with "travelling names."

The newspapers of Philadelphia in the years leading up to the Revolution were full, in fact, of this sort of meta-argument about language. A writer calling himself "C. M. Scævola" had written on July 20, 1774, also in the *Pennsylvania Journal,* against those who "take upon themselves the name of moderate men — prostituting the term — and cloathing themselves with the sacred garb of prudence." He ended his letter with the familiar slogan, "VOX PO-PULI: VOX DEI."[60] In reply to these charges, "A Moderate Man" made the following claim: "By a strange corruption of language in these degenerate days, Moderation and Prudence imply the most unspeakable degree of vice; the store-houses of Billingsgate are ransacked to find terms sufficiently opprobious and '*detestable*' to denominate them."[61] And the argument had been going on in previous issues of the paper, with "Anglus Americanus," for instance, addressing himself "To the Citizens of Philadelphia":

> I have observed with some concern, that certain cant terms are growing fashionable in this city, which, though unintelligible, may to a common ear sound plausible, but which to the wary, announce the defection of those who adopt them. *Moderation* and *moderate men,* is at present the Countersign or Badge of this party, who find their interest (or fancy they find their

59. "To the Inhabitants of Pennsylvania," *Pennsylvania Journal,* Aug. 31, 1774, p. 1.

60. "To the Inhabitants of Pennsylvania," *Pennsylvania Journal,* July 20, 1774, p. 7.

61. *Pennsylvania Journal,* August 3, 1774.

interest) in betraying the common cause. . . . *Moderation, moderate men* and *moderate measures* are therefore the spells which are to charm us into a destructive supineness; and most dangerous spells they are.[62]

A year later in the *Pennsylvania Journal,* "Antoninus" discussed a new set of words of which the meanings were contested:

> When the words faction, sedition, and oppugnation to government have entirely lost their force with the people, we are now plagued with a new *Shiboleth* or *Witch of Endor* conjured up to set the lazy, timid, ignorant, ambitious and corrupt at variance with the men whose disinterested wisdom and spirit have long labored for the deliverance of this oppressed and devoted country. This dreadful, this alarming sound is nothing less than the long word *Independence.* A word, which I confess, was grating to the ears of every devotee to the shrine of power in church or state, longer than any now living can remember.[63]

Antoninus shrewdly turned around the charge of linguistic innovation here, as Sidney had done, maintaining that the "alarming sound" of the word *Independence,* while it did have a "grating" effect, did so not because it was new; in fact, he claimed, it was old, and had been grating on the ears of the corrupt for a long time. He claimed for it an historical legitimacy, without wanting to sacrifice its powerful revolutionary aural effect. And he attacked the legitimacy of the language of loyalists: "To have a thorough understanding of these matters it becomes necessary to analize this chaos of Tory-jargon." One device of this "Tory-jargon" was to "[harp] on the string of religious domination," that is, to predict that after independence a new state church would be established. On the contrary, Antoninus wrote, "the major voice of the continent would be *no particular establishment* whatever."[64] This refer-

---

62. "To the Citizens of Philadelphia," *Pennsylvania Journal,* June 29, 1774, p. 2.
63. "To the Printers of the Pennsylvania Journal," *Pennsylvania Journal,* Oct. 11, 1775, p. 1.
64. Ibid., p. 1.

ence to a putative "major voice" was one that would have been familiar to readers of the time, who often saw what in other places might have been called the "general will" instead figured as the "general voice," "collective voice," or "vox populi."

A patriot writer in the *Pennsylvania Gazette* of May 18, 1774, signing himself "A Philadelphian" and addressing his argument "To the Freemen of America," worked a slight change on the linguistic theme. "Liberty — Property and Life — are now but *Names* in America. Liberty is levelled by the declarative Act of Parliament to tax us without our Consent — Property is now annihilated by the late Act of Parliament, which destroys the Trade of Boston."[65] This was to claim for the patriot cause the credit of attaching to the mere "*Names*" of things real signifieds, their proper and legitimate referents. In early 1775, again in the *Pennsylvania Gazette*, an exchange between "An Anxious By-Stander" and "Philadelphus" concerned several lexical definitions. The By-Stander on January 4 had written in support of nonimportation, but regretted that the Congress, unjustly, had not made allowance for goods already ordered from England.[66] Philadelphus responded a week later, charging that "impeaching the justice and wisdom of the last [Congress]" would dangerously "slacken the zeal, weaken the authority, and destroy the usefulness of every future Congress."[67] The By-Stander indignantly rejected the implied charge of undermining Congressional authority: "Let the man that can prove me an enemy to my country strike off my *hand*."[68] Whereupon Philadelphus after another week quite slyly expressed his "uncertainty whether *his* country means America" — or might, traitorously, mean England.[69] He returned to the attack on February 8, alleging both that "our Author grows angry, cavils at Expressions, and almost calls Names," and, the proverbial pot calling the kettle

---

65. "To the Freemen of America," *Pennsylvania Gazette*, May 18, 1774, p. 3.
66. "To the Printers of the Pennsylvania Gazette," *Pennsylvania Gazette*, Jan. 4, 1775, p. 2.
67. "To the Printers of the Pennsylvania Gazette," *Pennsylvania Gazette*, Jan. 11, 1775, p. 1.
68. "To the Printers of the Pennsylvania Gazette," *Pennsylvania Gazette*, Jan. 18, 1775, p. 1.
69. "To the Printers of the Pennsylvania Gazette," *Pennsylvania Gazette*, Jan. 25, 1775, p. 2.

black, questioning his adversary's understanding of economics, advising him to "look into his Dictionary, and see whether Demand means an Accumulation of Price."[70] The By-Stander soon came back rather weakly, and not quite to the point:

> It may be needless to enter into a disputation about the true meaning of the word "*compensation*." Doctor Johnson, the compiler of the dictionary, and Messieurs ABC, and Company, merchants, will most probably form very different conceptions of the matter; and whether I explained it agreeable to the common acceptation in the mercantile world, of which Philadelphus is a *professed* member, may be left to *them* to determine. . . . He accuses me "of cavilling at words, growing angry, and almost calling names." — As to playing upon words, I confess I little expected a charge on that score, from a man who, in his second performance, had tortured my honest and innocent declaration of a love to *my* country, into a quibbling doubt of *what* country I meant.[71]

In the *Pennsylvania Evening Post*, "A Reasonable Whiggess" asked its editor on November 16, 1775, if "any of your correspondents would favor me with a clear definition" of the terms "Whig" and "Tory," since she had been called both, to her confusion.[72] She waited for a reply until January 2, 1776, when a correspondent signing himself simply "B." offered his extended characterization of the true meaning of "Whig."[73] In the same paper, "The Apologist" on February 29, 1776, mitigated the alleged "backwardness in the cause of liberty" of the members of the Pennsylvania House of Representatives by quoting from the oath of loyalty to the King

70. "To the Printers of the Pennsylvania Gazette," *Pennsylvania Gazette*, Feb. 8, 1775, p. 2.
71. "To the Printers of the Pennsylvania Gazette," *Pennsylvania Gazette*, Feb. 15, 1775, p. 2.
72. "Dear Mr. Towne," *Pennsylvania Evening Post*, Nov. 16, 1775, p. 4.
73. "Mr. Towne," *Pennsylvania Evening Post*, Jan. 2, 1776, p. 3. The response is too long to quote here.

that they had sworn. An oath was a serious matter, he averred: "As religious men, they must consider the oath sacred." But the particular oath in question, from which he quoted an extract, "is so full of words of uncertain sense and import, so crammed with expressions the extent of whose signification is so undefined, and ill-limitted, that a conscientious man may readily be at a loss to know how far he may proceed with safety, and where he must stop, or be perjured."[74]

In the *Pennsylvania Evening Post* once again, on the following May 9, an unsigned letter waxed ironic at the expense of the moral and political dishonesty betrayed by the habitual use made of the word "expedient" by the King and his defenders.

> Doctor Johnson defines the word "expedient," as a thing necessary to be done, which implies, that it cannot be expedient to do evil; therefore the word "expedient" can only be applied to the promoting a good purpose, but you will find it frequently mentioned in the King's speeches; and in Parliament Ministerialists make a monopoly of it, and apply it altogether to the use and service of his Majesty, to wit, "it is become expedient to shut up the American ports;" "it is expedient to destroy their trade;" "quite expedient to take their vessels;" "expedient to bring them under our feet;" "expedient to humble them;" and highly "expedient to reduce them to absolute submission."[75]

The writer observed, therefore, that "it seems to be a court favorite word, and become high treason for an American to use it, or apply it. What would the Ministry and Parliament have done had there been no such word?" But if they had illegitimately claimed use of the word as their exclusive privilege, they had in the process also deformed it to their nefarious purposes, and Americans should henceforth shun it lest it had acquired from British misuse an irreversible taint of corruption. "We hope the Americans will

74. *Pennsylvania Evening Post*, Feb. 29, 1776, pp. 1–2.
75. "Mr. Towne," *Pennsylvania Evening Post*, May 9, 1776, p. 2.

not adopt their language, and instead of the word 'expedient,' say 'necessary;' and that it is now become highly necessary to oppose those Ministerial GRAMMARIANS, lest they should also attempt to defile our language, as they have defiled our land with blood."[76] The appeal to Dr. Johnson—a British authority—may seem at odds with the writer's protonationalist American argument, but the political-logical inconsistency is a measure of the difficulty American patriots had in making the charge of "abuse of words" stick, without borrowing from an English authority a standard of correctness.

My purpose in quoting extensively from the newspaper polemics of the period of the agitation for independence in Philadelphia is to establish how persistently language was thematized in the course of those polemics. And I have wanted to establish as well that, as nearly as surviving printed sources can suggest, such self-consciousness about language as a contested site of political action did not belong only to a more reflective elite, but was part and parcel of popular propaganda. Many scholars, in France but also in Germany and America, have recently traced such linguistic thematization in the propaganda of the French Revolution, and the effectivity of semantic innovation in the French context has been noted ever since Edmund Burke's dismayed recognition of the fact. There is no comparable body of scholarship on the linguistic dimension of the American Revolution, however. The literature on the Revolution's ideological origins, while it has in some cases taken the form of discourse analysis, has mostly been descriptive in nature, and committed to the dubious task of recovering the "true" definitions of such words as "virtue" and "liberty," rather than tracing the complex process of their semantic transvaluation.

Very recently a number of historians and political scientists, taking their cue from the massive research on French Revolutionary semantic innovation, have begun to adapt the methods of the German school of *Begriffsgeschichte* (history of concepts) to the political arguments of the period of the American Constitution. This work, while carefully done and of considerable value, still takes for the most part a fairly mechanistic view of such innovation, and

76. Ibid.

rests with describing, in a before-and-after manner, two semantic states, with the space of transformation between those states left implicit. Such an approach betrays a lack of understanding of the abstract, formal power of semantic transformation *per se,* apart from the specific content of the words being transformed. It also conflates language and concept, signifier and signified, focusing on the latter without granting the relative autonomy of the former: it is quite possible, for instance, that words may change, but the concepts they customarily signify may not—that a new word may come into an old concept, thus leaving the structure of political understanding intact while effecting an audible transformation that may yet have a decided impact.

The important lesson of post-Saussurean linguistics is that language as a differential system, in which individual terms are not essentially integral, but rather determined by their mutual interdependence with other terms, is always subject, as it were, to subtle shocks and tremors. When the meaning of one word changes, the meanings of all other words must also, however undetectably, alter. These effects are, of course, often exceedingly delicate; they may take place over long stretches of time; and they are difficult to trace with any local precision. But they are just as likely to occur in the least obvious places as in such conspicuously political words as those discussed in the extant scholarship—for instance, in the essays in a collection titled *Conceptual Change and the Constitution,* which trace shifts in the meanings of several politically charged terms (e.g., "constitution," "sovereignty," "republic," "virtue"), and in Terence Ball's *Transforming Political Discourse,* where another set of such terms is likewise traced ("power," "authority," "party," "republic," "justice," "democracy").[77]

But semantic-conceptual drift is as likely, it seems, to be detected with respect to quasi-political words like 'moderate,' 'expedient,' 'compensation,' 'demand,' and 'my country,' as it is with 'whig,' 'tory,' and other politically salient terms. And it is as likely to be found in the propaganda of the American Revolution as it

---

77. Terence Ball and J. G. A. Pocock, eds., *Conceptual Change and the Constitution* (Lawrence, Kansas: Univ. Press of Kansas, 1988); Terence Ball, *Transforming Political Discourse: Political Theory and Critical Conceptual History* (Oxford: Basil Blackwell, 1988).

is in the analogous French literature, despite the otherwise sensible and acute claims made by, for instance, Lynn Hunt in her study of the discursive and symbolic dimensions of French Revolutionary practice. Hunt distinguishes the American and French Revolutions according to several criteria: the lapsed charismatic authority of the king was replaced in America by mythic founders like George Washington, while in France "charisma came to be most concretely located in words"; in America "the written instrument of the Constitution acquired supremacy" while in France "the spoken word retained its supremacy"; American revolutionaries drew on historically legitimated British political traditions, while in France "the emphasis [was] on rejecting all models from the national past"; the "rhetoric of conspiracy . . . continued to dominate political discourse in France even after the break with the Old Regime," while in America such fears abated after the Revolution, and "American revolutionaries became much more concerned with the problems of representing the interests of different regions and social groups."[78]

All of these distinctions contribute to Hunt's central claim that "American revolutionary rhetoric did not foster the development of a revolutionary tradition; instead it fed into constitutionalism and liberal politics."[79] Conversely, French revolutionary rhetoric, on this analysis, had no self-limiting principle, no inner equilibrium, but only proceeded to greater and greater excesses; therefore the French Revolution betrayed itself in reaction, while the American Revolution created a viable republic. The obvious truth of this last fact does not, however, mean that Hunt's other claims are correct. For one, George Washington's construction as a charismatic symbolic presence was largely a posthumous, retroactive phenomenon, part of a long and contested process of creating out of an ambiguous revolutionary past usable political myths and traditions;[80] and to the extent that the cult of Washington existed during Washington's life and during the immediate postrevolutionary consolidation, it was a deeply ambivalent phenomenon,

---

78. Hunt, *Politics, Culture, and Class in the French Revolution*, pp. 26, 44, 51, 39.
79. Ibid., p. 51.
80. Michael Kammen, *A Season of Youth: The American Revolution and the Historical Imagination* (New York: Knopf, 1978).

marked by bombastic inflations and the widespread dissemination of his idolized image on the one hand, and on the other hand by such public demurrals as that of John Adams, who in Congress in 1777 said he was "distressed to see some of our members disposed to idolize an image which their own hands have molten. I speak here of the superstitious veneration which is paid to General Washington."[81] Americans, who had been schooled in monarchical forms, certainly continued to use the cognitive schemas inherited from the monarchical past even when monarchy had been repudiated, and the way in which the old forms were filled with new content is nowhere better illustrated than in Irving's concise depiction of this process of symbolic substitution in "Rip Van Winkle," where we are told that Rip, upon waking up from his sleep through the war and finding the "quiet little Dutch inn of yore" replaced by the "Union Hotel," detected nevertheless that the hotel preserved the signboard from its predecessor establishment: Rip "recognized on the sign, however, the ruby face of King George . . . but even this was singularly metamorphosed," with the old red coat now changed to blue and buff, a scepter changed to a sword, the crown replaced by a cocked hat, "and underneath was printed in large characters GENERAL WASHINGTON."[82] The decisive detail is Rip's *recognition* of the change as one of semiotic substitution, his immediate demystification of the new order of signs of authority. Barry Schwartz, in his study of the making of Washington as an American symbol, has found that despite the "presence of monarchical elements in America's veneration of Washington," Americans "contemplated their own venerational passions," evidenced a "capacity for reflexive deliberation, . . . self-inhibiting and self-correcting inner reflection" on the madeness of their symbols, and that this skepticism about their own hero-worship distinguished them in degree if not in kind from their hero-worshipping European contemporaries.[83]

The argument that the spoken word in America retained (and

81. Quoted in Barry Schwartz, *George Washington: The Making of an American Symbol* (New York: The Free Press, 1987), p. 22.

82. Washington Irving, *History, Tales and Sketches* (New York: The Library of America, 1983), p. 779.

83. Schwartz, *George Washington,* pp. 38–39.

perhaps even amplified) its charismatic authority even after the making of the written Constitution will be part of the general burden of the present study; despite recent arguments that the legitimacy of constitutional authority was intimately dependent upon the *textuality* of that instrument (which is true enough), the widespread cultural investment of authority in vocal forms like political oration and sermons created a counterpoint of anxiety about the sufficiency of textuality as a ground of authority, and inspired a widespread enchantment with vocal forms as necessary supplements to if not alternative grounds for authority.[84] Fear of conspiracy was, if anything, exacerbated in the post-Constitutional period in the United States. In general, after the Declaration of Independence, the customary authority of inherited political models no longer automatically obtained, and only a voluntary, discursively legitimated, elective adoption of old models and norms had any force. The American Revolution shared with the French Revolution, then, a thorough dependence upon vocal performance, discursive delegitimation of inherited authority and discursive institution of new authority, and other forms of linguistic and symbolic practice. The difference between the power of language in the American and French Revolutions, then (if there was a difference), was one of degree, not of kind; the persistent wish in the historiography to distinguish the two revolutions on these grounds seems to be a willful disparagement of the American Revolution as insufficiently radical, a disparagement that cooperates

84. Michael Warner, *The Letters of the Republic: Publication and the Public Sphere in Eighteenth-Century America* (Cambridge, Massachusetts: Harvard Univ. Press, 1990); see also Larzer Ziff, *Writing in the New Nation: Prose, Print, and Politics in the Early United States* (New Haven: Yale Univ. Press, 1991). Jay Fliegelman in his recent *Declaring Independence,* has demurred from Warner's argument, holding instead that Americans continued to be invested in the affective and personal powers of voice. In a subsequent essay Warner concedes, with respect to New England, that "in an important ideological way it was an oral society," but rejects as "sentimental" what he claims is the usual equation of *oral* with *preliterate* and *innocent.* I don't think scholars who recognize the widespread affective investment in orality in colonial New England or in the early national United States are necessarily as obtuse as Warner would have it. Rather, in a literate, text-oriented polity, voice would by virtue of its difference from print forms have an exceptional and new quality of authority. See Warner, "The Public Sphere and the Cultural Mediation of Print," in *Ruthless Criticism: New Perspectives in U.S. Communication History,* ed. William S. Solomon and Robert W. McChesney (Minneapolis: Univ. of Minnesota Press, 1993), p. 26.

(from a different point of view) with a reactionary historiography that seeks to contain the American Revolution within the frame of moderate politics, and that ignores the discursive continuity of the two revolutions.[85] In the pages that follow I will describe some further aspects of the discursive dimension of American Revolutionary experience, as well as trace in some measure the recognition, by such observers as Jefferson, Paine, and Tocqueville, of the ways in which language mediated historically the relation between the two revolutions.

III. Neology
The limits of my language *mean the limits of my world.*
Whatever we can describe at all could be other than it is.
Ludwig Wittgenstein

Writing to Richard Price from Paris on January 8, 1789, Jefferson acknowledged with pleasure the news that "our new Constitution . . . has succeeded beyond what I apprehended it would have done," and took this success as evidence that "whenever the people are well-informed, they can be trusted with their own government; that, whenever things get so far wrong as to attract their notice, they may be relied on to set them to rights."[86] This was when eleven states had finally ratified the Constitution, and it had gone into effect. He went on to inform Price "about the nature and circumstances of the present struggle here," having been "on the spot from its first origin" as ambassador from the American republic.[87] He testified as to the causal role the American Revolution had played in inciting the French Revolution:

> Though celebrated writers of this and other countries had already sketched good principles on the subject of government, yet the American war seems first to have awakened the thinking part of this nation in general from the sleep of despotism in which they were sunk.

85. See, in this regard, Gordon S. Wood, *The Radicalism of the American Revolution* (New York: Alfred A. Knopf, 1991).
86. Jefferson, *Writings*, p. 935.
87. Ibid., p. 935.

The officers too who had been to America, were
mostly young men, less shackled by habit and prejudice, and more ready to assent to the dictates of common sense and common right. They came back impressed with these. The press, notwithstanding its
shackles, began to disseminate them; conversation,
too, assumed new freedom; politics became the theme
of all societies, male and female, and a very extensive
and zealous party was formed, which may be called the
Patriotic party, who, sensible of the abusive government under which they lived, longed for occasions of
reforming it.[88]

Jefferson was, of course, a great partisan of the French Revolution,
and would, in August 1789, report to Diodati that it was "impossible to conceive a greater fermentation than has worked in Paris
. . . I have been thro' it daily, have observed the mobs with my
own eyes in order to be satisfied of their objects, and declare to
you that I saw so plainly the legitimacy of them, that I have slept
in my house as quietly thro' the whole as I ever did in the most
peaceable moments."[89] He conflated American and French experience by means of a version of the metaphor already cited: "The
National Assembly have now as clean a canvas to work on here as
we had in America."[90] He thus disputed the contention that
France had disowned its history, while the United States built
upon its past: both nations, on his account, secured for themselves
a new beginning. He conceded that French writers had helped
make the French Revolution possible — that it was in some measure an effect of prior French intellectual causes — and he would
also concede, as we have seen, that the American Revolutionary
utterance was to some extent a repetition of the formulas of prior
political philosophy. Thus we see here that Jefferson located in
both France and the United States the same dilemma that afflicts
all descriptions of revolutionary moments: the simultaneous recognition and denial of determination by the past. This recognition
is complicated here by the attempt to fix the causal relation be-

88. Ibid., p. 936.
89. Ibid., p. 957.
90. Ibid., p. 957

tween two revolutions: the American Revolution caused the French Revolution, but the American itself was caused (partly) by the same partly French political philosophy that also (in part) caused the French Revolution—and yet *both* of them represented absolute punctual departures from all past determinations, "clean slates" that allowed total freedom of social and political innovation. How does one uncaused effect, then, cause another uncaused effect?

Informing this double dilemma, as Jefferson represented it, was a recurrent attention to verbal phenomena: "writers," "dictates," the "press," "conversation," and so forth. Forms of linguistic "disseminat[ion]" propel, as it were, the engine of revolution, and mediate—like linguistic jumper cables—the association between the two revolutionary engines. What I wish to draw attention to now is a peculiar effect of retrodiction that operates in the writings of several authors—Jefferson, Paine, and Tocqueville especially—an effect whereby their observations of the discursive dimension of the French Revolution led them to revise, after the fact, their understandings of the American Revolution. Each of these writers noticed that the French Revolution had involved some deliberate linguistic transformations. And this led them to ask, in retrospect, if it had also been the case that the American Revolution had done so. To state it directly, the common theme I want to draw out of their writings is this: They asked themselves if, given that the American Revolution in some measure caused the French Revolution, and given that the French Revolution was explicitly and conspicuously linguistic, then must not the American Revolution have been linguistic too?

Writing in 1813 to the grammarian John Waldo, Jefferson expressed his delight at Waldo's willingness to approve of linguistic change: "I have been pleased to see that in all cases you appeal to usage, as the arbiter of language; and justly consider that as giving law to grammar, and not grammar to usage."[91] This was a direct translation of the Revolutionary theory of popular sovereignty into the domain of language. Jefferson went on to lament the efforts of "Purists" who inhibited change in English usage, and he applauded the French who had embraced change in language, and

91. Ibid., p. 1295.

even more he praised the ancient Greeks, who "were sensible that the variety of dialects, still infinitely varied by poetical license, constituted the riches of their language, and made the Grecian Homer the first of poets, as he must ever remain, until a language equally ductile and copious shall again be spoken."[92] English might well be that language, except that in Great Britain a "dread of innovation . . . and especially of any example set by France, has . . . palsied the spirit of improvement."[93] The French example, he held, was one that should be imitated — if not in England, then in the United States:

> If we wish to be assured from experiment of the effect of a judicious spirit of Neology, look at the French language. Even before the revolution, it was deemed much more copious than the English; at a time, too, when they had an academy which endeavored to arrest the progress of their language, by fixing it to a Dictionary, out of which [i.e., outside of which] no word was ever to be sought, used, or tolerated. The institution of parliamentary assemblies in 1789, for which their language had no apposite terms or phrases, as having never before needed them, first obliged them to adopt the Parliamentary vocabulary of England; and other new circumstances called for corresponding new words; until by the number of these adopted, and by the analogies for adoption which they have legitimated, I think we may say with truth that a Dictionaire Neologique of these would be half as large as the dictionary of the academy.[94]

This former president's conception of the linguistic dimension of political practice, and the analogy between the way both language and politics were structured in their transformations by questions of usage and custom, legitimation and judicious delegitimation, are impressive. They are surprising, however, from one whose

92. Ibid., p. 1296.
93. Ibid., p. 1299.
94. Ibid., pp. 1298–99.

own utterances were probably the most charismatic in all the mass
of revolutionary propaganda. Jefferson's call for a "Dictionaire
Neologique" indicates that he may not have known that Charles
Brockden Brown had published in the *Monthly Magazine* an essay
called "New French Political Nomenclature" which assembled and
defined the new political vocabulary of Revolutionary France.
"The French revolution curiously exemplifies the influence of new
situations to give birth to new ideas and to new terms," the essay
claimed. "The history of language is an important part of the history of man; and, to be unacquainted with the former, is to
be ignorant of the latter."[95] The author then listed 210 words,
phrases, and titles that qualified as "new terms," and offered definitions of them. This glossary followed immediately, in the pages
of the *Monthly Magazine,* an essay called "Statements of destruction produced by the French Revolution," which included another
list, but one that gave numerical totals of violent deaths, conspiracies, castles and villas destroyed, deaths by famine, suicides, and
so forth. This catalogue of violence was plainly an attempt to dis-
credit French political innovation, despite the essay's expressed intention of presenting "nothing but the display of an historical
fact."[96] Several months later, in the same magazine (of which
Brown was the editor, and of which he is said to have produced
most of the content),[97] an essay entitled "On the Scheme of an
American Language" appeared. This essay, signed "C.," took the

95. "New French Political Nomenclature," *The Monthly Magazine and American
Review* 2, 3 (Philadelphia, March 1800): 165. Neither this essay nor the following
one can be securely attributed to Brown himself, but I am assuming that either he
wrote them or that he approved them editorially. Their sentiments are generally in
keeping with Brown's expressed opinions on the French Revolution; on this subject see Steven Watts, *The Romance of Real Life: Charles Brockden Brown and the Origins of American Culture* (Baltimore: The Johns Hopkins Univ. Press, 1994), pp.
160–61. Both articles, the catalogue of political violence and the political lexicon,
were signed with the initials "C. D.," and their pairing was clearly meant to suggest
a grand analogy between two kinds of "destruction."
96. "Statements of Destruction Produced by the French Revolution," *The
Monthly Magazine and American Review* 2, 3 (Philadelphia, March 1800): 165.
97. Harry Warfel, in his chapter on Brown's editorship of the *Monthly Magazine,* asserts that he wrote most of the content. See Warfel, *Charles Brockden Brown:
American Gothic Novelist* (Gainesville, Florida: Univ. of Florida Press, 1949), pp.
165ff. Others have assumed the same, and the sentiments that these articles on the
French Revolution expressed are compatible with those in others of Brown's essays. See Warner Berthoff, "Brockden Brown: The Politics of the Man of Letters,"
The Serif 3, 4 (1966): 3–11.

position that while *"amor patriae,* the national spirit" may have
some valuable uses, it was "totally out of place in relation to science. Language is the vehicle of knowledge; but diversity of language is the greatest obstacle to its progress."[98] The writer — probably Brown himself — then recalled the "sublime lesson, taught in
the Hebrew scriptures, that diversity of language was introduced
to weaken, disperse, and annihilate the power, by retarding the
knowledge, and by disuniting the efforts of the species."[99] The
contrast with Jefferson's celebration of "the variety of dialects"
could not be more stark. Brown admitted, with regret, that language inevitably changed, and he was willing that new words like
"Congress, President, Capitol" and *"phlogiston* and *caloric"* should
be accepted.[100] Utterly new phenomena must find new words to
stand for them, but other innovations were unnecessary and therefore repulsive: "Diversities have risen from the nature of man,
who is at once a slave to novelty and to habit; from Indian vicinity; from intermixture of emigrants of different nations, and, particularly in the southern states, from converse with negroes; but
these diversities every one will admit to be *gross corruptions."*[101] The
contrast with Jefferson's attitude implicitly points up the contrast
that existed in the post-Revolutionary period between those who
remembered the war with satisfaction and wished its effects to lin-
ger (e.g., Jefferson), and those who recalled it with resentment
and sadness and wished its effects to be limited (e.g., Brown).
What both Jefferson and Brown recognized was that linguistic
change may be an instrument of political revolution, and that perhaps it is *after* a revolutionary war that language's instrumentality
is most powerful. Benjamin Rush, whose statement that the Revolution was fought as much with the pen as with the sword has
been adverted to above, also insisted that the war was only the
beginning of a larger, extended process of social and conceptual
change.[102]

Jefferson, as Hannah Arendt astutely noted, was unique among

98. [Charles Brockden Brown], "On the Scheme of an American Language,"
The Monthly Magazine and American Review 3, 1 (Philadelphia, July 1800): 1.
    99. Ibid., p. 1.
    100. Ibid., p. 4.
    101. Ibid., p. 3.
    102. Rush, "An Account," p. 243.

the founders in his attempt to preserve and extend the experience of revolution beyond the actual war that was its most obvious manifestation.

> The failure of post-revolutionary thought to remember the revolutionary spirit and to understand it conceptually was preceded by the failure of the revolution to provide it with a lasting institution. The revolution . . . had come to an end with the establishment of a republic which, according to the men of the revolution, was "the only form of government which is not eternally at open or secret war with the rights of mankind."[103]

The "revolutionary spirit" as defined by Arendt was a fascination with "the potentialities of action and the proud privilege of being beginners of something new."[104] But the new gets old, and the privilege of beginning is temporary.

> In this republic, as it presently turned out, there was no space reserved, no room left for the exercise of precisely those qualities which had been instrumental in building it. . . . If foundation was the aim and the end of revolution, then the revolutionary spirit was not merely the spirit of beginning something new but of starting something permanent and enduring; a lasting institution, embodying this spirit and encouraging it to new achievements, would be self-defeating.[105]

Jefferson, as Arendt recounts, was "more concerned with this perplexity than anybody else,"[106] and thus was given to take a more sanguine view of recurrent revolutionary upheaval than were most of his contemporaries. His tolerant view of Shay's rebellion and his enthusiasm for the French Revolution reflected his desire not

---

103. Hannah Arendt, *On Revolution* (Harmondsworth: Penguin Books, 1973), p. 232; embedded quotation from Jefferson's letter to William Hunter, March 11, 1790.
104. Ibid., p. 232.
105. Ibid., p. 232.
106. Ibid., p. 232.

to disown or forget the heady thrill of political innovation. Such
a desire was evident, for instance, when in writing to Adams in
1820 he proclaimed himself "a friend to *neology*," as he had also
described himself to Waldo.[107] The fabrication of new words returned him to the imaginary new beginning which he on some
occasions liked to claim the founding of the United States to be:
neology was a ritual reenactment of revolution. The practice of
improvising new words rejected the authority of the inherited, established lexicon. "If Dictionaries are to be the Arbiters of language, in which of them shall we find *neologism*. No matter. It is a
good word, well sounding, obvious, and expresses an idea which
would otherwise require circumlocution."[108] Gleefully Jefferson
experimented with the combinatory powers of language:

> And give the word neologism to our language, as a
> root, and it should give us it's fellow substantives, ne-
> ology, neologist, neologisation; it's adjectives neolo-
> gous, neological, neologistical, it's verb neologise, and
> adverb neologically. Dictionaries are but the deposit or-
> ies of words already legitimated by usage. Society is
> the work-shop in which new ones are elaborated.
> When an individual uses a new word, if illformed it is
> rejected in society, if wellformed, adopted, and, after
> due time, laid up in the depository of dictionaries.[109]

Writing on the same theme to John Waldo in 1813, in the letter
already cited, Jefferson had insisted on the utter necessity of such
improvisation in America, also reflexively using the word *neology*
as its own illustration.

> I am no friend . . . to what is called *Purism*, but a zeal-
> ous one to the *Neology* which has introduced these two
> words [i.e., "purism" and "neology"] without the au-
> thority of any dictionary. I consider the one as destroy-
> ing the nerve and beauty of language, while the other
> improves both, and adds to its copiousness. I have not

107. Jefferson, *Writings*, p. 1442.
108. Ibid., p. 1442.
109. Ibid., p. 1443.

been a little disappointed, and made suspicious of my own judgment, in seeing the Edinburgh Reviews, the ablest critics of the age, set their faces against the introduction of new words into the English language; they are particularly apprehensive that the writers of the United States will adulterate it. Certainly so great growing a population, spread over such an extent of country, with such a variety of climates, of productions, of arts, must enlarge their language, to make it answer its purpose of expressing all ideas, the new as well as the old. The new circumstances under which we are placed, call for new words, new phrases, and for the transfer of old words to new objects. An American dialect will therefore be formed.[110]

What is interesting here is not only that new American circumstances should be thought to require new names, but that a thoroughgoing analogy makes of the lexical system a figure for the nation. Each specific new thing requires a specific new word, and these new coinages will cumulatively expand the lexicon; but the growth and expansion of the nation *per se* requires an unmotivated burgeoning of language *in toto* as well. Language as a productive machine must realize its own inherent capacity for growth and mutation simply as a correlative of the growing and spreading of the American people. "Its enlargement must be the consequence, to a certain degree, of its transplantation from the latitude of London into every climate of the globe."[111] But this determination is only "to a certain degree." Aside from this practical necessity, its enlargement will be due merely to a "freedom of employing its elements," an "encouraging and welcoming new compositions of its elements," "a free use of its faculties," that is, to an abstract principle of change for change's sake.[112] It is this pleasure of sheer unnecessary creative performance that is most striking in Jefferson's "visions on the improvement of the English language."[113]

110. Ibid., pp. 1295–96.
111. Ibid., p. 1299.
112. Ibid., p. 1299.
113. Ibid., p. 1299.

IV. History and Language

History exists only in and through 'language' (all sorts of languages), but history gives itself this language, constitutes it and transforms it.

Cornelius Castoriadis

There has lately been considerable scholarly interest in the various ways in which the French Revolution realized itself by means of linguistic and symbolic transformations.[114] But the linguistic turn in understanding that event first took place during and immediately after its occurrence, and has been a theme of historians ever since. According to Tocqueville, "A study of the connection between the history of language and history proper would certainly be revealing," and he observed that the "word 'individualism,' which we have coined for our own requirements, was unknown to our ancestors."[115] Michelet mentioned the advent of "new

114. See, for instance, Marc Eli Blanchard, *Saint-Just & Cie: La Révolution et les mots* (Paris: Libraire A.-G. Nizet, 1980); François Furet, *Interpreting the French Revolution,* trans. Elborg Foster (Cambridge: Cambridge Univ. Press, 1981); Hans Ulrich Gumbrecht, *Funktionen parlamentarischer Rhetorik in der Französischen Revolution: Vorstudien zur Entwicklung einer historischen Textpragmatik* (München: Wilhelm Fink Verlag, 1978); Patrice L.-R. Higonnet, "The Politics of Linguistic Terrorism and Grammatical Hegemony during the French Revolution," *Social History* 5 (1980): 41–69; Hunt, *Politics, Culture, and Class in the French Revolution;* Hunt, "The Rhetoric of Revolution in France," *History Workshop* 15 (1983): 78–94; Martyn Lyons, "Politics and Patois: The Linguistic Policy of the French Revolution," *Australian Journal of French Studies* 18 (1981): 264–81; Mona Ozouf, *Festivals and the French Revolution,* trans. Alan Sheridan (Cambridge, Massachusetts: Harvard Univ. Press, 1988); Ronald Paulson, *Representations of Revolution 1789–1820* (New Haven: Yale Univ. Press, 1983); Judith Schlanger, *L'Enjeu et le Débat: L'invention intellectuelle* (Paris: Denoël/Gauthier, 1979); Jean Starobinski, *1789: The Emblems of Reason,* trans. Barbara Bray (Charlottesville: Univ. Press of Virginia, 1982).
See as well the three reference works in the mode of *Begriffsgeschichte:* Otto Brunner, Werner Conze, and Reinhart Koselleck, eds., *Geschichtliche Grundbegriffe: Historisches Lexikon zur politisch-sozialen Sprache in Deutschland,* 7 vols. to date (Stuttgart: Klett-Cotta, 1972–); Rolf Reichardt and Eberhard Schmitt, eds., *Handbuch politisch-sozialer Grundbegriffe in Frankreich, 1680–1820,* 2 vols., Heft 1/2 and 3/4 to date (München: R. Oldenbourg Verlag, 1985–); Joachim Ritter and Karlfried Gründer, eds., *Historisches Wörterbuch der Philosophie,* 8 vols. to date (Basel: Schwabe & Company, 1971–). Melvin Richter's two essays, "Conceptual History (*Begriffsgeschichte*) and Political Theory," *Political Theory* 14 (1986): 604–37, and "*Begriffsgeschichte* and the History of Ideas," *Journal of the History of Ideas* 48 (1987): 247–63, survey this field usefully.
115. Alexis de Tocqueville, *The Old Régime and the French Revolution,* trans. Stuart Gilbert (Garden City, New York: Doubleday/Anchor, 1955), pp. 83, 96.

forms and new words" in France in the 1780s.[116] Burke, in his celebration of the "prejudices" that secured man's connection to his forebears, the "sullen resistance to innovation, . . . the cold sluggishness of our national character," repeatedly emphasized the way the whole symbolic order of a national culture derived its meaningfulness from its sedimented, thickly interconnected nature, and not from abstract significations.[117]

What is a revolution? A revolution is what it turns out to have been. This is true in the simple sense that the American Revolution, say, if it had failed, would not have been the American Revolution, but the unsuccessful revolt or uprising in the British American colonies. It is what it is on account of its consequences; it was what it was on account of what it effected. And one of the American Revolution's effects, according to a certain interpretation, was the French Revolution. According to this interpretation, the American Revolution, as it turned out to have succeeded, was a condition (perhaps a necessary condition, though obviously not a sufficient one) for the French Revolution.[118] And if this is so, then the French Revolution, as an effect of the American Revolution, is part of what the American Revolution turned out to be, and it redefines retroactively what the American Revolution was, in effect (as we say). Countless Francophobe Americans in the 1780s and 1790s took just this view, as they fashioned theories of French-inspired conspiracies threatening to destroy the Union.[119] Despite their paranoid fantasies of Illuminati and other subversive groups, they had a point: a revolution is a meaningful event, a product of intentional activity, and what it means depends upon

116. Jules Michelet, *The History of the French Revolution,* ed. Gordon Wright, trans. Charles Cocks (Chicago: Univ. of Chicago Press, 1967), p. 18.

117. Edmund Burke, *Reflections on the Revolution in France* (with Thomas Paine, *The Rights of Man*) (Garden City, New York: Anchor/Doubleday, 1973), pp. 100, 99.

118. A good general article on the importance of the American model for French revolutionaries is Joyce Appleby, "America as a Model for the Radical French Reformers of 1789," *William and Mary Quarterly,* 3d ser., 28 (1971): 267–86.

119. A selection of contemporary American paranoid responses to the French Revolution is included in David Brion Davis, ed., *The Fear of Conspiracy: Images of Un-American Subversion from the Revolution to the Present* (Ithaca, New York: Cornell Univ. Press, 1971), pp. 35–65.

what it will come to mean, and what the American Revolution came to mean was, in part, the French Revolution. Jefferson, as we have seen, recognized this effect, and he also played an actual role in creating it. He had had a decisive role in precipitating the American Revolution, and then, as Washington's ambassador to France, actively promoted the French Revolution, conferring with Lafayette and other political leaders. It was precisely the glamour of his American Revolutionary role that authorized him, in French eyes, to advise the French in effecting their Revolution; and it was, in some degree, his glamour (and stigma) as a "Jacobin" that authorized him, upon his return to America, to lead the "French" party in the first national electoral contests, and eventually to lead what came to be referred to as the "revolution of 1800"[120] — the second American Revolution, which brought him to the presidency. And the "revolution of 1800" had a retroactive effect on the American Revolution of 1776 — made it, in effect, what it came to have been.

In the phenomenalism of historical understanding, effects precede causes, and they do so because, unlike poems, historical events cannot just be, but must mean. That is, they must have a meaning imputed to them, and this can be done most effectively in hindsight, when history is written. The meaning of an event is not intrinsic to it, but is attributed to it, both near to the time of its occurrence and later (and earlier). "In the phenomenalism of the 'inner world' we invert the chronological order of cause and effect. The fundamental fact of 'inner experience' is that the cause is imagined after the effect has taken place."[121] Such historical hindsight may pay some respect to what historical foresight or prophecy would have liked a projected or anticipated event to mean, or what contemporaries and agents of the event may have taken it to mean. But if a historical event sometimes comes to mean what it had been expected or intended to mean, it also sometimes turns out to have meant something else. Or it may happen that an historical event turns out to have meant a little of all

---

120. Jefferson, *Writings,* p. 1425.

121. Friedrich Nietzsche, *The Will to Power,* ed. Walter Kaufman, trans. Walter Kaufman and R. J. Hollingdale (New York: Vintage Books/Random House, 1968), p. 265.

of these: what it was expected to mean, what it was intended to mean, and what it happens to have meant. In any case, there is no escaping the necessity of an historical event's meaning being an effect of deferral and consequence.

I outline these mildly bewildering possibilities and structures of reversal of cause and effect since one of the ways the French Revolution figured in the literature of Federalist and Republican America was as the deferred action of the American Revolution, and as the relay station (as it were) between the revolutions of 1776 and 1800. The extent to which the politics of the new American nation was defined in terms of the French Revolution is notorious, and it is one aspect of this definitional or figurative power to which I have been attending: the way the linguistic aspects of the French Revolution came to inform the way the American Revolution came to be understood.

This was an aspect of the debate over the conservative or radical nature of the American Revolution, a debate that has traditionally been cast in terms of a purported difference between the French and American Revolutions. This was a sticking point between, for instance, Adams and Jefferson. Adams's comment on the matter, in a letter of July 13, 1813, is to the point:

> The first time, that you and I differed in Opinion on any material Question . . . was [on] the french Revolution.
>
> You was well persuaded in your own mind that the Nation would succeed in establishing a free Republican Government: I was as well persuaded, in mine, that a project of such a Government, over five and twenty millions people, when four and twenty millions and five hundred thousands of them could neither write nor read: was as unnatural irrational and impracticable; as it would be over the Elephants Lions Tigers Panthers Wolves and Bears in the Royal Menagerie, at Versailles. Napoleon has lately invented a Word, which perfectly expresses my Opinion at that time and ever since. He calls the Project Ideology.[122]

122. Cappon, ed., *Adams-Jefferson Letters,* vol. 2, pp. 354–55.

It is not quite true that Napoleon invented the word "ideology" — that honor belongs to Destutt de Tracy[123] — but Adams's contention, that the French Revolution was just such an event as to require the coining of new descriptive terms, remains valid. It is essentially the same contention as that of Jefferson, except that Adams gave it a negative valuation, while Jefferson thought it a good thing. And just as Jefferson's observation of the agency of neology in the French Revolution led him to reinterpret the American Revolution as having also been a linguistically performed event, so Adams's dislike of the French Revolution led him, retrospectively, to question the value of its American precedent, and to deplore the linguistic innovations that informed both. When Benjamin Rush wrote to him (August 20, 1811) attempting to soothe his wounded pride by assuring him that his patriotic heroism would in the end be credited by history, Adams was both flattered and unbelieving, and worried that if his revolutionary agency was to be known by its fruits, he might just as soon disclaim credit:

> Like Louis the 16, I said to myself, "Qu'est ce que J'ai fait pour le meriter?" [What have I done to merit this?] Have I not been employed in mischief all my days? Did not the American Revolution produce the French Revolution? And did not the French Revolution produce all the calamities and desolations to the human race and the whole globe ever since? I meant well however.[124]

If the French Revolution, then, was a matter of "ideology" — a matter, as it were, of speaking with a misplaced rationality to uncomprehending illiterates — and if, as such, it was an effect of the American Revolution, then must not the American Revolution have been ideological too, that is, an irrational effect of a rational cause?

Adams did not trust that words would call into being their adequate objects: the reasoned discourse and responsible arguments of republican theorists might have instigated the American Revolution, but the American Revolution did not produce a society that could live according to the precepts of that discourse. Rush's purpose in flattering Adams was to persuade him to set the historical record straight by writing his own history of the Revolution, his own interpretation of its meaning.

> Suppose you avail yourself while in health of the sensibility which awaits the public mind to your character soon after your death by leaving behind you a posthumous address to the citizens of the United States, in which shall be inculcated all those great national, social, domestic, and religious virtues which alone can make a people free, great, and happy.[125]

The deferred effect of such a message would be, Rush stated, to correct the contemporary misunderstandings of the Revolution and Adams's role in it. "I fancy I hear a cry for a sight of your voice from the tomb such as was excited by Mark Antony for the reading of Caesar's will."[126] Rush's double prosopopeia — imagining he heard a voice from the future, summoning Adams's voice from its grave (strangely, a "sight" of that voice) — is a brilliant figure for the way history is constructed in the interpenetration of prolepsis and metalepsis, expectation and remembrance. Adams was no more willing to believe that his posthumous pronouncements would have their intended effect — would be received and understood as he wished them to be — than he was willing to believe that his pre-Revolutionary utterances had eventuated in the effects they were meant to produce. In justification of his reluctance to gratify Rush's request, Adams ran through a whole catalogue of the misunderstandings and misrepresentations to which his utterances and actions had been subject throughout his public career; but, as if to correct for such distorting mediations homeopathically, he volunteered to put his name to any such address that Rush should have composed, or that Jay or Trumbull or Hum-

125. Ibid., p. 190.
126. Ibid., pp. 190–91.

phreys or ("perhaps") Jefferson should have written. In any case,
such an address would have needed to be "revised, corrected,
obliterated, interpolated, amended, transcribed twenty times, pol-
ished, refined, varnished, burnished,"[127] as if to exhaust the possibilities of deferral and deviation to which such a message was ordinarily subject, and thereby preempt such deformations as those to
which he feared it would be prone after his death.

No writer's attitude toward these questions could be more opposed to Adams's than was Paine's. Adams, in fact, regularly invoked Paine as an example of the kind of abuser of words who
thereby disrupted the communicative order and made unexpected
disasters occur. But Paine, on the contrary, seems to have willfully
promoted such assaults on the canons of language precisely as a
means of subjecting history to a salutary indeterminacy. And in
this he, too, found the space between the two revolutions to be a
crucial field in which such coimplications of language and history
were observable and manipulable.

Paine's *The Rights of Man* (1791–92), in reply to Edmund
Burke's scathing attack on the goals and methods of the French
Revolution, claimed that one of those methods — the extravagant
use of language — was perfectly legitimate. At the same time, and
somewhat inconsistently, it described the language of the old regime as unnatural, and credited the Revolution with restoring a
natural language. Among the words that fell into the former cate-
gory were titles: "The French Constitution says, *there shall be no
titles;* and of consequence, all that class of equivocal generation,
which in some countries is called '*aristocracy*,' and in others '*nobility*,' is done away, and the *peer* is exalted into *man*."[128] Having "out-
grown the babyclothes of *count* and *duke*," France had "breeched"
itself. "The insignificance of a senseless word like *duke, count*, or
earl, has ceased to please."[129] Paine's assumption that childhood
was governed by words, while adulthood required that the subject
be released from the sway of language, inverts the tenet of recent
linguistic and psychological theory, which holds that subjecthood
is precisely the interpellation of the individual into the order of

127. Ibid., p. 194.
128. Thomas Paine, *The Rights of Man* (with Edmund Burke, *Reflections on the Revolution in France*) (Garden City, New York: Anchor/Doubleday, 1973), p. 318.
129. Ibid., p. 318.

language. But Paine held it to be otherwise. "The genuine mind of man, thirsting for its native home, society, contemns the gew-gaws that separate him from it. Titles are like circles drawn by the magician's wand, to contract the sphere of man's felicity. He lives immured within the Bastille of a word, and surveys at a distance the envied life of man."[130] The "Bastille of a word" calls to mind the modern critical commonplace of the prison-house of lan-guage, the sense of language as a confining structure, determining patterns of thought and enforcing social norms. Paine traded on a similar intuition, and intensified its power by naming that sym-bol of old-regime tyranny, the Bastille. But what the imprisoned imagination of man saw through the bars of that linguistic prison was not nature — the world of natural things — but "society," the "life of man," only a society of a more natural sort. "Through all the vocabulary of Adam, there is no such an animal as a duke or a count; neither can we connect any idea to the words."[131] (A crown, he would say, was merely a "metaphor," a "name," and hence a "fraud.")[132] Paine's linguistic allegory condensed the gen-eral theme of a society founded on natural relations — a theme that had been immensely important to the political theory of both Revolutions — and gave it a characteristic linguistic coloration.

Throughout *The Rights of Man,* figures of language reappeared, sometimes in the context of describing the historical relation be-tween American political independence and the French Revolu-tion. In refuting Burke's claim that the French Revolution had been a sudden irrational eruption, Paine claimed that it had only "*apparently* burst forth like a creation from a chaos, but it is no more than the consequence of a mental revolution previously ex-isting in France."[133] And that previous mental revolution had been precipitated by the textually embodied influence of American events.

> As it was impossible to separate the military events which took place in America from the principles of the American Revolution, the publication of these events

130. Ibid., p. 319.
131. Ibid., p. 319.
132. Ibid., p. 364.
133. Ibid., p. 332 (italics added).

in France necessarily connected themselves with the
principles which produced them. Many of the facts
were in themselves principles; such as the declaration
of American independence, and the treaty of alliance
between France and America, which recognized the
natural right of man, and justified resistance to op-
pression.[134]

The chain of circumstances connecting American political upheaval with its French effects included as one of its links the
agency of Franklin's diplomacy, which obtained an "influence"
over Count Vergennes.[135] It was Franklin who persuaded Vergennes to allow the translation and publication of the state constitutions of the United States, and in relating this textual event
Paine elaborated another linguistic metaphor:

Count Vergennes resisted for a considerable time the
publication in France of the American Constitutions,
translated into the French language; but even in this
he was obliged to give way to public opinion, and a
sort of propriety in admitting to appear what he had
undertaken to defend. The American Constitutions
were to liberty, what a grammar is to language: they
define its parts of speech, and practically construct
them into syntax.[136]

Thus American political experience became, as it were, *langue* to
the French Revolution's *parole,* competence to its performance.
The linguistic system of American political liberty, once acquired,
could not then be unlearned, according to Paine. In refuting
Burke's and others' wish for a counter-revolution, Paine developed
the same metaphor: "There does not exist in the compass of language, an arrangement of words to express so much as the means
of effecting a counter-revolution. The means must be an oblitera-
tion of knowledge; and it has never yet been discovered how to

134. Ibid., pp. 333–34.
135. Ibid., p. 334.
136. Ibid., p. 334.

make a man *unknow* his knowledge, or *unthink* his thoughts."[137] Or unsay what has been said, we might add. The claim is debatable, of course, but its expression by means of the vehicle of Paine's metaphor is evidence of how thoroughly his understanding of historical processes was informed by the model of linguistic action.

A further variation on this figure came when Paine addressed the question of the authority of precedent. Burke had, of course, centered his arguments on the necessity of a positive valuation of precedent. Paine thought otherwise: "Governments now act as if they were afraid to awaken a single reflection in man. They are softly leading him to the sepulchre of precedents, to deaden his faculties and call his attention from the scene of revolutions."[138] This "sepulchre of precedents," he wrote, was like a dictionary: "If every thing that can happen is already in precedent, legislation is at an end, and precedent, like a dictionary, determines every case."[139] The implication of this figure is clear: If precedent is like a dictionary, which "determines every case" — that is, establishes the correctness of usage — then revolution is like *in*correct usage, a deformation of language, refusing determination by received canons of propriety. Revolution would necessarily involve ungrammaticality, neology, and other kinds of deviation from the linguistic norm.

* * *

In construing the American and French Revolutions in these linguistic terms, Paine may have been remembering his own practice as a propagandist in 1776 in Philadelphia. Writing as "The Forester," he had contended in print with a "typographical Cato,"[140] as he called him, who had been debating in the newspapers, principally with another anonymous writer called "Cassandra." Cato had started a controversy in the *Pennsylvania Packet* on March 11, 1776, by urging that the British peace commissioners, then re-

137. Ibid., p. 358.
138. Ibid., p. 432.
139. Ibid., pp. 432–43.
140. Paine, *Complete Writings,* vol. 1, p. 61.

ported to be on their way to America, be greeted with a sincere disposition on the part of the colonists to negotiate in good faith. Immediately suspected as a secret loyalist, he was attacked by many respondents, who often reflected upon his use of language. The Forester, in his first letter, quoted Cato's remark that "the true interest of America lies in *reconciliation* with Great Britain on *constitutional principles*," but he found these words suspiciously vague:

> This is a curious way of lumping the business indeed! And Cato may as well attempt to catch lions in a mousetrap as to hope to allure the public with such general and unexplained expressions. It is now a mere bugbear to talk of *reconciliation* on *constitutional principles* unless the terms of the first be produced and the sense of the other be defined; and unless he does this he does nothing.[141]

And more: "Cato is exceedingly fond of impressing us with the importance of our '*chartered constitution*.' Alas! We are not now, Sir, to be led away by the jingle of a phrase."[142] Paine decried Cato's "little popular phrases" which were "only the gildings under which the poison is conveyed," and deplored his use of a "stale and hackneyed phrase," that is, Cato's claim "*that the eyes of all Europe are* upon us."[143] This phrase, Paine wrote,

> has had a regular descent, from many of the king's speeches down to several of the speeches in Parliament; from thence it took a turn among the little wits and bucks of St. James's; till after suffering all the torture of senseless repetition, and being reduced to a state of vagrancy, it was charitably picked up to embellish the second letter of Cato. It is truly of the bugbear kind, contains no meaning, and the very using it discovers a barrenness of invention. It signifies nothing.[144]

141. Ibid., vol. 1, p. 62.
142. Ibid., vol. 1, p. 63.
143. Ibid., vol. 1, pp. 64, 65.
144. Ibid., vol. 1, p. 65.

Here not grammar or usage, but cliché was the sign of attachment to the status quo—signified historical precedent or repetition. Against "senseless repetition" Paine proposed "invention," and this term carried with it a traditional connotation of rhetorical invention as well as a political connotation of new fabrication; in fact, it conflated the two, identifying political innovation with rhetorical creation.

Paine continued to criticize Cato's linguistic expression: "Cato's manner of writing has as much order in it as the motion of a squirrel."[145] But he admitted that his own language had grown extravagant: "He [Cato] frequently forces me out of the common track of civil language, in order to do him justice; moderation and temper being really unequal to the task of exposing him."[146] Quoting a particularly unintelligible passage from one of Cato's letters, Paine responded with exasperation: "Art thou mad, Cato, or art thou foolish—or art thou *both*—or art thou *worse* than both? In this *passage* thou hast fairly gone beyond me. I have not language to bring thee back."[147] Cato himself criticized in his fourth letter (March 27, 1776) the language of Paine's *Common Sense:* its doctrines were "out of the common way—bold, marvellous, and flattering," and hence belied the title: "Is this *common sense* or common nonsense?"[148] He particularly quarreled with the notion of a declaration of independence: "I am not able, with all the pains I have taken, to understand what is meant by a Declaration of Independence; unless it is to be drawn up in the form of a solemn abjuration of *Great Britain,* as a nation with which we can never more be connected."[149] Paine then replied, in the Forester's second letter (April 8, 1776):

> Cato seems possessed of that Jesuitical cunning which
> always endeavors to disgrace what it cannot disprove;
> and this he sometimes effects, by unfairly introducing
> *our* terms into *his* arguments, and thereby begets a
> monster which he sends round the country for a show,

145. Ibid., vol. 1, p. 69.
146. Ibid., vol. 1, p. 71.
147. Ibid., vol. 1, p. 73.
148. Peter Force, ed., *American Archives,* 4th Series, 6 vols. (Washington, D.C.: Published by M. St. Clair Clarke and Peter Force, 1837–46), vol. 5, pp. 514, 515.
149. Ibid., vol. 5, p. 516.

and tells the good people that the name of it is *independence.* . . . Such an unfair and sophistical reasoner doth
not deserve the civility of good manners. He creates
. . . confusion by frequently using the word *peace* for
union.[150]

In his third Forester letter, Paine claimed falsely "that I scarcely
ever quote," but his motive for this claim is important: "The reason is, I always think."[151] In the fourth letter, he formulated the
attack on precedent that, as we have seen, he would later elaborate
in *The Rights of Man:* "When precedents fail to spirit us, we must
return to the first principles of things for information; and *think,*
as if we were the *first men* that *thought.*"[152] To think in this way
was never to quote; to abjure cliché, stale repetition; to invent,
and if necessary to break the linguistic rules, to go verbally "out
of the common track"; to close the dictionary of received ideas
and verbal formulas and speak into being an unprecedented
nation.

Paine's figuration of revolution as linguistic action was, as we
have seen, a constant presence in his political writing, as his writing was a constant instance of the phenomenon the figure represented. His observation of the French Revolution, with its prominent linguistic dimension, led him to recall his own involvement
in the propaganda of the American Revolution, and his figuration
of its enactment as a matter of linguistic deformation. Having established the agency of language in both revolutions, he was led to
describe the historical relation between them as itself a linguistic
relation: *langue* to *parole,* grammar to enunciation, competence to
performance. Implicitly, however, the order of cause and effect
was not unidirectional: the French Revolution, as an effect, was
the cause of Paine's reformulation of the American Revolution as
a linguistic precedent, just as Jefferson's observation of the French
Revolution had made him a convert to neology, and to the agency
of language in the perpetuation of the revolutionary moment in
America.

150. Paine, *Complete Writings,* vol. 1, p. 73.
151. Ibid., vol. 1, p. 78.
152. Ibid., vol. 1, p. 83.

V. Letters

In history, this is my hypothesis, epistolary fictions multiply when there arrives a new crisis of destination.

Jacques Derrida

Benjamin Franklin's understanding of the discursive dimension of revolutionary action was formed, in part, by his experience in one of the most revealing episodes of his political career, the affair of the so-called Hutchinson letters. What he discovered during this affair, as his statements on it show, was that the political tie that subsisted between Great Britain and the colonies was a tie constructed of words. There was, in the eighteenth century, no other way for an imperial power to govern far-flung dominions except by the protracted and uncertain means of messages sent on ships across oceans. Such messages were long in transit, dangerously susceptible to diversion, and equally susceptible to misconstruction when they reached their destination. Such messages (for example, instructions to royally appointed governors) might miss their mark for various reasons: perhaps the conditions they addressed might be already irrelevant by the time the circuit of communications was traveled. Despite such risks, however, there was no other route for power to take than that of language stretched over time and space.

If words were the form that the exercise of imperial power must have taken, then resistance to that power also necessarily took the form of linguistic performance. Franklin's interference, in the affair of the Hutchinson letters, with the transmission of messages between colony and crown is a promising site for the examination of these issues. The editors of the Franklin *Papers,* it seems, recognized implicitly that this was so when they repeatedly referred, in their annotations of documents having to do with this episode, to the missives in question as "purloined" letters, and to their mysterious deviation from their proper itinerary as their "purloining."[153] This adjective and this gerund allude, it seems, to Poe's famous tale, and they characterize the enigmatic qualities of this episode

---

153. Benjamin Franklin, *The Papers of Benjamin Franklin,* ed. Leonard W. Labaree, William B. Willcox, Barbara B. Oberg et al., 30 vols. to date (New Haven: Yale Univ. Press, 1959–) 19: 399, 402, 405; 21: 38.

in Franklin's public career by borrowing some of the glamour of Poe's tale of senders, receivers, and displacements. But they take the adjective, as it happens, directly from Thomas Moffatt, the Rhode Island loyalist, some of whose letters were among the stolen correspondence, and who wrote on a copy of a letter of Franklin's that came into his possession (a letter that discussed the Hutchinson letters affair) that the correspondence was "purloined from the Collection of the late Mr. Whatley."[154] A point Franklin would make in extenuation of his own role in the theft of the letters was that his own correspondence had been stolen, too, and Moffatt's notation confirms this. The symmetry of thefts can be taken as a figure of reciprocity: the reciprocity of miscommunication. For as I shall try to show, the deviation of a letter in its travels from writer to addressee acts, in the texts that record this event, as a figure for the uncertainty of communication between imperial sender and colonial receiver (and vice versa). It was characteristic of Franklin to conceive of the political relationship as a communicative or linguistic relationship, and of course that is what it largely was; so the affair of Hutchinson's letters functioned synecdochically, one instance of imperial-colonial miscommunication standing for political miscommunication in general.

Rather than elaborate upon the analogy between Poe's tale and Franklin's experience, I will outline the basic features of the notorious episode in Franklin's life, and describe some of the terms of Franklin's attitude toward it, terms which help to specify Franklin's troubled, uncertain, conflicted, but prescient conceptualization of the historical situation of the American colonies in the 1760s and 1770s, and the prospects for political reconciliation or revolution. The facts: In 1772, Franklin clandestinely obtained some letters that Massachusetts Governor Thomas Hutchinson and Lieutenant Governor Andrew Oliver had written to English authorities (principally Thomas Whately, a member of Parliament and former Secretary of the Treasury who had been involved in drafting the Stamp Act) from 1767 to 1769, when Hutchinson and Oliver had been lieutenant governor and province secretary, respectively. In their letters they urged that repressive measures be taken to maintain colonial subjection. Whoever it was who gave Franklin the

154. Ibid., 19: 399n.

letters would not permit copies to be taken, but did allow Franklin to send the original letters to the Committee of Correspondence of the Massachusetts House of Representatives on the condition that they should not be copied or printed in Boston either, but carefully returned after perusal. The Massachusetts legislators who read them were alarmed to find their governor, as they saw it, plotting against the welfare of Massachusetts. Eventually the letters were copied, against Franklin's relayed instructions, and then printed. The identity of the person who had obtained them in England was made an issue: Franklin, as the agent of the Massachusetts legislature, was an obvious suspect, but only when a duel was fought between John Temple and William Whately after Temple accused Whately of having leaked the letters, did Franklin publicly avow his role in the matter. (William Whately was the brother and executor of Thomas Whately, who died in June 1772.) The duel was fought inconclusively in December 1773, and in order to prevent another duel Franklin published a statement acknowledging his responsibility for sending the letters to America. He therefore exculpated the duelists, but brought a load of scorn upon his own head.

In justifying his leaking of the letters, Franklin had to rationalize the obvious impropriety of his actions, and this gave him cause to rethink his attitude toward British power. During much of 1773, while rebellion was forming in Massachusetts and repressive measures were being formulated in the royal administration, Franklin, as London agent for the Massachusetts House, corresponded regularly with Thomas Cushing, Speaker of the House. In his letters, he regularly conceived of the growing conflict in oral and aural terms. On January 5, 1773, he urged Cushing to try to limit agitation in Massachusetts. It was Lord Dartmouth's "Opinion that if the Americans continued quiet," offensive administrative measures "would be reconsidered," and Franklin therefore concluded with his own firm advice: "I think our Prudence is mean while to be quiet."[155] In March he again urged restraint: "I must hope that great Care will be taken to keep our People quiet."[156] When Cushing replied, he attributed Franklin's recommendation of verbal re-

155. Ibid., 20: 8, 10.
156. Ibid., 20: 99.

straint to the court: "It is in Vain for administration to flatter themselves that the People here will rest quiet."[157] This was not really a misattribution, however; Franklin was, in fact, voicing the fondest wishes of the court. And when the Massachusetts House adopted a declaration asserting independent powers, Franklin urged Lord Dartmouth not to take it seriously: it was "*Words* only*,*" and Parliament, he said, should "turn a deaf Ear" to it.[158] He did, however, insist that Dartmouth should not expect the declaration to be withdrawn, since the colony "is all of one Mind upon the Subject" and "there was not . . . a single dissenting Voice" when it was approved.[159] Quietness, in all of this, meant social peace; and the insurrectionary voices, though unanimous, were uttering "*Words* only." In this scene of royal-colonial political dialogue, Franklin exhibited at once a nervous fear of utterance, and an equally nervous bad-faith denigration of it.

He soon persuaded himself, however, that the publication of the letters would not necessarily have the dire effects he feared. In August 1773 he proposed to Lord Dartmouth that the colonists, "having lately discovered, as they think, the authors of their grievances to be some of their own people, their resentment against Britain is thence much abated."[160] This represented wishful thinking, and Franklin may not have believed it, but only meant it as a strategic lie to induce the ministry to put the blame on Hutchinson and Oliver, as the colonists (according to Franklin) had done, and thereby restore good will between the colonies and the crown. In a letter to a newspaper at the end of August he made the same recommendation. Of the British government he said, "It is in their Power to make an honourable Sacrifice of the wicked Authors of this dangerous Deception."[161] That is, Franklin proposed to use the time-honored scapegoating device to reconcile the colonies and the crown.[162]

157. Ibid., 20: 124.
158. Ibid., 20: 201.
159. Ibid., 20: 202.
160. Ibid., 20: 373.
161. Ibid., 20: 381.
162. Bernard Bailyn's biography, *The Ordeal of Thomas Hutchinson* (Cambridge, Massachusetts: The Belknap Press of Harvard Univ. Press, 1974), has a chapter on the scandal of the letters that is the best general treatment of the episode; called

The scapegoats would be Hutchinson and Oliver, but in a more fundamental sense the scapegoat would be miscommunication.[163] In the letter to the *Public Advertiser*, he anonymously suggested that the scandal of the Hutchinson letters provided, paradoxically, an opportunity for "re-establishing Peace and Harmony between Great Britain and her Colonies" by removing the "Falshoods" and "Misrepresentation" that had interfered with understanding. He went so far as to propose that all "confidential Letters" between public officials in America and their superiors in London be made public: if the "Seal of Secrecy" were broken, and all private communications made public, a new transparency would obtain between sender and receiver, one that would ensure renewed political unity.[164] Sender and receiver would reunite in the ritual sacrifice of "Falshood" and "Misrepresentation."

At about the same time that he was propounding this theory of communicative transparency as a political panacea, however, Franklin was himself creating some static on the lines of communication by sending contradictory messages along other routes, pursuing a strategy of communicative opacity. I refer to Franklin's anonymous newspaper satires, some of the best of which were appearing concurrently with the Hutchinson letters scandal. In those letters to the press Franklin employed his powerful arsenal of witty rhetorical devices, and by means of such deflections, distortions, and deformations of language, he sought, ostensibly, to reconcile the parties, but in effect to separate them. Chiefly he was ironical: he said what he meant by saying what he didn't mean, and he did so in at least one case so effectively (or ineffectively)

"The Scape-Goat," it foregrounds the metaphor that Franklin deployed to such effect. Instances of Franklin's use of the metaphor may be found in his *Papers* at 20: 381 and 21: 430, 431.

163. The work of Michel Serres, for instance *The Parasite,* trans. Lawrence R. Schehr (Baltimore: Johns Hopkins University Press, 1982), provides an interesting conflation of the scapegoating device and the theory of communicational disturbance via the figure of the parasite (*parasite* in French means "static"), who acts as a disruptive, noisy third party to an otherwise symmetrical exchange (economic, communicational). The exclusion of the interference, in the interest of restoring communicational transparency, is analogous to the sacrifice of the scapegoat in the interest of restoring political/economic stasis. It isn't possible to explore this matter here, but the conflation of these two functions in the figure of the parasite is fairly prevalent in Franklin's writing.

164. Franklin, *Papers* 20: 381.

that what he thought he meant was almost lost. In "An Edict by
the King of Prussia" (September 22, 1773), Franklin's own message almost went astray—got purloined, if you will—when his
irony was so fine as to go almost undetected.

The "Edict" first appeared in the *Public Advertiser,* and was then
quickly reprinted (as was customary in the London press at
that time) in other newspapers. One of the reprintings was in the
London Chronicle, and about this reprinting Franklin made some
comments to his son William, the royal governor of New Jersey.
Writing to William, he repeated his theory that the king and his
American subjects could be reunited over the dead body, as it
were, of certain sacrificial victims: the ministers and Parliament
were obstructions preventing communication between the king
and the colonists. "I know your sentiments differ from mine on
these subjects," Franklin wrote to his son; "You are a thorough
government man, which I do not wonder at, nor do I aim at con-
verting you." He recognized that his son was in the same position
with respect to the fraught political situation as had been Hutchinson, and he urged William only to avoid the "duplicity" that had
led Hutchinson into trouble.[165]

Franklin's own communications with his son, he recognized,
were disrupted by a kind of static on the wires, and his letter represented a final attempt to reinstitute understanding between them.
But at the same time he again introduced new elements of communicative obstruction between them: he enclosed in his letter
copies of several of his newspaper satires, which, despite his
avowal of a desire to reconcile, had the effect of inciting distrust.
These writings, he admitted to William, were cast in "out-of-the-
way forms,"[166] their language distorted by powerful rhetorical
effects which were far from transparent: "Lord Mansfield I hear
said of it, that it *was very* ABLE *and very* ARTFUL indeed, and
would do mischief by giving here a bad impression of the measures of government."[167] When discussing the material form these
satires took, Franklin admitted as much:

165. Franklin, *Writings,* p. 886.
166. Ibid., p. 886.
167. Ibid., p. 886.

> It is reprinted in the Chronicle, where you will see it,
> but stripped of all the capitalling and italicing, that in-
> timate the allusions and marks the emphasis of written
> discourses, to bring them as near as possible to those
> spoken: printing such a piece all in one even small
> character, seems to me like repeating one of Whitfield's
> sermons in the monotony of a school-boy.[168]

The essay was, in fact, cast in the elaborate typographical manner
Franklin preferred: particular words printed in italics, or in all capitals or all small capitals, or large capitals and small capitals, and
so forth. Such baroque typographical devices attract attention to
the graphic form of the utterance, and detract from its simple verbal meaning. These mannerisms of printing style probably looked
less busy to readers in 1773 than they do to us now, but their
elimination by the *Chronicle* when it reprinted the article is a sign
that such devices were going out of favor. And even to an eye
accustomed to them, they must have been conspicuous: otherwise
they would not have had the effect they aimed to create. In Franklin's view, this foregrounding of the graphic surface, as it were, of
the utterance, was intended precisely to conjure the phonic image:
to bring the "written discourses . . . as near as possible to those
spoken." They represented the cadences, emphases, and other
paralinguistic qualities that supplement the strictly linguistic features of the discourse. There is an obvious analogy between such
graphic exorbitances and vocal inflections, but it is nevertheless
paradoxical that *visual* static should have the task of restoring an
imaginary *vocal* effect.

Franklin assumed here, of course, the traditional valuation of
the imputed presence, fullness, authenticity, and truth of speech,
and the correlative devaluation of writing as a derived, supplementary, corrupt, and possibly false translation of speech. He also attributed to spoken language a quality of transparency, but suggested that quality by means of graphic opacity. Thus two formal
structures of the "Edict" reinforced one another: rhetorical com-

168. Ibid., p. 886.

plication (irony) was meant to restore clarity of communication, and typographical complexity was meant to reinstate simple vocal expression. And each of these analogous structures found another analogy in Franklin's belief that by stealing letters — interrupting the flow of messages — transparency and clarity might be restored between George III and the American colonies. Ironical indirection and typographical noise were, in this perspective, self-consuming artifacts that magically erased the interferences they embodied, and mail theft similarly reestablished (Franklin hoped) the lines of communication.

* * *

The King of Prussia, in the "Edict" that Franklin's satire represented, was himself a parodist. He parodied the claims that the British government made in justifying its taxation. He recalled that "the first German Settlements made in the Island of *Britain,* were by Colonies of People, Subjects to our renowned Ducal Ancestors," and that these colonies "have flourished under the Protection of our august House, for Ages past, [and] have never been *emancipated* therefrom."[169] The German "colony" of Great Britain had been draining resources from its political parent for years, without paying the cost of military protection. Therefore these "Descendants of our antient Subjects"[170] still owed obedience to the German crown, and owed money too; thus new taxes were ordered. England's trade with other countries, according to this "Edict," would be required to pass through German ports, and raw materials from England would have to be taken to Germany for manufacture. In return for this monopoly of the metal ores, wool, furs, and other natural resources of England, certain products would be sent in return: the German jails would be emptied,

---

169. Ibid., p. 699. Franklin calls here upon the so-called Saxon myth, of which I will have more to say with respect to Brown's use of it in *Wieland* (see chapter 2). On the use made by American revolutionary leaders of this historical myth see H. Trevor Colbourn, *The Lamp of Experience: Whig History and the Intellectual Origins of the American Revolution* (Chapel Hill: Univ. of North Carolina Press, 1965), pp. 28, 30–31, 48, 55–56, 183–84, 191, 194–98.

170. Ibid., p. 699.

and the criminals transported to Great Britain. The laws enacted for these purposes, according to the "Edict," would be copied verbatim from various English laws enacted there in respect of British colonies in America and Ireland.[171] Here the irony was made rather obvious, but in case anyone had missed the point, Franklin spelled out the satire at the end:

> Some take this Edict to be merely one of the King's *Jeux d'Esprit:* Others suppose it serious, and that he means a Quarrel with England: But all here think the Assertion it concludes with, "that these Regulations are copied from Acts of the English Parliament respecting their Colonies," a very *injurious* one: it being impossible to believe, that a People distinguished for their *Love of Liberty,* a Nation so *wise,* so *liberal in its Sentiments,* so *just and equitable* towards its *Neighbours,* should, from mean and *injudicious* Views of *petty immediate Profit,* treat *its own Children* in a Manner so *arbitrary* and TYRANNICAL![172]

Franklin's intellectual strategy was brilliant: the legitimacy of Great Britain's abusive rule of America was put into question by attributing the identical policies to Germany and making England the abused colony. In doing this, however, Franklin didn't only delegitimate the abuses; he implied, additionally, that as legitimate political authority was historically inherited, Great Britain's sovereignty over America was not original, but depended in turn upon putative German authority over Great Britain. Franklin instituted a series of derivations, a logic of dependency, that effectively disintegrated the whole project of guaranteeing political legitimacy by reference to a potentially infinite regression of historical origins: British authority was imaginatively demolished by the recursive pattern. The historical series that Franklin described — the genealogy of authority — was itself, on his account, constructed of a train of verbal performances, a *textual* history. Just as British authority over America was exercised via words — declarations, edicts, letters

171. Ibid., p. 702.
172. Ibid., pp. 702–703.

of instruction, and so forth — so too did German authority over Great Britain take the form of performative utterance.

This conceptualization of the genealogy of authority was repeated in Franklin's statements on the affair of the Hutchinson letters. We should remember that during the entire affair, Franklin was still deputy postmaster of the colonies, earning his commission on the profits of the postal service. Thus it was the postmaster — the man whose responsibility was to ensure that messages reached their destination and that their privacy was preserved — who diverted these letters, who opened someone else's mail. It should come as no surprise, then, that on the day following the hearing before the Privy Council — the famous encounter in the Cockpit when Solicitor General Wedderburn excoriated Franklin as "*a man of letters; homo* trium *literarum*" (i.e., *fur,* "thief")[173] — Franklin was stripped of his postmastership. Franklin did not seem to understand this punishment: as he wrote in a letter published in American newspapers shortly after his humiliation, "The Post Office in America thro' *his* care and management of it alone, is rais'd from *nothing,* to produce £3000 sterl. annually, *clear* to the treasury. This comes out of the pockets of the Colonists. Though it is not a revenue in principle, it is in effect. It grows daily more and more valuable by the increase of correspondence."[174] That Franklin should conceive it to be an injustice that the postmastership be denied to a man who received stolen mail and circulated it illicitly was rather odd; that he should protest the supposed injustice by bragging of the money he produced for the mother country was even odder. When we remember that it was precisely the efficiency and reliability of the American post office, along with its expanded network of routes and frequency of delivery, that helped create colonial union by knitting the separate colonies together communicatively — well, the ironies multiply. Franklin had curried favor with the crown in 1755 by setting up mail communications for Major-General Edward Braddock, commander of British forces in North America,[175] when Braddock and his army had been sent to defend the colonies and by their presence inhibit the formation of a union of the colonies of the sort Franklin had

173. Franklin, *Papers,* 21: 49.
174. Ibid., 21: 82.
175. Franklin, *Writings,* p. 1435.

proposed in his Albany Plan. What he was unable to establish politically, then, he helped to establish by this other means, under
the guise of aiding Braddock's efforts to forestall such unification.
Franklin's position as postmaster, more or less from start to finish,
then, was an enactment of his political ambivalence: he was simultaneously the British placeman boasting of his service to the
crown, and he was the patriotic American warning his comrades
that once the postal service was out of his hands, the security of
communications between the various colonial committees of correspondence would be at risk. Newly appointed postal officials,
sent from England, might even open the mail of the committees
of correspondence, Franklin warned.[176]

There is an obvious analogy between the tactics of the committees of correspondence — which sought to exclude the British third
party from the circuit of colonial communications — and those of
Franklin, as he sought to exclude the royal officials from the chain
of communication between colony and crown. Much of the thinking — and the fantasies of conspiracy — of both the committees of
correspondence and Franklin was governed by the metaphor of
correspondence. Letters from colonies addressed to the king were
intercepted by ministers and not transmitted to the crown, they
thought. If only the mail were delivered, the king would reply
favorably. Franklin's own letters to Cushing and the Massachusetts
Assembly were frequently intercepted — by Hutchinson himself
among others — and their contents divulged. Franklin, needless to
say, was no proponent of openness when it was his own communications being published. Each of Franklin's letters to Cushing
cited the dates of his previous letters, as did Cushing's to Franklin,
to enable each of them to know if some of the letters had been
stolen — as, it turned out, many of them had. Such divulgence
might be endemic to the project of long-distance imperial rule:
the very exercise of government is committed to the mail, and
to the deferrals and disruptions occasioned by packet boats crossing the Atlantic. Thus there were reasons why — literally, so to
speak — the British Empire could be represented in terms of relations of communication.

What emerges from such conceptions is a master metaphor:

176. Franklin, *Papers*, 21: 83.

The relation of historical descent, mother country or patria to colonial offspring, is refigured as a transmitting of messages. These
messages are the carriers of political legitimacy. The letters sometimes go undelivered, or their delivery is refused, or the mail is
diverted from its appointed destination. And if destination here
has a connotation of destiny, then it stands to reason that the
divergence of history accomplished by revolution is quite well
figured as the purloining of letters.

VI. Words

*The generality of the word institutes a common world. The
ethical event at the basis of generalization is the underlying
intention of language.*

                                              Emmanuel Levinas

Among the most acute observations of American society in the
decades following independence were those that Washington Irving made in *Salmagundi* (1807–8),[177] particularly in the letters
ascribed to the Tripolitan prisoner, Mustapha Rub-a-Dub Keli
Khan. Irving's use of the device of an oriental persona, whose bewilderment and astonishment in the face of the alien American
culture nicely relativized its norms, was a great stroke: it achieved
a powerfully defamiliarizing effect.[178] As Emmanuel Levinas has
written, "The absolutely foreign alone can instruct us."[179] What
was otherwise taken for granted in American political culture,
what went unremarked by a member of that society, seemed remarkable and nearly unaccountable to the fascinated Muslim

177. For convenience I will adopt the convention of speaking of Irving as the
author of *Salmagundi,* although it was, of course, a collaboration between him, his
brother William Irving, and James Kirke Paulding. Although the authorship of the
individual parts cannot be determined absolutely, Bruce I. Granger and Martha
Hartzog, the editors of the 1977 Twayne edition (of which the text I quote is a
reprint), venture some attributions; their attributions to Washington Irving are
given in Irving, *History, Tales and Sketches,* (New York: The Library of America,
1983), p. 1104. They suggest that the Mustapha letters in *Salmagundi* XI, XVI,
and XIX were by Irving. The first of those concerns logocracy. My guess is that,
given the prominence of similar satire in *The History of New York,* the theme of
"windy war" was Irving's primarily, even if his collaborators were responsible for
the earlier Mustapha letters.
178. Irving very likely encountered this device in Montesquieu's *Persian Letters*
(1721), if not elsewhere.
179. Levinas, *Totality and Infinity,* p. 73.

stranger. Irving's reader was then allowed to see his own country from the perspective of that stranger, who had an outsider's privileged vantage point, and could tell things about America that Americans didn't know.

Here is the first of these revelations: "I find that the people of this country are strangely at a loss to determine the nature and proper character of their government."[180] Even their "dervises" (leaders) were ignorant on this point, and yet "continually indulging in the most preposterous disquisitions on the subject; some have insisted that it savors of an *aristocracy;* others maintain that it is a *pure* democracy; and a third set of theorists declare absolutely that it is nothing more nor less than a *mobocracy*" (p. 143). Such an observation undoubtedly offended American common sense in 1807, as did Mustapha's representation of Americans as "in the dark," "poor infidels," "unenlightened by the precepts of Mahomet," and so forth (pp. 143, 144). This would be the constant theme of these oriental letters: the Americans were self-deluded, "totally ignorant of their own true character" (p. 144). And this method of conceptual inversion, whereby Mahometanism became enlightenment and Enlightenment became darkness, would also be Mustapha's constant practice. Although the American nation was more like a mobocracy than either of the other alternatives, according to this foreign observer, the truth was otherwise:

> To let thee at once into a secret, which is unknown to these people themselves, their government is a pure unadulterated LOGOCRACY or *government of words.* The whole nation does everything *viva voce,* or, by word of mouth, and in this manner is one of the most military nations in existence. Every man who has, what is called, the *gift of the gab,* that is, a plentiful stock of verbosity, becomes a soldier outright, and is forever in a military state. The country is intirely defended *vi et lingua,* that is to say, by *force of tongues.* (p. 144)

This is an immensely condensed presentation of a number of related themes having to do with language and authority. Every-

180. Irving, *History, Tales and Sketches,* p. 143. Further page references will be given parenthetically.

thing is done "*viva voce,* or, by word of mouth": this is Irving's claim, as I take it, for the supersession, in the American republic, of traditional forms of political legitimation by discursive legitimation. Nothing can be taken for granted; everything must be justified. After "the modern democratic revolution," according to Claude Lefort, a theorist of this modern historical transition,

> Power appears as an empty place and those who exercise it as mere mortals who occupy it only temporarily or who could install themselves in it only by force or cunning. There is no law that can be fixed, whose articles cannot be contested, whose foundations are not susceptible of being called into question. . . . Democracy inaugurates the experience of an ungraspable, uncontrollable society.[181]

Or, in the idiom of Jürgen Habermas, social norms can now be routinely thematized, challenged, and contested; hence they must be rationalized, tested, and argumentatively justified. Their universal (or at least general) validity must be asserted and supported with reasons, so as to engineer consent; and this can only be done verbally.[182] Irving's Mustapha claimed, first, that Americans did not agree as to the location of political authority—it might be vested in the few (aristocracy), the many (pure democracy), or the unlettered multitudes (mobocracy). But in fact—given this fundamental disagreement, which needed to be mediated—it could only be located in words (logocracy), since only words could mediate such normative dissensus.

The basic legitimacy deficit of the new nation, on this account, meant that fundamental differences were always threatening to erupt dangerously. Mustapha reported that the Americans "are the most warlike, and I must say, the most savage nation that I have as yet discovered among all the barbarians. They are not only at war (in their own way) with almost every nation on earth, but

---

181. Claude Lefort, *The Political Forms of Modern Society: Bureaucracy, Democracy, Totalitarianism,* ed. John B. Thompson, trans. Alan Sheridan, Terry Karten, and J. B. Thompson (Cambridge, Massachusetts: The MIT Press, 1986), p. 303.

182. Jürgen Habermas, *Legitimation Crisis,* trans. Thomas McCarthy (Boston: Beacon Press, 1975), pp. 105–110.

they are at the same time engaged in the most complicated knot of civil wars that ever infested any poor unhappy country on which ALLA has denounced his malediction" (p. 144). And their remedy for the fragility of social norms that produced both their internal differences and their external enmities was to produce a constant hum of difference-mediating utterance. "Every offensive or defensive measure is enforced by *wordy battle,* and *paper war; he* who has the longest tongue, or readiest quill, is sure to gain the victory" (p. 144). Beneath the illusion of social coherence yawned an abyss of total conflict. Irving seems to have sensed that language was not necessarily a pacifying medium: its mediations of social differences might very well sometimes exacerbate conflict, or perhaps they usually did. Throughout his writing there appeared an implicit claim that utterance was essentially domination, that interlocution was never an experience of perfect equality and reasonable exchange, but rather one of terror, intimidation, or deception.

The military metaphor was retained throughout Mustapha's letters. "There has been a civil war carrying on with great violence for some time past," he wrote, the logomachy occasioned by the alleged skepticism of the American "bashaw" respecting both the biblical account of the deluge, and the story of Balaam's ass; the bashaw (Jefferson) "maintaining that this animal was never yet permitted to talk except in a genuine logocracy, where it is true his voice may often be heard, and is listened to with reverence as 'the voice of the sovereign people'" (p. 145). For seven years (the length of time Jefferson's administration had then been in office), the president's supporters and detractors had carried on "a most inhuman war, in which volumes of words have been expended, oceans of ink have been shed," with various "slang-whangers" (editorialists) making "furious attacks upon each other and upon their respective adherents, discharging their heavy artillery, consisting of large sheets, loaded with scoundrel! villain! liar! rascal! numskull! nincompoop! dunderhead! wiseacre! blockhead! jackass!" (p. 146). Irving was, of course, referring to the violent quarrels between Republicans and Federalists during Jefferson's administration. Jefferson himself was the object of much of Irving's satire, as he would be in *A History of New York* (1809), where the same themes would be rehearsed. What was important in *Salmagundi*, however, was not Irving's opinion of Jefferson, but rather the notice he took of the unprecedented verbal violence of the period, and the massive quantity of volatile political utterance that attended the inception of new political norms. What amazed Mustapha (and, presumably, Irving too) was that despite the conflicts tearing apart the fabric of the nation, it yet endured. The social conflict was substantially limited to the realm of spoken and written communication; the discussion was violent, but it did not end in violence. It just went on and on. Language provided a medium which established, at least formally, a common ground where opposed parties could meet. They might meet there only to disagree, but they were joined there in at least the minimal sense of confronting one another. It would not be too much to claim that Irving's denomination of America as a "logocracy" was meant to suggest that in the endemic legitimation crises that beset the new nation — in the absence of established institutions of social control and traditional means of securing consent — the *only* social institution readily available to the young republic was language itself.

* * *

The extraordinary verbosity of the American nation, according to Mustapha, was exemplified by the Congress:

> This is a blustering windy assembly where every thing is carried by noise, tumult, and debate; for thou must know, that the members of this assembly do not meet together to find out wisdom in the multitude of counsellors, but to wrangle, call each other hard names and hear *themselves talk.* When the congress opens, the bashaw first sends them a long message (i.e. a huge mass of words — *vox et preterea nihil*) all meaning nothing; because it only tells them what they perfectly know already. Then the whole assembly are thrown into a ferment, and have a *long talk,* about the quantity of words that are to be returned in answer to this message. (p. 147)

The talking went on in "little juntos of *talkers*, called committees," and then went on some more when the full Congress reconvened; the talking went on so long that by the time debate was finished, the moment had passed when action might be taken on the matter at hand. And "it is an even chance that the subject of this prodigious arguing, quarreling, and talking, is an affair of no importance" anyway, and that therefore "the whole nation have been talking to no purpose" (pp. 147–48). Even so, the logocracy was bitterly divided by the words that were exchanged.

> Unhappy nation — thus torn to pieces by intestine talks! never, I fear, will it be restored to tranquility and silence. Words are but breath — breath is but air; and air put in motion is nothing but wind. This vast empire, therefore, may be compared to nothing more nor less than a mighty windmill, and the orators, and the chatterers, and the slang-whangers, are the breezes that put it in motion; unluckily, however, they are apt to blow different ways, and their blasts counteracting each other — the mill is perplexed, the wheels stand still, the grist is unground, and the miller and his family starved. (p. 148)

This extended metaphor was marvelously apt: in the post-Revolutionary period, it was precisely the contested status of social norms and values that gave rise to the vigorous verbal contention that Mustapha noted. Every verbal exchange — every conversation or debate — contains as its implicit goal the creation of understanding or agreement. It contains, that is, an implicit teleology. What Irving lamented was not so much the talking as the "talking to no purpose" or talking at cross-purposes. Consequently the practical activities of the nation were inhibited, economic development was stalled, and the citizenry deprived of the benefits that would result from rational coordination and cooperation among individuals. At the time of Irving's writing, the deprivation that was most on his mind was doubtless that resulting from the Jeffersonian policy of economic embargo, which caused numerous shortages of manufactured goods and considerable domestic economic hardship. But the image referred more generally

to the problems of an emerging capitalist state and the legitimation problems attendant upon its uncertain power to regulate the
economy. Jefferson figured conspicuously in Irving's satire: he was
the "reigning bashaw . . . at the very top of the logocracy." According to Mustapha, "He is a man of superlative ventosity, and
comparable to nothing but a huge bladder of wind. He *talks* of
vanquishing all opposition by the force of reason and philosophy;
throws his gauntlet at all the nations of the earth and defies them
to meet him—on the field of argument!" (p. 149). Alluding to a
series of recent political issues in the United States, Mustapha
claimed that Jefferson's response to each was an ineffectual verbal
challenge: American commerce was molested by British ships, and
Jefferson "utters a *speech.*" American citizens were forcibly removed
from American ships and detained on board British warships—
the reference, of course, was to the Chesapeake-Leonard affair—
and Jefferson "utters a *speech.*" Aaron Burr and his alleged cocon-
spirators plotted an insurrection in the west, and Jefferson "utters
a speech!—nay, more, for . . . he most intrepidly dispatches a cou-
rier on horseback, and orders him to ride one hundred and twenty
miles a day, with a most formidable army of *proclamations,* (i.e. a
collection of words) packed up in his saddle-bags" (p. 149). It was
as if he could "speechify and batter by words the conspiracy and
the conspirators out of existence" (p. 150). Naturally, Jefferson's
own account of the effectiveness of his verbal measures was
different: he marveled that "a simple proclamation informing the
people of these combinations, and calling on them to suppress
them," had entirely succeeded in stopping the progress of Burr's
insurrection.[183] No matter the accuracy of Irving's and Jefferson's
respective evaluations; what is striking is their mutual recognition
of the historical situation in which they found themselves, a situation which required that popular consent be manipulated rhetorically. Jefferson thought it the easiest thing in the world to do, and
a very good thing to be done; Irving thought otherwise on both
counts. For both of them, however, "tranquillity and silence" signified social consensus, and "the noise and tumult of debate" was
an indication of dangerous social crisis. Jefferson wrote to Thomas

183. Thomas Jefferson, *The Writings of Thomas Jefferson*, ed. Paul Leicester Ford,
10 vols. (New York: G. P. Putnam's Sons, 1892–99), 9: 66.

Cooper in 1802, "A noiseless course, not meddling with the affairs of others, unattractive of notice, is a mark that society is going on in happiness."[184] In the same year he agreed with Dupont de Nemours' assertion that "Il y a dans les etats unis un bon sens silencieux, un esprit de justice froide" ("There is in the United States a silent good sense, a spirit of cool justice"), and in corroboration quoted a "plain country farmer [who] has written lately a pamphlet on our public affairs. . . . His words are 'The tongue of man is not his whole body. So, in this case, the noisy part of the community was not all the body politic.'"[185] Thus, according to the "reigning bashaw," the "noise and tumult of debate" that Irving had found to be endemic to the logocracy was actually a superficial phenomenon, a surface effect created by a disgruntled minority of Federalist partisans.

The theme of unanimity Jefferson had announced in his first inaugural address—"We are all Republicans, we are all Federalists"[186]—became his great article of faith.

> During the contest of opinion through which we have passed the animation of discussions and of exertions has sometimes worn an aspect which might impose on strangers unused to think freely and to speak and to write what they think; but this being now decided by the voice of the nation, announced according to the rules of the Constitution, all will, of course, arrange themselves under the will of the law, and unite in common efforts for the common good.[187]

He would thereafter refer confidently, as in his first annual message to Congress, to "that progress of opinion which is tending to unite [the American people] in object and will."[188] He would periodically reassure others—and himself—that this was not mere wish-fulfillment, as when in 1805 he wrote to Volney that "the two parties which prevailed with so much violence when you were here, are almost wholly melted into one," even though the Feder-

---

184. Jefferson, *Writings,* p. 1110.
185. Ibid., p. 1099.
186. Ibid., p. 493.
187. Ibid., p. 492.
188. Ibid., p. 509.

alist leaders "still make as much noise as if they were the whole nation."[189] In the letter to Dupont de Nemours already cited, Jefferson supported his claim of unanimity by an "appeal to the testimony of my farmer, who says 'The great body of the people are one in sentiment. If the federal party and the republican party, should each . . . frame a constitution of government or a code of laws, there would be no radical difference in the results of the two conventions.'"[190] It was not himself, as Irving would have had it, but the few remaining "royalists or priests" who were *"vox et preterea nihil,* leaders without followers."[191]

VII. Orator Mums

Language is perhaps to be defined as the very power to break the continuity of being or of history.

                         Emmanuel Levinas

It is notable, that Irving should have chosen Jefferson to exemplify "ventosity," when Jefferson was wont to refer frequently to his intense personal aversion to verbal contention, what he called, in a letter to Washington in 1791, "my love of silence & quiet, & my abhorrence of dispute."[192] It was, as I have said, Jefferson's habit, as it was Irving's, to conceive of society and politics in terms of voice, speech, and language, and his own reticence and pauciloquence were notorious. When writing to his grandson Thomas Jefferson Randolph in 1808, at the end of his presidency, his accumulated exasperation with the violence of political discourse in America prompted him to pass on to the young man some considered advice:

> In stating prudential rules for our government in society I must not omit the important one of never entering into dispute or argument with another. I never yet saw an instance of one of two disputants convincing

189. Ibid., p. 1158.
190. Ibid., p. 1100.
191. Ibid., p. 1100.
192. Jefferson, *Writings,* p. 978.

the other by argument. I have seen many on their getting warm, becoming rude, and shooting one another. . . . It was one of the rules which above all others made Doctr. Franklin the most amiable of men in
society, 'never to contradict any body.'[193]

Franklin, as we shall see in the next chapter, imagined consistently
throughout his career that such verbal self-constraint would have
the effect, if practiced generally, of mitigating the fissiparous tend-
encies of the American body politic. Social and political differences, when they remained unspoken and unheard, would be as
good as nonexistent. Thus Jefferson was following the true Frank-
linian model when he urged his grandson to practice not merely a
calculated reticence when he found himself among the "illtemp-
ered and rude men in society who have taken up a passion for
politics," but even an undeviating taciturnity: "Be a listener only,
keep within yourself, and endeavor to establish with yourself the
habit of silence, especially in politics."[194]

Jefferson recommended silence not merely as a means of self-
protection, a way of removing oneself from the arena of verbal
combat; he believed that in a political context of noisy commo-
tion, a studied silence could gain for one a special authority. This
was something Franklin had discovered early in his career and had
used to great advantage, and Jefferson had made it his practice too.
George Washington was notoriously quiet in company as well.
Jefferson wrote of them both in his *Autobiography:* telling of the
"trifling but wordy debate" in Congress on the ratification of the
Treaty of Paris, when he was asked by a fellow representative, John
F. Mercer (who was himself "afflicted with the morbid rage of
debate, of an ardent mind, prompt imagination, and copious flow
of words"), how he could remain quiet, Jefferson justified his silence by citing his "willing[ness] to listen" and his satisfaction if
others made the necessary arguments.[195] If they didn't, he would
"suggest the omission" but refrain from "going into a repetition
of what had been already said by others."

193. Ibid., p. 1195.
194. Ibid., p. 1196.
195. Ibid., p. 52.

And I believe that if the members of deliberative bodies were to observe this course generally, they would do in a day what takes them a week, and it is really more questionable, than may at first be thought, whether Bonaparte's dumb legislature which said nothing and did much, may not be preferable to one which talks much and does nothing. I served with General Washington in the legislature of Virginia before the revolution, and, during it, with Dr. Franklin in Congress. I never heard either of them speak ten minutes at a time, nor to any but the main point which was to decide the question.[196]

All of them—Washington, Jefferson, and Franklin—qualified, therefore, as what Irving called "*orator mums*" (p. 181). Mustapha Rub-a-Dub Keli Khan, having witnessed "innumerable contests of the tongue in this talking assembly" (p. 180)—the Congress— noticed that during one particularly trivial debate "several gentlemen . . . who had never been known to open their lips in that place except to say *yes* and *no*" had finally weighed in with their thoughts. In the critical circumstances of this "most strenuous and eloquent debate about patching up a hole in the wall of the room," a debate that was carried out into the public sphere where it "came well nigh producing a civil war of words throughout the empire," dividing the country into parties of "the *holeans* and the *anti-holeans*," these silent orators had, by virtue of their very silence, acquired a powerful charismatic authority (pp. 180, 181). "These silent members are by way of distinction denominated *orator mums*, and are highly valued in this country on account of their great talents for silence—a qualification extremely rare in a logocracy" (p. 181). Irving may not have considered Jefferson an orator mum—he was rather more inclined to consider him the opposite, not only in *Salmagundi* but in *The History of New York* as well, where he presented him in the guise of Wilhelmus Kieft, or William the Testy, whose comical magniloquence essentially repeated the portrait of the Jeffersonian bashaw drawn in *Salmagundi*. Wil-

196. Ibid., p. 53.

liam the Testy also had a ridiculous misplaced faith in the performative power of utterance. In response to the encroachment of the Yankees upon the territory of New Netherlands, his decision was to utter a proclamation, explaining in his first address to the legislature "that he had taken measures to put a final stop to these encroachments — that he had been obliged to have recourse to a dreadful engine of warfare, lately invented, awful in its effects, but authorized by direful necessity. In a word, he was resolved to conquer the Yankees — by proclamation!"[197] This "engine" was "perfect in all its parts, well constructed, well written, well sealed and well published — all that was wanting to insure its effect, was that the Yankees should stand in awe of it" (p. 519), which they unaccountably failed to do. A second proclamation, "written in thundering long sentences, not one word of which was under five syllables," ordering a cessation of all commerce between the nations, was equally ineffective (p. 520). When a frontier fortress of the Dutch was surrounded by Yankee settlements, it was plain to William the Testy — "the rage of the little man was too great for words, or rather the words were too great for him" — that more decisive action was required, and so he indulged himself in "enormous execrations . . . anathematizing the Yankees" (p. 525), with equally dire results. When the Yankees appeared to be preparing to invade New Amsterdam itself, William the Testy defended the city with a trumpeter, Anthony Van Corlear, "who as the story goes, could twang so potently upon his instrument, as to produce an effect upon all within hearing, as though ten thousand bagpipes were singing most lustily i' the nose" (p. 526). Finally the legislature, despairing of William the Testy's verbal measures, sent an army under the command of Stoffel Brinkerhoff to meet the enemy at Oyster Bay on Long Island, where they found the Yankees "armed with no other weapons but their tongues, and . . . with no other intent, than to meet him on the field of argument" (pp. 529–30). The Dutch army's nonverbal measures defeated the New Englanders easily.

William the Testy's trust in the material efficacy of words was further satirized, in a manner that again reflected fairly undis-

197. Irving, *History, Tales and Sketches,* p. 517. Further page references to *The History of New York* will be given parenthetically.

guisedly on Jefferson, when Irving stated that among the many books William had read, "he unluckily stumbled over a grand political *cabalistic word*" (p. 535), which determined all of his policies. Such was the magical power of this word that Irving, in the character of his narrator, Diedrich Knickerbocker, searched the literature of theology, witchcraft, and philosophy to find its origin, but to no avail. "In all my cabalistic, theurgic, necromantic, magical and astrological researches, from the Tetractys of Pythagoras, to the recondite works of Breslaw and mother Bunch, I have not discovered the least vestige of an origin of this word, nor have I discovered any word of sufficient potency to counteract it" (p. 536). The word was "no other than *economy*—a talismanic term, which by constant use and frequent mention, has ceased to be formidable in our eyes, but which has as terrible potency as any in the arcana of necromancy" (p. 536). The spell cast by this word had led William to ignore the expensive military needs of the nation, and hence leave it undefended—which was a standard Federalist criticism of Jefferson's notorious resistance to a standing army and attendant dislike of government spending.

In *The History of New York,* this critique of Jefferson as a man charmed by words, and hence unconscious of real material exigencies of statecraft, was a local instance of a general treatment of the priority of language in American political culture and United States history. This theme was introduced at the very beginning of the book, where the necessary metalepsis of historiographical reconstruction was brilliantly parodied. Knickerbocker discussed the various available conflicting accounts of the origin of the world, each of which was unimpeachably self-consistent and none of which (as far as he could tell) had any greater claim on belief than any other. He therefore decided to recognize that causes follow from effects, "that this globe really *was created*" since "the formation of the globe and its internal construction, were first necessary to the existence of this island [Manhattan], as an island—and thus the necessity and importance of this part of my history, which in a manner is no part of my history, is logically proved" (pp. 398–99). Again, Knickerbocker reasoned from present facts to necessary preconditions to assert that while all the various discrepant accounts of the European discovery of the American continent

were attractive, he would rest with the logical fact "that this country *has been discovered*" (p. 403). Likewise with the origin of the
natives: "this part of the world has actually *been peopled* (Q. E. D.)"
(p. 411). This recognition that historical necessity was an illusion
of retrospection led Knickerbocker to the further assumption that
historical truth was an effect of retrodiction: "For after all, gentle
reader, cities *of themselves,* and in fact empires *of themselves,* are
nothing without an historian," and even "the world — the world,
is nothing without the historian!" (pp. 379, 380). Knickerbocker
would thereafter in his narrative maintain the conceit that what
happens — what happened — was an effect of his writing, was
made to have happened by the present acts of his linguistic performance. It then became one of Irving's standard comic devices to
identify the historian's written performance with the action he was
describing. Having narrated the first transatlantic migration (the
Puritans came over to enjoy "the inestimable luxury of talking"
on "this loquacious soil" [p. 494]), Knickerbocker expressed his
expectation that his readers would then be eager to dispense with
further preliminaries. But to explain and justify his intention to
disappoint such impatience, he constructed an elaborate analogy
between the historical writer's work with his pen and the colonists'
work with their axes and plows, and the analogy was one example
of this identification of historical writing with the past events written of.

> Think you the first discoverers of this fair quarter of
> the globe, had nothing to do but go on shore and find
> a country ready laid out and cultivated like a garden,
> wherein they might revel at their ease? No such
> thing — they had forests to cut down, underwood to
> grub up, marshes to drain, and savages to exterminate.
>
> In like manner, I have sundry doubts to clear away,
> questions to resolve, and paradoxes to explain, before
> I permit you to range at random; but these difficulties,
> once overcome, we shall be enabled to jog on right
> merrily through the rest of our history. Thus my work
> shall, in a manner, echo the nature of the subject, in the
> same manner as the sound of poetry has been found by

certain shrewd critics, to echo the sense—this being
an improvement in history, which I claim the merit of
having invented. (p. 404)

The semantic double duty of the word *history*—referring at once
to the discourse and the thing discoursed of—here nicely condensed the theme of performative retrodiction. Further instances
of narrative self-reflection abound in the book. The theme culminated, however, when Knickerbocker explained in Book VI that
his method of research and writing was proof against the intrusion
of false teleology into his story. Writing of Peter Stuyvesant's
march against the Swedes and their governor, Jan Risingh, at Fort
Christina, he professed his ignorance of what would ensue:

> Thus I have fairly pitted two of the most potent chief-
> tains that ever this country beheld, against each other,
> and what will be the result of their contest, I am
> equally anxious with my readers to ascertain. This will
> doubtless appear a paradox to such of them, as do not
> know the way in which I write. The fact is, that as I
> am not engaged in a work of imagination, but a faith-
> ful and veritable history, it is not necessary, that I
> should trouble my head, by anticipating its incidents
> and catastrophe. On the contrary, I generally make it
> a rule, not to examine the annals of the times whereof
> I treat, further than exactly a page in advance of my
> own work; hence I am equally interested in the prog-
> ress of my history, with him who reads it, and equally
> unconscious, what occurrence is next to happen. (p.
> 643)

He thus tried, he claimed, to recreate the uncertainty that the historical actors themselves would have faced as they encountered
the openness of the future. Irving exposed the bad faith of Knickerbocker's pretension, however, fairly clearly. Again the crucial semantic multivalence of "history" was brought into play, and the
retrodictive agency of the historian's "trembling pen and anxious
mind" was invoked (p. 643). Situating himself imaginatively in
"the very nick of time," as Knickerbocker repeatedly called it (pp.

381, 527, 640), collapsing the time of his writing and the time of the historical event, he nevertheless conceded that he had "one advantage [ad-vantage: a superior position or point of view, fig-urally *before* but literally *after* something else] over [his] reader." Though he "cannot save the life" of his hero, "nor absolutely con-tradict the event of a battle," yet he can "make" him give blows to his enemy, or "drive" his enemy around the field, "or if my hero should be pushed too hard by his opponent, I can just step in, and with one dash of my pen, give him a hearty thwack over the sconce" (pp. 643–44). Past historical events were here the direct objects of present-tense active verbs, and this violation of the grammar of historical discourse enacted the transgression of com-mon sense cause-and-effect relations that Irving's purposes re-quired.

Irving's reflections on the inscrutability of relations of cause and effect, and on the relations of priority between writing and event, were many and varied. The deception that attended publication, for instance — when he perpetrated a newspaper hoax intended to lend credence to the existence of his fictional narrator, placing ar-ticles in newspapers seeking information on Knickerbocker's dis-appearance, telling of the manuscript Knickerbocker's landlord discovered in his abandoned room, and so forth — was meant to insert the fictionalized historical text itself into the real history of 1809 America.

It may be that, as Martin Roth has written, Irving's *History of New York* was a "counter-history," informed by an "imaginative na-tionalism, which attempts to destroy the history that is in order to create a culture."[198] That is to say, Irving's deconstruction of the epistemological assumptions and causational structures of histori-cal writing was meant to diminish the power of accumulated his-torical understanding, to destroy precedent, and reopen historical time to creative possibilities. Historical creation would be, on this account, determined by linguistic action: if past history was an effect of retrodiction, then what else would future history be but an effect of protodiction? This theory of historical semiosis found

198. Martin Roth, *Comedy and America: The Lost World of Washington Irving* (Port Washington, New York: Kennikat Press, 1976), p. xi.

its most effective expression in "Rip Van Winkle," slyly subtitled "A Posthumous Writing of Diedrich Knickerbocker." If Knickerbocker was writing into being his own prehistory, then why shouldn't he be writing posthumously too? This tale was, of course, largely about the vagaries of historical time and the conditions of historical understanding. Rip's perplexity in the face of the alterations that had, to his mind, occurred within the merest nick of time — during his twenty-year nap, in which time the American Revolution came and went — was emblematized when, upon awakening, he repaired to his ancestral village. "The very village was altered," inexplicably, even his own house: approaching it, "expecting every moment to hear the shrill voice of Dame Van Winkle," he found it "empty, forlorn and apparently abandoned." Its silence was equal to the emptiness of time, and his speech seemed to want to overcome the discontinuities of those unfilled moments: "He called loudly for his wife and children — the lonely chambers rung for a moment with his voice, and then all again was silence."[199]

If Van Winkle's voice could not fathom or bridge the abyss of time, nevertheless only signs could make time intelligible.

> He now hurried forth and hastened to his old resort, the village inn — but it too was gone. A large, ricketty wooden building stood in its place, with great gaping windows, some of them broken, and mended with old hats and petticoats, and over the door was printed "The Union Hotel, by Jonathan Doolittle." Instead of the great tree, that used to shelter the quiet little Dutch inn of yore, there now was reared a tall naked pole with something on top that looked like a red night cap, and from it was fluttering a flag on which was a singular assemblage of stars and stripes — all this was strange and incomprehensible. He recognized on the sign, however, the ruby face of King George under which he had smoked so many a peaceful pipe, but even this was singularly metamorphosed. The red coat was

---

199. Irving, *History, Tales and Sketches,* p. 778. Further page references to "Rip Van Winkle" will be given parenthetically.

changed for one of blue and buff; a sword was held in
the hand instead of a sceptre; the head was decorated
with a cocked hat, and underneath was printed in large
characters GENERAL WASHINGTON. (p. 779)

There may be no text of the early national period in which the
mysteries of time, change, and national inception were more preg-
nantly addressed than this. The allegorization of historical process
as semiotic substitution is acute. But the substitution of one
"sign" for another is at the same time a repetition: the new face of
Washington was the same old face of George III. Red went to
blue and buff, sceptre went to sword, crown went to cocked hat;
only this chain of signifiers made the passage of time intelligible.
Where a great tree once stood — a symbol of rootedness, tradition,
organic continuity — there now stood another symbol, a liberty
pole, with a United States flag attached. The character of the
people had changed too, and its change was also represented by
an alteration of verbal phenomena: "There was a busy, bustling
disputatious tone about it, instead of the accustomed phlegm and
drowsy tranquility." And the vocabulary of politics had undergone
a decisive modification, as evidenced by the speech of a man hand-
ing out broadsides in front of the hotel, who was "haranguing
vehemently about rights of citizens — elections — members of Congress — liberty — Bunker's hill — heroes of seventy six — and other
words which were a perfect babylonish jargon to the bewildered
Van Winkle" (p. 779).

The invocation of Babylon immediately glossed American history as the equivalent of the biblical myth of Babel, in which human history was the hostage of the disseminating energies of
language. The multiplication and confusion of tongues followed
from an original linguistic unity. The hotel might be named
"Union," but the audible facts belied the claim. And while Rip
Van Winkle might soon accustom himself to the new language of
American politics, his own linguistic performances took on the
discrepant qualities of the universe of words into which he entered: his "story" would "vary on some points, every time he told
it," and even if it eventually ceased its variations and became a
stable utterance, "the reality of it" would still depend upon other
utterances (pp. 783–84). Diedrich Knickerbocker's subjoined

note, attesting to the truth of the tale, was itself hostage to the chain of utterances that attested in turn to Knickerbocker's authenticity: it invoked, as corroboration, a certificate "taken before a country justice and signed with a cross in the justice's own hand writing." This constant regression from one utterance to another, the truth of each continually deferred along the chain of utterances, and the truth of the nation's existence depending all along the series, was thrown into high relief by the massive irony of Knickerbocker's final subjoined claim, his unearned q.e.d.: "The story therefore is beyond the possibility of doubt" (p. 784).

Appendix to Chapter 1

This appendix presents the text of the broadside referred to in footnote 58. It is entitled "We have long since lost the right names of Things from amongst us," and is included in the collection of the Historical Society of Pennsylvania (Evans 13545).

PHILADELPHIA, SEPTEMBER 1st, 1774

This is true *Liberty,* when free born Men, Having t'advise the Publick, may speak free, Which he who can, and will, deserves his Praise; Who either can, or will, may hold his Peace; What can be juster in a State than this?

EURIPIDES translated by MILTON.

"We have long since lost the right Names of Things from amongst us: the giving of what belongs to other People is called Generosity; and the Courage to venture upon Wickedness is named Fortitude;" is an Observation, if I mistake not, of a noble Roman: how far it is applicable to the present Time may not be amiss for such among the People, who really mean uprightly, to consider. One Thing, I may venture to say, is most observable, that where any one attempts Admission to the publick Attention, with an honest Anxiety that Truth may appear, and the People may be shewn wherein they are abused by hot brained Impostors, every possible Difficulty and Discouragement is thrown in their Way; and they are sure to be treated as Enemies to their Country, by a Set of riotous Spirits whose

"Unruly Murmurs, and ill-tim'd Applause"
"Wrong the best Speakers, and the justest Cause."
  ILIAD.
Those "*partial Spirits,*" who "aloud complain:
"Think themselves injur'd that they cannot reign:
"And own no Liberty but where they may
"Without Controul upon their fellows prey."
  WALLER.

MODERATION and Justice are exploded as inimical to the publick
Cause; whoever professes Moderation must expect to be stigmatized as an Advocate for "Submission to the British Parliament,"
and for this good reason, because moderate Men are generally
against being unlawfully forced into a Sacrifice of their Rights as
free Men; notwithstanding this is contended for as the alone Measure to be relied on "for a Redress of American Grievances."

    Thus "mighty Blusterers impeach with Noise
    "And call their Private Cry the publick Voice."

NON-IMPORTATION is the Word of the Day; you must submit to
it, fellow Subjects, the great Patriots tell you so; those very Patriots who tickle your Ears with the *Words* ["]SALVATION OF
AMERICA," to whom alone the grand Secret is communicated:
Can you doubt their absolute Right to save you in their own Way?
If you do, dare you express such a Doubt? beware how you provoke their generous Spirits; remember their Mercy in the midst
of their Might, who, though they "could name your Persons" are
yet disposed "to spare you the Weight of popular Vengeance."
What though you may fondly imagine you have sufficient Reason
to think the generality of those brave Spirits who claim a Right to
ride upon your Necks, are such as made a gainful Job of the last
nonimportation Farce, or have taken Care to provide themselves
for another; Will you dare to suppose these noble Souls (however
great Cheats they might have been a few Years past) are not the
only Men of untainted Virtue now? Do you not know that there
is a Body of bold Men (you know Men that are very wicked and
very ignorant may be bold) who hold it as a constitutional Principle that they have a Right to fill their Pockets, or, in any Way,

give themselves Consequence at your Expence; and that they have the further Right of sacrificing you to "popular Vengeance" if you will not believe it is all for your good? Do you not know that such have a Power to chuse Committees, and that you must acknowledge said Committees to be your true and lawful Representatives, whose Decrees and Edicts are to be binding on you IN ALL CASES WHATEVER; and that these bold Men only have an exclusive Right of Exemption from the said Decrees and Edicts, or such Part of them as do not suit their particular Purposes; in which Case it is their peculiar Privilege to tell you, your said Representatives have not conformed to "the Sentiments of above Fifty Men in the whole Province." What though this may appear to be an impudent Assertion, unsupported by the least Shadow of Probability; yet, clap your Hands upon your Mouths, forget not ["]the Weight of popular Vengeance."

My Countrymen, I sincerely wish you well; it is a hot Season; there are unwholesome Vapours abroad; may you be preserved from the mal-influence of these double Dog-Days.

A TRADESMAN.

CHAPTER TWO

"The Affairs of the Revolution Occasion'd the Interruption": Self, Language, and Nation in Franklin's *Autobiography*

I. Authorship and Revolution

"I DO NOT PRETEND to the gift of prophecy," Benjamin Franklin wrote to the Massachusetts House of Representatives Committee of Correspondence in May 1771. "I think," he nevertheless stated, "one may clearly see, in the system of customs to be exacted in America by act of Parliament, the seeds sown of a total disunion of the two countries, though, as yet, that event may be at a considerable distance." The distance was not, in the event, as great as Franklin hoped; the consequences that he predicted would follow from Parliament's tax policies — ultimately, "ruin to Britain by the loss of her colonies" — ensued quite rapidly, to his dismay. "I cannot but wish to see . . . that the fatal period may be postponed," he wrote, and that "both countries might thence much longer continue to grow great together, more secure by their united strength, and more formidable to their common enemies."[1]

When Franklin, several months after writing this letter, began to write his *Autobiography,* his wish to defer the anticipated conflict governed his act of composition. His *Autobiography,* perhaps the central major utterance of his life, consequently exhibits in its formal and linguistic features certain traces of the revolutionary conflict, but also (and more significantly) certain traces of Franklin's deeply felt wish to defer the onset of revolution. That is, the first part of his text, written in 1771, manifests this desire; the subse-

---

1. Benjamin Franklin, *The Papers of Benjamin Franklin,* 30 vols. to date, ed. Leonard W. Labaree, William B. Willcox, Barbara B. Oberg et al (New Haven: Yale Univ. Press, 1959–), 18: 102–104.

quent parts, the writing of which he deferred until after the Revolution had taken place, express his retrospective misgivings with respect to the recent revolutionary struggle, and his desire to repress the memory of it in the interest of ensuring a return to social and political order. And just as he characteristically conceived of the social realm as linguistically constituted in the process of speech interaction (and therefore considered verbal aggression as the paramount offense against social peace), so too he conceived of this desired return to order as something to be achieved linguistically. In his *Autobiography* he represented this return in the guise of his own personal assumption of a particular style of verbal action, a conciliatory style that he associated with the authority of his father. Franklin's initial rebellion against his father's authority, and then his eventual imitation of his father's role, figure in the *Autobiography* as a model that he proposed not only to other individuals, but also to the nation that had recently founded itself in a revolution against the authority of British institutions and now needed to establish institutions of its own.

Franklin's *Autobiography* is in large part an explicit record of an individual's accession to language. It is also (since Franklin claims a representative status for himself, presenting his life as an allegory of American national experience) an account of the nation's self-constitution in language. For just as Franklin encountered language as the vehicle of a social given — a complete system of relationships and values, a symbolic order into which he was required to enter in order to acquire individuality — so too did the American colonies struggle to achieve, largely by means of rhetorical assertions and semantic transformations, the singularity and autonomy that are, for nations as well as persons, largely effects of language. In the case of the American colonies, the polemics of the Revolution specifically negated certain particular features of the preexisting symbolic order; they posited, over against that imperial-colonial order, a new realm of freedom and independence, an imaginary reality that they would, by means of strategic redefinitions and revaluations, call into being.

Franklin's *Autobiography* addressed itself directly to the postrevolutionary social and cultural situation, and offered a model of discursive activity that he believed would help to establish the new postcolonial social and political order. The rhetorical excesses of the Revolution had disordered the realm of intersubjective communication; this demanded, as Franklin thought, a return to order: a new set of rules for verbal behavior that would effectively govern social life.[2] The hallmark of this new order, as Franklin imagined it, and as his prescriptions for speech sought to create it, was a profound antirevolutionary bias.

Franklin enlarged his personal concern with language and speech into a national issue, and enlarged the autobiographical text (which dramatized that concern) into a national performance; the resolution of his own anxieties thereby became a program for America. The *Autobiography* prescribed, for a postrevolutionary society, restrictions on linguistic behavior that reflected a very unrevolutionary frame of mind. If, as Franklin's friend Benjamin Vaughan believed, "the immense revolution of the present period, will necessarily turn our attention towards the author of it,"[3] we will find that this author chose not only to record his conviction that the Revolution was an avoidable mistake, but also to provide a pattern that would operate to prevent another such mistake in the future. Vaughan's conflation here of revolutionary historical agency and Franklin's act of writing, in the 1783 letter he wrote to Franklin to urge him to resume his *Autobiography*, a letter Franklin then embedded in his text, is thus deeply at odds with the facts (Franklin was by no means the "author" of the Revolution, nor does he claim such authorship) and with the drift of the text.

A chief motive guiding Franklin's composition of the *Autobiography*, as I have said, was a desire to contain the disruptive power of the Revolution. The War of Independence is conspicuously absent from his text. What is present in its place is a program for the institution of an order of language that would, he believed, establish a new ground of social coherence.[4] This *coherence* stands in stark opposition to the social *rupture* that the Revolution repre-

2. Franklin's most resolute and meticulous attempt to re-order society by means of language was his design of a reformed alphabet. See Christopher Looby, "Phonetics and Politics: Franklin's Alphabet as a Political Design," *Eighteenth-Century Studies* 18 (1984), pp. 1–34.

3. Franklin, *Writings*, p. 1378. Further page references to the *Autobiography* will be given parenthetically.

4. My argument here is close to that of James M. Cox, who has observed that in the *Autobiography* "the history of the revolution . . . is displaced by the narrative

sented. Franklin's presentation of this program took the form of
an Oedipal drama in which he first opposed himself to, and then
identified himself with, the exercise of paternal authority. That the
narrative should have taken this form is not surprising, since members of the Revolutionary generation habitually represented the
conflict by means of familial tropes. In the words of a recent
scholar, "a call for filial autonomy . . . echoes throughout the rhetoric of the American Revolution. It is its quintessential motif."[5]
What is particularly interesting about Franklin's *Autobiography* is
that, as he presented it, the Oedipal conflict was largely about language. And as Franklin's Oedipal tale ends with his resumption,
in a new form, of the authority he at first rebelled against, so, his
narrative implied, the nascent nation-state, having emerged from
its revolution, would need to reinstitute in a new form the structures of authority it had only recently destroyed.

II. Fathers and Sons

Franklin began his *Autobiography* by addressing to his son a series
of "Anecdotes of my Ancestors" (p. 1307). The mode of direct
paternal address, and the pronounced emphasis on ancestry, together constituted an assertion of the power and value of genealogical continuity. The insistence with which Franklin made this
assertion might seem out of place in a text that has attained paradigmatic status in a culture founded on an act of radical discontinuity with the past. But Franklin wrote the first part of the *Autobiography* in 1771, when he was 65 years old, at a time when he
was exercising his diplomacy in an effort to prevent a political rupture; he was on particularly bad terms at that moment with Lord
Hillsborough (Secretary of State for Colonies) and the Ministry,
but his discouragement had not yet led him to lose hope of preserving the imperial-colonial connection. Not until late 1775,
after he had returned to Philadelphia, and after one last petition

---

of Franklin's early life, so that Franklin's personal history *stands in place of the revolution.*" Cox, "Autobiography and America," *Virginia Quarterly Review* 47 (1971),
p. 259.
    5. Jay Fliegelman, *Prodigals and Pilgrims: The American Revolution Against Patri-
archal Authority, 1750–1800* (Cambridge: Cambridge Univ. Press, 1982), p. 3.

to the crown had been rejected, did Franklin conclude that "a sep-aration will . . . be inevitable."[6] As Jack Greene has written, "the relinquishment of his attachment to Britain had been . . . a long and painful process that he would have much preferred to avoid."[7] So if Franklin, when beginning his *Autobiography,* recounted in considerable detail his familial connection to England, and did so, ostensibly, for the benefit of his son (who would, ironically, learn the intended lesson all too well: William Franklin remained, to his father's chagrin, loyal to the crown during the war), the political context of this personal affirmation of English descent is clear. Franklin's assertion of the authority of the father is the expression of a political desire. And the voice of paternal authority that speaks here is all the more urgent, we may surmise, since the son who is addressed is illegitimate.

Franklin took care to emphasize certain conspicuous repetitions in his account of his ancestry. He recalled that when he went some years previously to Ecton, the village in Northamptonshire where his ancestors had lived for three centuries (a trip on which he was accompanied by his son William), he discovered while examining the parish register that he was "the youngest Son of the youngest Son for 5 Generations back" (p. 1309). His father, he related, hav-ing been another youngest son, was apprenticed to an older brother, John, a dyer; Franklin himself, we will learn, was also apprenticed to an older brother, James, a printer. Apparently this was the fate of youngest sons whose fathers were unable to pro-vide for them the advantages they had bestowed on other, earlier offspring.[8] Oldest sons, too, were fated to repeat a traditional pat-tern: in the Franklin family, "the eldest Son," in addition to inher-iting the "Freehold of about 30 Acres," was "always bred" to the "Smith's Business," which supplemented the livelihood generated

6. Franklin, *Papers,* 22: 217.

7. Jack P. Greene, "The Alienation of Benjamin Franklin — British American," *Journal of the Royal Society for the Encouragement of Arts, Manufactures and Commerce* 124 (1976), p. 70.

8. Franklin's resentful sense of deprivation is evident in a letter he wrote to his cousin Mary Fisher in 1758, in which he anticipated what he would later write in the *Autobiography:* "I am the youngest Son of the youngest Son of the youngest Son of the youngest Son for five generations; whereby I find that had there origi-nally been any Estate in the Family none could have stood a worse Chance for it." Franklin, *Papers,* 8: 118.

by the farm—"A Custom," Franklin observes, "which he [Uncle Benjamin, whose notes on the family history provided much of Franklin's information] & my Father both followed as to their eldest Sons—" (p. 1309).

The affirmation of familial continuity was further strengthened—and its linguistic element stressed—by the brief essay, grafted here onto the text, concerning the family name: Franklin guessed that his ancestors were probably living in Ecton long before the date, three hundred years past, that his uncle's notes specified as the earliest known time of their residence there—"perhaps," he speculated, they were there "from the Time when the Name *Franklin* that before was the Name of an Order of People, was assum'd by them for a Surname, when others took Surnames all over the Kingdom—" (p. 1308). This inserted note on the patronymic adduces, as "proof that FRANKLIN was anciently the common name of an order or rank in England," a fifteenth-century legal treatise written by Sir John Fortescue, *De Laudibus Legum Angliae,* and some lines from Chaucer's *Canterbury Tales.* (William Temple Franklin, the illegitimate son of the illegitimate son of the author of the *Autobiography,* would later add to this note, when he published the second edition of his grandfather's text, three lines from the *Faerie Queen* as additional legitimation, so to speak, of the family name.)[9] What Franklin's note on his name did, in addition to extending the ancestral line further back in time—that is, enlarging the claim of unbroken succession—was to appeal to a mythical moment of inscription, an original naming of the family, and to claim an uninterrupted (if attenuated) connection with that origin. It also, and not incidentally, identified Franklin with the particular class of citizens that would, when it was transported to America, constitute what Jefferson, in *Notes on the State of Virginia,* would call "the chosen people of God" whom "he has made his peculiar deposit for substantial and genuine virtue," the smallholding peasants or yeoman farmers central to American political mythology.[10] But most important for present purposes, Franklin's note on his name established for him

    9. See *The Autobiography of Benjamin Franklin: A Genetic Text,* ed. J. A. Leo Lemay and P. M. Zall (Knoxville: Univ. of Tennessee Press, 1981), pp. 175–77.
    10. Jefferson, *Writings,* p. 290.

a link, crucial to the narrative program of the *Autobiography,* between political order, paternal authority, filial submission, and the linguisticality of the individual subject: the name Franklin, as it is explicated here, referred to a place in a particular social hierarchy; also, it was inherited from father to son; and, as a word—a name—it determined a particular personal identity.

The conscious assertion of the value of continuity and the fact of repetition was, however, subtly and (it seems) unwittingly subverted, even this early in the text, by certain of the details of his ancestry that Franklin chose to mention. He began to rewrite, as it were, his own genealogy, making significant substitutions.[11] There was an irregularity in his own relation to his father that produced a problematic dispersal of the paternal function. Paternal authority in Franklin's own family was divided and distributed among several men; consequently Josiah Franklin, the biological father, was displaced in some degree from the ordinary position of paternal authority, and his role as representative of the moral law and custodian of language was divided among several of Franklin's male relations and mentors. This dissociation of paternal authority can be attributed to the fact that Franklin was, as he recalls in the text, the son of his father's second wife, and that his father was nearly fifty years old when Franklin was born. Josiah Franklin's first wife bore him seven children (three in England, four more after emigration to Boston); his second wife, Abiah, bore him ten more, among them Benjamin, "the youngest Son," as he reminds us yet again, "and the youngest Child but two" (p. 1312). When Benjamin was a young child, as he tells it, there were at one time thirteen siblings and half-siblings at his father's table; that is, he grew up in a household that included a number of grown siblings, among them several who were not his mother's offspring. A degree of ambiguity therefore marked the order of generations in the household, and a definite duality marked the system of filiation. This ambiguity and duality experienced in the intimacy of the family home was also, not incidentally, a living reminder of

11. Hugh J. Dawson has observed that "In the person of Josiah Franklin and his surrogates, the image of the father is a continual presence in Part I of the *Autobiography.*" Dawson, "Fathers and Sons: Franklin's 'Memoirs' as Myth and Metaphor," *Early American Literature* 14 (1979/80), p. 270.

the way the family was conspicuously marked by the experience of transatlantic emigration. In addition to this irregularity, the presence in the household of Franklin's Uncle Benjamin — Josiah's widowed older brother — added to the uncertainty of authority, since Uncle Benjamin evidently assumed a considerable degree of paternal authority over the nephew who was, as we learn, "nam'd after this Uncle"; and several of the poems Uncle Benjamin wrote "to My Name," as he put it (pp. 1311, 1310), were inserted by Franklin into the text of the *Autobiography*. In this irregular family environment, it is not surprising that Franklin should have elected to identify imaginatively with several other ancestors who, like his Uncle Benjamin, more adequately performed for him the function of paternal authority, especially, as we shall see, in the matter of initiation into the order of language.[12]

Franklin also chose to affiliate himself with another of his father's brothers, Thomas. The reason is given in the text: Thomas, who was the oldest son, and was therefore according to custom at first "bred a Smith under his Father," nevertheless disrupted the family pattern by educating himself to be a "Scrivener." He did so by attaching himself to "an Esquire Palmer then the principal Gentleman in that Parish," who, recognizing that Thomas was "ingenious," encouraged the young man in "Learning" (p. 1309). By choosing this other uncle as one more symbolic father, Franklin identified with someone who also had had recourse to a substitute paternal figure; in turning aside imaginatively from his own father, Franklin repeated the maneuver of an uncle who had also turned aside from *his* father. But by this elective, willful repetition of his Uncle Thomas's innovation, he broke the customary pattern of repetition; he repeated, instead, his uncle's divagation.

Franklin, like this Uncle Thomas, would find a local patron — "an ingenious Tradesman* [*Mr Matthew Adams] who had a pretty Collection of Books, & . . . took Notice of me, invited me to his Library, & very kindly lent me such Books as I chose to read" — who would assist him in his effort to acquire, by indepen-

---

12. Jacques Lacan described the phenomenon of a "dissociation of the Oedipus relation" as an effect of "discordances in the father relation" in *Ecrits: A Selection* (New York: Norton, 1977), p. 67. I should make it clear that the *nom du père*, as Lacan has described it, is not necessarily identical with actual empirical fathers such

dent means, linguistic competence (p. 1318). Uncle Thomas was
enabled by his literacy to become "a considerable Man in the
County Affairs," and also to be "much taken Notice of and
patroniz'd by the then Lord Halifax" (pp. 1309–10, 1310). So
closely did Uncle Thomas's career imitate the later career of the
nephew he never met, but who would take careful note of the
likenesses between them, that the fact that he "died in 1702 Jan.
6. old Stile, just 4 Years to a Day before I was born" seemed to
Franklin the least noteworthy of the similarities (p. 1310). He
nevertheless recorded the coincidence, and further recorded for
his son that "the Account we receiv'd of his Life & Character from
some old People at Ecton, I remember struck you as something
extraordinary from its Similarity to what you knew of mine. Had
he died on the same Day, you said one might have suppos'd a
Transmigration" (p. 1310). If Franklin was unwilling to suppose
that he reincarnated his Uncle Thomas, he was pleased nevertheless to record certain facts concerning yet another ancestor — his
maternal grandfather, Peter Folger — that might have struck a
more credulous person as grounds to suppose a different transmigration. Abiah Franklin, Benjamin's mother, was "a Daughter of
Peter Folger, one of the first Settlers of New England, of whom
honourable mention is made by Cotton Mather, in his Church
History of that Country, (entitled Magnalia Christi Americana)
as a *godly learned Englishman,* if I remember the Words rightly — "
(p. 1312).[13] Franklin's reference to Mather's *Magnalia* is one of
the more curious features of the text, but one of the most intriguing. His pretended uncertainty of memory was quite disingenuous, since it was straight out of the *Magnalia* that he drew the

---

as Josiah Franklin; it is nevertheless the case that Franklin, in this text, assigned to
his actual father the role of language master — that is, he invested his biological
father with the authority over language that Lacan would later assign to an abstract principle.

13. Franklin didn't remember the words quite rightly: as J. A. Leo Lemay
points out, Mather's words had been "an Able Godly Englishman." *Benjamin
Franklin's Autobiography,* ed. J. A. Leo Lemay and P. M. Zall (New York: Norton,
1986), p. 5n. Herman Melville, in whose imagination Franklin figured persistently,
seems to have had Franklin's genealogical pride in mind when in *Moby-Dick* he
cited Franklin's descent from the Folgers of Nantucket as qualifying Franklin for
the honorific title "noble Benjamin." Herman Melville, *Redburn, White-Jacket,
Moby-Dick* (New York: The Library of America, 1983), p. 911.

metaphor that is prominent on the first page of the *Autobiography,* and to which he returned at several later places in the text: the conceit that his life was a book (and a first edition at that) the "Faults," "sinister Accidents," and untoward "Events" of which were but "Errata" that would be corrected in a "second Edition" (pp. 1307, 1325, 1307). Although the book topos is a fairly common one in Western literature,[14] it appears from close verbal parallels that Franklin adapted it from Mather's chapter on John Cotton, where it is the central image in the elegy by John Woodbridge that Mather quotes at the conclusion of the chapter; Franklin's stated familiarity with the *Magnalia* makes the source more likely. John Cotton, according to the elegy, was a "living, breathing Bible,"

> His head an index to the sacred volume;
> His very name a *title-page;* and next,
> His life a *commentary* on the text.
> O, what a monument of glorious worth,
> When, in a *new edition,* he comes forth,
>
> Without *erratas,* may we think he'll be,
> In *leaves* and *covers* of eternity![15]

Franklin would very likely have found the whole account of John Cotton an appealing one, since Mather treated his maternal forebear as a latter-day Augustine, whose early fascination with rhetoric and excessive fondness for disputation were later to be rejected and to be distasteful to his memory. Mather's life of Cotton reads now, in this respect and in other particulars, as a virtual premonition of Franklin's account of his own life.[16] How consciously

14. Ernst Robert Curtius, *European Literature and the Latin Middle Ages,* trans. Willard Trask (New York: Pantheon Books for Bollingen Foundation, 1953), pp. 302–47.

15. Cotton Mather, *Magnalia Christi Americana: or, The Ecclesiastical History of New England,* 2 vols. (Hartford, Connecticut: Silas Andrus and Son, 1855, 1853), 1: 284.

16. John Cotton's father, Roland Cotton, was credited by Mather with "two most imitable *practices*": "One was, that when any of his neighbours desirous to sue one another, addressed him for *council,* it was his manner, in the most perswasive and obliging terms that could be, to endeavour a *reconciliation* between both parties; preferring the *consolations* of a *peacemaker,* before all the *fees* that he might have got by blowing up *differences*" (Mather, *Magnalia,* 1: 253). This is very nearly exactly how Franklin described his own father, and also how he described the Phil-

Franklin used the *Magnalia* as a literary model cannot be established very confidently, but the *Autobiography* is, to a degree surpassing most such texts, a synthetic work, constructed largely of
borrowed and adapted motifs and ideas. Much of its literary effect
derives from the success with which it answers to the conventional
expectations that readers bring to an encounter with the autobiographical genre; and, as Daniel Shea has written, "In England and
in America, the Puritan background contributed to these expectations."[17] The most compelling evidence of such a contribution in
Franklin's text is in the way in which, by appealing to his grandfather, and by emphasizing the earliness of that forebear's presence
in New England and his respectable position among the worthies
who figured in the official history of the Puritan errand, Franklin
grounded his own writing in a prior text which was, in a general
way, its literary model. More important than specific plagiaries,
however, is the implied identification with the literary tradition
that the *Magnalia* inaugurated, what Sacvan Bercovitch has called
"auto-American-biography": a mode of writing that conflates individual experience and national destiny in a celebration of representative American selfhood.[18] Franklin did for himself what

---

adelphia lawyer, Andrew Hamilton, whom he admired greatly. Another of John
Cotton's characteristics, as related by Mather, must have struck Franklin forcibly:
"Every *night* it was his custom to *examine himself*, with reflections on the transac-
tions of the day past; wherein, if he found that he had not either *done* good unto
others, or good unto his own soul, he would be as much grieved as ever the famous
Titus was, when he could complain in the evening, *Amici, Diem Perdidi!*" (Mather,
Magnalia, 1: 276). Cotton's moral account-keeping prefigures Franklin's quite obviously. Mather further asserted that Cotton was "patient and *peaceable,* even to a
proverb"; that he "learned the lesson of Gregory, 'It is better, many times, to fly
from an injury by silence, than to overcome it by replying:' and he urged that
practice of Gryneaus, 'To revenge wrongs by Christian taciturnity'" (Mather,
Magnalia 1: 277). Franklin very often professed his disinclination to reply to those
who criticized or abused him, and his habitual taciturnity was often commented
on by acquaintances.
    17. Daniel Shea, *Spiritual Autobiography in Early America* (Princeton: Princeton
Univ. Press, 1968), p. 239. As Shea has written, "Ben Franklin, the archetypal
apprentice studying hard to make good, is at least as much a product of English
literature and society as of the American Dream"(ibid., p. 235).
    18. Sacvan Bercovitch, *The Puritan Origins of the American Self* (New Haven:
Yale Univ. Press, 1975), p. 134. Mitchell Robert Breitwieser has discussed Franklin's "aspiration to representative personality" and the continuity of this aspiration
with Puritan ideas of self-discipline in his *Cotton Mather and Benjamin Franklin:
The Price of Representative Personality* (Cambridge: Cambridge Univ. Press, 1984).
This point has also been made with specific reference to Franklin by J. A. Leo
Lemay, who finds that in the *Autobiography* "ontogeny recapitulates both American
history and the American Dream"; see "Benjamin Franklin," in Everett Emerson,

Mather did for the spiritual and civil leaders of seventeenth-century New England: he rehearsed in the story of his life both the past and the (predicated) future of America.

Placed in the literary tradition commenced by Mather's history, it becomes especially significant that Franklin should have recalled with such evident pride that his family "was early in the Reformation, and continu'd Protestants thro' the Reign of Queen Mary," that they "were sometimes in Danger of Trouble on Account of their Zeal against Popery," and that they possessed an English Bible and read it despite the risk that doing so might bring down upon them the ecclesiastical authorities (p. 1311). It was deeply important to Franklin, too, that his father and Uncle Benjamin, upon the visit of itinerant nonconforming preachers to Northamptonshire, "adher'd to them, and so continu'd all their Lives," removing to America in consequence, "where they expected to enjoy their Mode of Religion with Freedom—" (p. 1312). It was important to Franklin, in short—and it is one of the presiding assumptions of his text—that he was descended from Puritans both on the paternal and maternal sides, and that his *Autobiography* was governed by a metaphor of textualized selfhood that he borrowed from the work that consolidated, for America, a particular vision of corporate selfhood and of a special national mission. Franklin discovered that in Peter Folger he had found a maternal ancestor whose life anticipated his own in remarkable ways, just as Thomas Franklin's life had done. Peter Folger, too, was a writer. The only piece of his that was ever printed was a jeremiad in the "homespun Verse" of 1675, in which Folger "ascrib[ed] the Indian Wars & other Distresses, that had befallen the Country" to the persecutions of "Baptists, Quakers, & other Sectaries." In other words, according to Franklin's interpretation of Folger's poem, the "many Judgments of God" that were visited upon New England were so many signs that He was "in favour of Liberty of Conscience" (p. 1312). Such an interpretation enabled Franklin

---

ed., *Major Writers of Early American Literature* (Madison: Univ. of Wisconsin Press, 1972), p. 241. Two other recent articles of considerable interest make similar arguments: Elizabeth Davis, "Events in the Life and in the Text: Franklin and the Style of American Autobiography," *Revue Française d'Etudes Americaines* 14 (1982): 187–97; David Seed, "Projecting the Self: An Approach to Franklin's *Autobiography*," *Etudes Anglaises* 36 (1983): 385–400.

to find in his grandfather a forebear whose tolerant attitudes pre-figured and validated his own, and whose latitudinarian God would have approved of Franklin's ecumenical practices — for example, his contributing to every subscription for the erection of places of worship, "whatever might be the Sect" (p. 1383). "The whole" of his grandfather's poem, Franklin wrote, "appear'd to me as written with a good deal of Decent Plainness & manly Freedom." He particularly liked the final stanza:

> The six last concluding Lines I remember, tho' I have forgotten the two first of the Stanza, but the Purport of them was that his Censures proceeded from *Goodwill,* & therefore he would be known as the Author,
>
>> because to be a Libeller, (says he)
>> I hate it with my Heart.
>> From Sherburne Town where now I dwell,
>> My Name I do put here,
>> Without Offence, your real Friend,
>> It is Peter Folgier. (pp. 1312–13)

The sentiment here anticipates the attitude Franklin would later take himself, and repeatedly announce in the *Autobiography:* he would come to regret, he said, the reputation he acquired, in his youth, "as a young Genius that had a Turn for Libelling & Satyr" (p. 1324), and he would make a concerted effort to cultivate a habit of expressing himself in such a way as to convey an impression of goodwill. But if what Franklin called the "modest way in which I propos'd my Opinions" had, once he adopted it, the happy effect that it "procur'd them a readier Reception" and "more easily prevail'd with others to give up their Mistakes & join with me when I happen'd to be in the right" (thus enabling him to pursue, like those symbolic fathers whose careers prefigured his own, a career in public affairs), it was nevertheless true that he "put on" this conciliatory mask "with some violence to natural Inclination" (p. 1393). I will come back to this "natural Inclination," and the methods by which he redirected it — to his struggle with language, and in particular his struggle to overcome the "disputacious Turn" (p. 1318) that he was naturally inclined to take in conversation — at the end of this chapter. Next, however, I want to examine the prominence in the *Autobiography* of the cultural system of language — its institutional presence in the world that Franklin describes.

III. The Subject of Language

Among the poems Uncle Benjamin wrote to his namesake nephew was one which illustrated typographically the position of the child who assumes his place in the symbolic order of his culture on the condition that he submit to the laws governing it.[19] The simultaneous grounding of both the individual subject (as creature of language) and the social order (as effect of linguistically constituted intersubjectivity) was quite elegantly represented in Uncle Benjamin's acrostic poem, where Franklin's proper name (the sign of his individual subjectivity, or what is called in the poem his "Inward part") was made to emerge, as it were, from the system of rules and norms that formed the basis of the culture:

   Sent to B. F. in N. E. 15 July 1710

   B e to thy parents an Obedient Son
   E ach Day let Duty constantly be Done
   N ever give Way to sloth or lust or pride
   I f free you'd be from Thousand Ills beside
   A bove all Ills be sure Avoide the shelfe
   M ans Danger lyes in Satan sin and selfe
   I n vertue Learning Wisdome progress Make
   N ere shrink at Suffering for thy saviours sake
   F raud and all Falshood in thy Dealings Flee
   R eligious Always in thy station be
   A dore the Maker of thy Inward part
   N ow's the Accepted time, Give him thy Heart
   K eep a Good Consceince 'tis a constant Frind

---

19. In the precise formulation of Émile Benveniste, "Society is not possible except through language; nor is the individual. The awakening consciousness in the child always coincides with the learning of language, which gradually introduces him as an individual into society." *Problems in General Linguistics,* trans. Mary Elizabeth Meek (Coral Gables, Florida: Univ. of Miami Press, 1971), p. 23.

L ike Judge and Witness This Thy Acts Attend
I n Heart with bended knee Alone Adore
N one but the Three in One Forevermore (pp. 1310–11)[20]

This uncle (who also taught Franklin a system of shorthand, and offered to give him the many volumes of sermons he had heard and recorded in his shorthand, since Franklin would need "a Stock to set up with" if he were to become, as his father at one time intended, a minister) assumed, as the author of this poem, as the teacher of writing, and as the supplier of words, the paternal function of introducing the child into the symbolic order, initiating him into the interdependent systems of language and moral law.[21] But he did so in a way that must have made a four-and-a-half-year old boy feel, even more deeply than every child feels at that age, that he was powerless within that order.

The very first of the requirements among the many laws, rules, taboos, and beliefs that were listed in the poem, was the admonition to filial obedience. This reinforced, when Franklin quoted the acrostic in his *Autobiography,* the emphasis he had already placed on paternal authority and generational continuity. But it also alluded to the more general question of the system of marriage and kinship regulations as the basis of cultural order, as that which controls "natural Inclination" and organizes it according to socially sanctioned patterns. Cultural anthropologists have suggested that there is a structural identity between language and the laws of matrimonial alliance.[22] This identity is what has led Jacques Lacan to propose wittily that, in fact, "it is through sexual

20. This poem, an acrostic on his name written by the uncle whose name he inherited, gains a certain resonance when we recall that Franklin's earlier discussion of his genealogy centered precisely on the family name.

21. John Cotton's *New-England Primer* had established this interdependence in a most impressive fashion: children who, like Franklin, learned their letters from this abecedarium, were taught that the moral imperatives of their culture were inextricably tied to the order of letters in the alphabet; Uncle Benjamin's acrostic poem (like all acrostic poems, which were very popular at the time) operates to enforce the same linkage.

22. I refer, of course, to the well-known formulations of Claude Lévi-Strauss, who says that marriage regulations and kinship systems constitute "a kind of language" or "a certain type of communication," that they are among "aspects of social life . . . whose inmost nature is the same as that of language." *Structural Anthropology,* trans. Claire Jacobson and Brooke Grundfest Schoepf (New York: Basic Books, 1963) pp. 61, 62.

reality that the signifier came into the world,"[23] and to suggest that the father's role as original representative of the law governing sexual behavior coincides with his authority as legislator of language.[24]

The interdependence or identity of language and marriage regulations was acknowledged implicitly in Franklin's *Autobiography.* We may begin to see its presence in the text by noticing that when Franklin first attempted to write something for publication in his brother's *New England Courant,* he did so under a feigned name: "Silence Dogood." This was the name of a female persona, first of all, and thus set Franklin in at least a partly skewed relation to the normative masculine social role; but more to the point, it was a name that indicated insecurity concerning the speaker's emergence into speech: Franklin called his speaking "Silence." As he wrote, "being still a Boy, & suspecting that my Brother would object to printing any Thing of mine in his Paper if he knew it to be mine, I contriv'd to disguise my Hand, & writing an anonymous Paper I put it in at Night under the Door of the Printing House." He soon had the "exquisite Pleasure, of finding it met with . . . Approbation" from his brother's circle of aspiring litterateurs (p. 1323). Soon after, therefore, finding that his authorial ruse had succeeded, he dropped his disguise, and claimed the respect that he felt was due him as the author of the piece. His "exquisite Plea-

23. Jacques Lacan, *The Four Fundamental Concepts of Psycho-Analysis* (New York: Norton, 1978), pp. 150–51.

24. The father, by prohibiting his son's desire for his mother, deflects the son's desire onto another object; this object stands in a relation to the original object of desire as a signifier to a signified. The Oedipal conflict, in this account, is at once a matter of the son's acceptance of the limits within which he must choose a sexual object, and an accession thereby to semiotic competence. He has mastered the process of representation, and can now control language in some degree rather than merely being controlled by it. There is an interesting episode in the *Autobiography* in which Franklin reenacts the classic Oedipal drama, with his friend James Ralph in the paternal position this time. While Ralph was away from London teaching at a country school, having assumed Franklin's name because he was "unwilling to have it known that he once was so meanly employ'd" (p.1347), Franklin grew fond of Ralph's mistress. After loaning her money to help her out of her "Distresses," Franklin "attempted Familiarities, (another Erratum) which she repuls'd with a proper Resentment, and acquainted him with my Behaviour" (p. 1347). This was the Ralph whose identity Franklin assumed when he had read Ralph's composition aloud to the Junto back in Philadelphia, gathering the praise that Ralph's writing had earned (I discuss this episode below); when Ralph later assumed Franklin's identity, he was less willing to share the benefits.

sure" soon dissipated, however, as he incurred the wrath of James, who, "tho' a Brother . . . considered himself as my Master, & me as his Apprentice," and who "was passionate & had often beaten me, which I took extreamly amiss" (p. 1324).

Franklin took "the Blows his Passion too often urg'd him to bestow upon me" very badly; he determined to break his indentures and leave Boston. But since his brother and father would have tried to prevent his flight, he needed to depart secretly, and for this purpose he again assumed a disguise, one which casts the whole episode of the "Thing" he "put . . . in at Night," his "Hand," and his "exquisite Pleasure" in a different light. He had his friend Collins arrange "with the Captain of a New York Sloop for my Passage, under the Notion of my being a young Acquaintance of his that had got a naughty Girl with Child, whose Friends would compel me to marry her, and therefore I could not appear or come away publickly" (pp. 1325, 1325–26). That is, Franklin translated his first experience of gratifying literary performance into an infraction of the marriage regulations of his culture. He represented his desire to escape the authority of his father and brother — a desire that had its roots in his urge to write — in explicitly transgressive sexual terms. His desire to be an author, and the various obstacles to the gratification of that desire, acquired by his own account a distinctly Oedipal coloration.

It begins to appear at this place in the text that Franklin, in the act of utterance which was the assertion of his individuality, embarked on a course of self-alienation in language. His first published writing appeared pseudonymously as the utterance of a distinctive persona whose recognizable voice was very definitely not that of a seventeen-year-old boy. Franklin's flight from paternal authority, in its first motions, then, succeeded only by virtue of the fact that he represented himself as what he was not. He was able to individualize himself only by mediating himself to others, registering himself before them in the guise of a second, linguistically created self. This is one early instance of what became Franklin's highly developed sense of the possibilities of self-presentation, his knowledge of the difference that can separate the public persona from the subjective self. He learned to exploit that difference to considerable advantage, but the learning did not come without difficulty. Franklin's struggle with language, his own genesis as a speaking subject, was, as he recounted it in the *Autobiography,* chiefly a matter of coming to terms with the fact that language, although it seems to be a responsive personal instrument, is in fact something irreducibly other, something transindividual, something to which he had to submit at the cost of the attendant self-alienation.

This process of submission to language is illustrated in a number of places in the *Autobiography.* In one such place, Franklin told how, as a young man, he, along with his friend Collins, "sometimes disputed, and very fond we were of Argument, & very desirous of confuting one another" (p. 1318). One of their most memorable arguments, he recalled, had to do with "the Propriety of educating the Female Sex in Learning, & their Abilities for Study. [Collins] was of Opinion that it was improper; & that they were naturally unequal to it. I took the contrary Side, perhaps a little for Dispute sake" (p. 1319). They did not settle the point then, nor in the course of the ensuing correspondence in which they continued their argument. One thing Franklin did determine, however, was that linguistic skill was a considerable advantage in argument: Collins, he said, "was naturally more eloquent, had a ready Plenty of Words, and sometimes as I thought bore me down more by his Fluency than by the Strength of his Reasons." The abashed conviction of his own deficient verbal capital made Franklin resolve to be "more attentive to the *Manner* in Writing, and . . . to endeavour at Improvement" (p. 1319). This resolution was also motivated by his desire to respond to his father's criticisms: having examined the letters that Franklin and Collins exchanged, Josiah "observ'd that tho' I had the Advantage of my Antagonist in correct Spelling & pointing (which I ow'd to the Printing House) I fell far short in elegance of Expression, in Method and in Perspicuity" (p. 1319). This was not the first time Franklin's father had criticized his son's writing: only a short time before, having written a couple of occasional poems "in the Grubstreet Ballad Stile," and having "made a great Noise" by hawking them in the streets (the first poem "sold wonderfully"), Franklin was distressed to meet with his father's disapproval, who only "discourag'd me, by ridiculing my Performances, and telling me Verse-makers were generally Beggars" (p. 1318). Franklin's celebrated encounter with the *Spectator* followed: his attempt to reproduce the style of Addison and Steele was meant to forestall further ridicule, having been undertaken to correct just the deficiencies his father had cited. The procedures Franklin followed are best described by himself:

> I thought the Writing excellent, & wish'd if possible to imitate it. With that View, I took some of the Papers, & making short Hints of the Sentiment in each Sentence, laid them by a few Days, and then without looking at the Book, try'd to compleat the Papers again, by expressing each hinted Sentiment at length & as fully as it had been express'd before, in any suitable Words that should come to hand.
>
> Then I compar'd my Spectator with the Original, discover'd some of my Faults & corrected them. But I found I wanted a Stock of Words or a Readiness in recollecting & using them, which I thought I should have acquir'd before that time, if I had gone on making Verses, since the continual Occasion for Words of the same Import but of different Length, to suit the Measure, or of different Sound for the Rhyme, would have laid me under a constant Necessity of searching for Variety and also have tended to fix that Variety, in my Mind, & make me Master of it. (pp. 1319–20)

This rather strict discipline—which really amounted to a self-dissolution in the language of another—may seem an excessive abnegation, especially in view of the fact that Franklin's avowed intent was to become "Master" of language. But his method was, clearly, to *submit* himself to language—to become, as it were, an instrument of a language system and a discourse that he encountered ready-made; and the discourse he chose to conform himself to was the prose of Addison and Steele, the impersonal generality of which exactly met the requirements of Franklin's desire, which was for an evacuation of selfhood. Still, some kind of mastery was what he paradoxically expected to achieve by this means, and the evident resentment toward his father that he expressed here indicates that while he "saw the Justice" (p. 1319) of his father's remarks (the very phrase speaks loudly of the vivid presence to

Franklin's mind of an image of paternally invested legal authority), he wished very much nevertheless to put his father in the wrong. It was his father, after all, as he says, who discouraged his attempts at verse-making—efforts which, Franklin thought, would have benefitted him by enlarging his vocabulary, the personal "Stock of Words" for the deficiencies of which his father then unjustly belittled him. Franklin therefore returned (against his father's counsel) to versification exercises:

> I took some of the Tales & turn'd them into Verse: And after a time, when I had pretty well forgotten the Prose, turn'd them back again. I also sometimes jumbled my Collections of Hints into Confusion, and after some Weeks, endeavour'd to reduce them into the best Order, before I began to form the full Sentences & compleat the Paper. This was to teach me Method in the Arrangement of Thoughts. By comparing my Work afterwards with the original, I discover'd many faults and amended them; but I sometimes had the Pleasure of Fancying that in certain Particulars of small Import, I had been lucky enough to improve the Method or the Language and this encourag'd me to think I might possibly in time come to be a tolerable English Writer, of which I was extreamly ambitious. (p. 1320)

Here, significantly, Franklin's "Pleasure" in linguistic performance was no longer at odds with the social order; on the contrary, it was involved in the construction of that order. It was experienced in the reduction of promiscuous "Confusion" into "the best Order"—the restoration of structure, accomplished by means of "the Method or the Language."[25]

IV. Verbal Imposture

This attempt to install himself within the horizon of a preexisting discourse would be characteristic of Franklin's further efforts to

---

25. A similar experience would be recounted in the *Autobiography* when, one night, a case of type fell and broke on the floor of the print shop, and the individual characters were jumbled into confusion, not unlike the bits and pieces of scrambled

"improve" himself. On another occasion, having agreed with a circle of friends — all of whom were, like himself, ambitious to improve their "Language & Expression" (p. 1341) — to meet to read and criticize each other's compositions, Franklin found himself unprepared for the first meeting, having been unable to complete the assignment, which was to make a version of the eighteenth psalm. Thus unprepared, Franklin agreed to present his friend Ralph's composition as his own, since Ralph, who was "extreamly eloquent" — Franklin said he "never knew a prettier Talker" (p. 1340) — was afraid that another member of the group, named Osborne, would criticize his composition severely "out of mere Envy" (p. 1341). Ralph asked Franklin, therefore, to read his (Ralph's) version of the psalm at the meeting, so as to elicit Osborne's unprejudiced opinion of it, and the imposture succeeded perfectly: Osborne credited it as Franklin's own, and unstintingly showed his admiration by "applauding it immoderately." When the meeting adjourned, Osborne walked home with Ralph, and, still not knowing whose words he was actually praising, continued his effusions:

> As they two went home together, Osborne express'd himself still more strongly in favour of what he thought my Production, having restrain'd himself before as he said, lest I should think it Flattery. But who would have imagin'd, says he, that Franklin had been capable of such a Performance; such Painting, such Force! such Fire! he has even improv'd the Original! In his common Conversation, he seems to have no Choice of Words; he hesitates and blunders; and yet, good God, how he writes! (pp. 1341, 1342)

It is not clear that in relating this episode — a piece of narrative in which Franklin allowed himself, for the sake of recording the praise he received in his absence, the rare privilege of omniscience[26] — Franklin distinguished between his own performance

---

Addisonian prose. Franklin would spend the night recomposing the pages, restoring the linguistic order that had been momentarily threatened by mischance (p. 1363).

26. John Lynen, in one of the most thoughtful treatments of Franklin's artistry and thought, stresses Franklin's habitual limitation of his narrative viewpoint to

and the composition, belonging to somebody else, that he recited. He savored the success of the joke, of course; but he also frankly enjoyed the recognition he attracted by virtue of his borrowed eloquence. The "original" in question here, anyway, is elusive: is it Ralph's composition? or the words of scripture on which it was based? The search for an origin in this case is especially problematic, since from one point of view the original author of the Book of Psalms was uncertain (David?) and, as an inspired text, its ultimate author (God) could scarcely be thought to be improvable.

What this series of putative origins indicates, however—and this is also true of his imitation of the *Spectator*—is that Franklin understood keenly the way a particular subject was fashioned by the pregiven structures of language into which he inserted himself. There is a careful irony in Franklin's report of Osborne's assertion that Ralph's composition had "improv'd the original"—and the irony is present also in Franklin's claim that he had improved the *Spectator* when he rewrote it. For the original—the subject of any specific utterance—is, as Franklin by his irony tacitly recognized, fundamentally the emergence into being of a property of language itself; in the words of Benveniste, "It is in and through language that man constitutes himself as a *subject*, because language alone establishes the concept of 'ego' in reality, in *its* reality which is that of the being. . . . 'Ego' is he who *says* 'ego.'"[27]

When the deception was revealed to Osborne, he was accordingly "laught at" for his gullibility (p. 1342). Ralph remained fixed in his determination to become a poet. The muses did not aid him in this resolution, but he nevertheless became "a pretty good Prose Writer," according to Franklin (p. 1342). Osborne, ironically, went on to advance himself by means of the linguistic facility he always deprecated: he made a lot of money as a lawyer—that is, as a professional talker, one who speaks for others. The irony is heightened by Franklin's relation of a promise once made to him by Osborne. The two of them had agreed that whichever of them

---

that of the particular individual in his immediate experience, and contrasts this mundane point of view with the one chosen by Jonathan Edwards, which was that of the universal panorama as apprehended by God. See *The Design of the Present: Essays on Time and Form in American Literature* (New Haven: Yale Univ. Press, 1969), pp. 87–152.

27. Benveniste, *Problems,* p. 224.

died first would come back and inform the other "how he found things in that separate State." But although Osborne died first, and although he had been the one who deprecated mere talk and was careful to acquire the reputation of a man whose word could be credited, he "never fulfill'd his Promise" (p. 1342). His words, as it turned out, were empty. This small circumstance, casually related, acquires a broader meaning when we notice that Osborne's failure to fulfill his verbal promise paralleled another failure of a similar kind, detailed at length in the *Autobiography*. This was the failure of Governor William Keith to deliver on a promise he also made to Franklin.

The Keith episode is central to the *Autobiography's* purposes. In the *Autobiography*, Franklin, having embarked for London at the behest of Keith to buy the equipment and materials necessary to start a printing house, found that Keith's promise to underwrite the venture by providing letters of credit was worthless. The letters, supposedly sent on board the ship at the last moment, were not to be found when the mail sack was opened; and Franklin, finding himself in London completely without means, but with a new suspicion regarding the "Sincerity" (p. 1344) of utterances like those that had brought him to his unhappy position, had to shift for himself. Confiding his experience to his friend Thomas Denham, Franklin found that this confidant only "laught at the Notion of the Governor's giving me a Letter of Credit, having as he said no Credit to give" (p. 1344). Another of Franklin's ironies is here: having no credit to give, Keith was yet able to give *letters* of credit very easily; or, at one further remove, to give *promises* of letters of credit. That is, he was able to use words to represent himself as having the credit he actually lacked. And a "poor ignorant Boy" like Franklin readily credited those words (p. 1345). (The trip to London to purchase types is in itself an allegory of language acquisition; letters of one kind were to enable him to obtain letters of another kind.) In spite of having been so grossly imposed upon, however, Franklin seemingly harbored little resentment (perhaps because, by the time he wrote the first part of his text in 1771, he had long since learned to rely on the credit his own words could buy him); he concluded his account of his youthful credulity and Keith's insincerity by recalling that, after all, Keith was "a pretty good Writer" (p. 1345). Such, we recall, was Franklin's grudging final comment on his friend Ralph—who had also imposed upon him (by borrowing money and never repaying it, exposing likewise the absence of real credit behind his verbal promises) but who was, after all, "a pretty good Prose Writer" (p. 1342). This was, of course, Franklin's own dearest ambition, and by granting to these two otherwise stigmatized characters the talent he most desired for himself, Franklin considerably vitiated the punishment his memoir visited upon their reputations. But he actually had more in common with Ralph and Keith than talent as a prose writer, as his own narrative demonstrates; he, too, was adept at verbal imposture.

Franklin interrupted this account of the "Tricks" (p. 1345) played on him by Keith to give an account of what he also called a "Trick" (p. 1342)—one involving verbal deception as well—but which was not played *on* him but *by* him. This was the imposture, already described, which he and Ralph performed at the expense of Osborne. The two episodes, so nearly symmetrical, are embedded one within the other in the text; they thus comment on one another in an obvious, though perhaps unintended, way. They make it difficult for the reader to credit Franklin's description of himself as "a poor ignorant Boy" who was at the mercy of sophisticated verbal charlatans like Keith, since the narrative of that deception is interrupted by the narrative of the similar imposture in which Franklin was not the deceived but the deceiver. The reversal of roles, and the identity of crucial phrases in the two accounts—Denham "laught at" Franklin's naiveté just as Franklin and Ralph "laught at" Osborne; Keith's "Tricks" and the "Trick" played by Franklin and Ralph on Osborne beg to be compared—suggest an admission, making its way to the verbal surface of the text, of an internal inconsistency. For the two accounts—of the Franklin who deceives and the Franklin who is deceived—stand in a relation of contradiction which their proximity in the text serves to point out.

The contradiction received no overt examination, though; the two accounts, despite their symmetry and proximity, were not explicitly confronted with one another. There was no point of view from which Franklin the narrator would reconcile the knowing boy who tricked his friend with words and the innocent boy who was tricked by the governor's words. Although he was writing in retrospect, Franklin did not, for instance, represent himself as having passed from an innocent trust in words to a skeptical distrust of them: the deceiving act he perpetrated preceded the deception of which he was the victim, both in order of narration and in chronological time. We are hard put, as readers, to decide which of these Franklins to credit.

Unexamined contradiction is, in fact, a characteristic feature of the text. The moment when the text's inner disparities will be reconciled is repeatedly postponed. The real, integral Franklin is promised but never produced, just as the letters of credit promised by Keith were never delivered. As Franklin put it, "For these Letters I was appointed to call at different times, when they were to be ready, but a future time was still named" (p. 1342). This sentence could well stand as an emblem for the text as a whole, since Franklin's writing (to borrow a formulation of Barthes) "practises the infinite deferment of the signified."[28]

The text is, after all, an autobiography; it is meant to represent Franklin's self.[29] Critics have frequently commented on the plurality of Franklin's "masks," or they have referred to his "many sides." But they have felt obliged, in the end, to posit a unitary Franklin behind the masks, a single individual who is the locus of resolution of the several aspects in which he was represented. Such an insistence on Franklin's ultimate unity manifestly misconstrues the text. We would do better simply to accept the fact that a radically discontinuous, incomplete, patched-together text like that of the *Autobiography* cannot be made to produce an integral Franklin unless its most prominent formal features and its many internal inconsistencies are ignored. The self that such a text represents is, inevitably, disunified and incomplete; in the case of Franklin, this

28. Roland Barthes, *Image, Music, Text,* trans. Stephen Heath (New York: Hill and Wang, 1977), p. 158.

29. Louis Renza has said of autobiography that its aim is "to signify the autobiographer's nontextual identity or 'interiority'—to induce in the reader a belief that the words on the page originated in a real being." See "The Veto of the Imagination: A Theory of Autobiography," *New Literary History* 9 (1977): 7. But Franklin's text explicitly frustrates this expectation; it flaunts the *textual* self, in all its unstable variability, and conspicuously fails to produce the presence of the genuine subject.

is in keeping with his recognition that the self is a function of language, and is therefore (because of its necessary alienation in the otherness of language) fundamentally divided.

V. Revolution at a Distance

What is continually deferred in the text of the *Autobiography* is the American Revolution itself. If the Revolution is announced in Franklin's text, it is only by the vicarious means of a conspicuous division in the text's structure which refers obliquely to the definitive break with British authority. It is generally true that since revolution is a process, it resists representation. Representation seeks to fix its object, but revolution is motion and change; to represent it would necessarily be to distort it by closing it off. Franklin's text, although it manifestly avoids the Revolution as subject matter, nevertheless refers covertly, by means of its formal irregularities, to the very event it seeks to repress.

Overtly, however, Franklin avoided writing about the Revolution. His narrative breaks off at the events of 1757, and while it is usual among interpreters of the *Autobiography* to characterize the text's incompletion as an accident — to claim that Franklin just didn't get any farther along, having died before he could write more — this is not really an adequate explanation. (It is the alibi given by Franklin himself at various places in the text.) Any textual feature can be called an accident of circumstances, and can therefore be considered meaningless and uninteresting. While it is true that a literary text is produced under determinate conditions that may substantially affect the form it takes by limiting in certain ways the author's creative autonomy, even exhaustive enumeration of those conditions would not, obviously, give a complete account of the text's formation. So to say that Franklin died before he could write any more, while strictly true — he was, in fact, writing part four on his deathbed — is nevertheless trivial. The actual conditions in which he wrote — the heavy burden of official duties — did not prevent him from writing thousands of personal letters, pamphlets, broadsides, moral essays, and scientific reports, amounting to millions of words. It did not prevent him from flirting with French ladies, playing chess with friends, and calcu-

lating the number of candles that would be saved if daylight sav-
ings time were to be instituted. The essential question is why, in
a life full of so much accomplishment, Franklin repeatedly put
aside this particular piece of writing and left it unfinished; why, in
the most methodical of lives, in which few intentions, once
formed, were not carried out, did he find this particular project so
difficult to complete? Franklin formed the intention of writing his
Autobiography and began writing it in 1771, and spent the next
twenty years failing to complete it, repeatedly turning away from
it toward other endeavors. My hypothesis is that he did not want
to write about the Revolution. This is necessarily a speculative
contention, but given the premises of Franklin's narrative program, and considering his remarks in other places on the Revolution, it seems likely.

In fact, I believe his repeated deferral, as he composed the *Autobiography,* of the moment of the Revolution, was a manifestation
of a deep strategy of avoidance that joined his practice as a writer
to his policy as a diplomat. This deferral, I suspect, accounts for
the numerous interruptions of the narrative, and for the conspicuous breaks in the text which are the traces of Franklin's repeated
abandonment of the act of writing. The word revolution is one
that went unspoken in Franklin's text: he referred once to "the
War" (p. 1395), but only to regret that his personal papers were
lost in it; and he referred another time to "the bloody Contest"
(p. 1431), only to regret that his advice hadn't been taken when
it would have prevented the occurrence of the Revolution. Tem-
peramentally averse to precipitate action, Franklin was not a likely
revolutionary. He hesitated to commit himself to armed insurrection against British authority, and his diplomacy probably delayed
the war for several years, as he succeeded in getting Parliament to
repeal the Stamp Act and other measures that had contributed to
the growth of revolutionary consciousness in America. When he
wrote the third part of his *Autobiography* in 1788, he recalled with
evident distress that the compromise he had worked out in 1754
for the government of the colonies (the Albany Plan) had not
been adopted, since the British thought it too democratic and the
Americans not democratic enough. "The different & contrary
Reasons of dislike to my Plan, makes me suspect that it was really

the true Medium," he wrote; "& I am still of Opinion it would
have been happy for both Sides the Water if it had been adopted"
(p. 1431). Had it been adopted, Franklin reasoned, the colonies
so united would have been able to defend themselves in the Seven
Years War; then no troops would have been stationed by Britain
in the colonies; then the British would have had no pretense for
the taxes they laid on the colonies, taxes which were said to be
required to support the military forces stationed in America; and
then "the bloody Contest it occasioned, would have been
avoided" (p. 1431).[30] But if it was not avoided in fact, to Franklin's
permanent chagrin, it could certainly be avoided in the text; at
least, the text could be written in such a way as to make the Revolution's commanding presence in the author's life only vaguely and
indirectly felt.

The oblique indications of the Revolution's presence are the
gaps in the text. One way to describe the formal structure of the
Autobiography is by detailing precisely those fissures. The first appearance of the Revolution in Franklin's text is, as it happens, at
the first of the conspicuous discontinuities that are the text's most
prominent structural features — the gap between parts 1 and 2.
Here Franklin inserted a "Mem.o," which accounted for the space
in the text by reference to the intervention of time between the
composition of the parts. "Thus far was written with the Intention
express'd in the Beginning," Franklin noted; "What follows was
written many Years after" (p. 1372). The "Intention" governing
the writing of the first part, as he had said, was to convey to his
son and other descendants the method of his success in life so that
they might imitate it. His first intention, then, was the familiar
didactic one of reproducing the norms of a particular cultural system in the succeeding generation. The rhetoric of direct paternal
address served that end well. But the model of a text governed
by a single performed intention was, in the course of writing the
Autobiography, repeatedly subverted, not least by the visible inter-

30. At about the time Franklin was writing the third part of the *Autobiography,*
he wrote to a newspaper in a similar vein. Citing the Albany Plan, he claimed "that
if the foregoing Plan or some thing like it, had been adopted and carried into
Execution, the subsequent Separation of the Colonies from the Mother Country
might not so soon have happened, nor the Mischiefs suffered on both sides have
occurred, perhaps during another Century." Franklin, *Papers,* 5: 417.

ruptions that betrayed the author's shifting intentions. Most of these interruptions are relatively inconspicuous, but the large gaps between the four main sections declare the text's radical discontinuity quite unmistakably. In the space opened up by the lapse of time between 1771 (the time of composition of the first part) and 1784 (second part), Franklin wrote that "The Affairs of the Revolution occasion'd the Interruption" (p. 1372). This "Mem.o" was probably not meant to be printed; but its existence justifies us in saying that the Revolution first makes its presence felt in the space of its absence; in its first appearance it is blamed for having separated the author from his original intention, or for having diverted or dilated that intention. The Revolution, that is, effected a decisive *divergence* of the text, quite literally; and thereafter (in the second, third, and fourth parts of the text) the Revolution, and Franklin's skewed relation to it, determined further formal irregularities.

The text of the *Autobiography* as it exists is anything but a single coherent document. Its most salient formal features, as I have said, are its divisions or interruptions. Its next most prominent feature would probably be its incompletion, its lack of closure. Scholars and critics have labored diligently to process the text into coherence, to produce the requisite unity that is the object of much literary criticism; but in so doing they have obscured, I would argue, what are among the text's most meaningful features. The disunity of the text bears witness to the historical rupture of the Revolution. The text's discrepancies and contradictions, far from being mere surface phenomena that the critic does well to dismiss, are in fact among its most densely meaningful aspects, and demand critical attention and understanding. As I hope to show, the formal incoherence of the *Autobiography* is the sign of the failure of Franklin's narrative program, and that failure is the result of his tangential relation to the Revolution. Since the basic premise of the narrative is that Franklin is a representative figure, whose course of life stands in an allegorical relation to the historical course of the nation, his alienation from the Revolution—the founding event of the nation—presented him with a difficult narrative problem. How could he identify himself with America if he held that its founding act, the Revolution, was an avoidable mistake? How could he identify himself with America if he was in England trying to prevent the Revolution from happening, and then, once it did happen, spent its duration in France trying to put an end to it? How could he present himself as a representative figure when his doubts as to the Revolution's advisability or necessity were so serious?

The tangential nature of Franklin's relation to the Revolution was a product of other circumstances too: his son, to whom the *Autobiography* was first addressed, was a Loyalist.[31] Franklin could not very well, then, have carried out his initial formal intention and still have identified himself with the Revolution. His advice to his son had too obviously had the wrong effect. Franklin's role in the political agitations in Philadelphia in the decades preceding the Revolution also complicated his status as a revolutionary: his role had been actively to *seek* royal government for Pennsylvania, to replace the proprietary government of the Penns. This agitation, and the popular resentment it aroused against colonial administration by absent powers, fed directly into the popular protest against British rule in later years. Franklin's energies, then, had been exercised on behalf of the crown; and his business activities tied him to British authority as well, both as official printer to the government and as postmaster general (a royal appointment). All of this is not to cast doubt on Franklin's eventual attachment to the patriot cause; it is merely to show that in writing the *Autobiography* it was not a simple matter for him to portray himself as a representative figure, since in certain crucial respects he was quite *un*representative of a nation founded in revolution. The complex, equivocal nature of his relation to the Revolution left its mark on his *Autobiography* as he contended with it while writing.

31. William Franklin was at the time of this writing forty years old or older, and thus the salutation must not be understood literally to make of the following text a personal communication to Franklin's offspring; it is, as J. A. Leo Lemay has observed, a literary conceit, a convention with many precedents in advice literature. Nevertheless I would still hold that the political affiliation of this nominal addressee creates an ideological problem for Franklin's rhetorical program. See Lemay, "Lockean Realities and Olympian Perspectives: The Writing of Franklin's *Autobiography*," in James Barbour and Tom Quirk, eds., *Writing the American Classics* (Chapel Hill: Univ. of North Carolina Press, 1990), p. 4; also idem., "Benjamin Franklin," in Everett Emerson, ed., *Major Writers of Early American Literature* (Madison: Univ. of Wisconsin Press, 1972), pp. 238–39.

In the space opened up between parts 1 and 2 by the intervention of the Revolution, Franklin inserted two letters from his friends Abel James and Benjamin Vaughan. In these letters they advised him to continue his *Autobiography* and to write it for the edification of the broad public. In this way, at this place, the point of the text's first prominent dilation, two additional voices were permitted to be heard, displacing the single commanding voice of a father addressing his son. It is as though the text, having departed from its original intention, having been interrupted by the event of the Revolution, could now be written without the guarantee of its father, was now free of the didactic burden formerly dominating it. What was formerly a monologue became, at least momentarily, a conversation; and when Franklin's voice was again asserted, in the resumption of the narrative, it was heard at the invitation, so to speak, of James and Vaughan. They required him to reassume the representative role he had felt unable, after the Revolution, to reclaim for himself. Vaughan in particular engaged Franklin in this representative role: "All that has happened to you is also connected with the detail of the manners and situation of *a rising* people," he assured the hesitating autobiographer (p. 1374). Vaughan also very conveniently provided Franklin with a rationale (or alibi) for his hesitation: one of the things that will be demonstrated by the *Autobiography*, Vaughan said, "will be the propriety of every man's waiting for his time for appearing upon the stage of the world" (p. 1376). The enabling effect of this alibi consisted in its granting credit to Franklin for exactly the habit of deferral that had distanced him from the action of the Revolution. This habit of deferral — what Vaughan (paraphrasing Abel James) called "frugality, diligence, and temperance," that is, a talent for postponing the gratification of desires — made Franklin "a pattern for all youth" (p. 1377). Thus the very lack of precipitating desire that distanced Franklin from the Revolution was conveniently interpreted by Vaughan as a virtue that restored Franklin to his place as a "pattern" for "*a rising* people." Of course it was Franklin who inserted the Vaughan letter into the text, who absorbed it as his own utterance much as he had assimilated Ralph's version of the psalm or the *Spectator's* prose. In this case, however, the Vaughan letter re-established the representative status to which Franklin aspired, but which the Revolution made problematic; Vaughan placed Franklin once more at the center of the national drama, and this restoration took place at the very point in the text where his actual distance from the Revolution had disintegrated the allegorical equation.

The textual gap was bridged by virtue of the James and Vaughan letters, but the narrative problem was not so easily solved. Franklin was, after all, of a different generation from the Revolutionary leaders. If he was a founding father, as he is usually considered to have been, he stood in a relation to his Revolution-born children that was very much like the irregular relation in which his own father stood to him: Franklin was seventy years old when independence was declared by younger men. Even if we believe that he succeeded in his attempt to reestablish his representative status, he still never actually wrote about the Revolution. He wasn't *there* for it, and his narrative never explicitly addresses it. The *Autobiography,* after a series of interruptions, breaks off finally in 1757; it is entirely the story of a colonial subject of Great Britain. Why should the life of a colonial, and the autobiography that is its written rehearsal, have become the paradigm for lives and autobiographies in the independent American nation, as Franklin's has?

The question will find no simple answer. In part, the success of the *Autobiography* as a model had to do with the need in a postrevolutionary society for a pattern of unrevolutionary behavior. In the 1790s and thereafter, when Franklin's text became available and was widely reprinted and avidly read, his method of deferral conceivably served several useful purposes. In the years of nation-building, political consolidation and cultural order emerged only fitfully; a nation *founded* on revolution, propelled into existence by the human energy that revolution released, could not easily, afterwards, contain and control the individualistic forces it had stimulated. The Revolution created new expectations of social equality and individual freedom, and such expectations were not immediately satisfied. The promise of the Revolution — like the promise made to Franklin by Governor Keith — consisted of certain words that could not instantly call into being the imagined reality they sought to refer to. In particular, the expected end to social privilege was not immediately met; inequalities of wealth and status that had been slowly enlarged in the preceding decades were not to be reduced at a stroke. Those who were less equal than others were consequently impatient and frustrated. They had the word — *equality* — but they still awaited its referent. The Revolution, in short, had been an affair of the signifier; and as the reality was repeatedly withheld or postponed — as taxes were reimposed, as local insurrections were quashed by military force, and as economic privileges were left in place and even reinforced by government policy — many who had fought for what the Revolution promised were restless and dissatisfied. Franklin's text taught such people the virtue of patience in the face of such deferral; it taught the necessity of frugality and diligence at a time when, for instance, the poor were wondering why, now that British authority had been removed, their condition was substantially unchanged. And it recommended, in its prescriptions for behavior (particularly verbal behavior), special methods for avoiding social conflict when possible and suppressing it when it threatened to erupt.

VI. Textual Self-Difference

It is an interesting coincidence that at the place where the Revolution's absence created a space in Franklin's text — a space into which Franklin inserted the claim (assigned to the voice of another) that he was, as Vaughan implausibly said, the "author" (p. 1378) of the Revolution, who was only too full of "modesty" (p. 1377) to advance the claim himself — at that place, Franklin chose (despite the recommendations of both James and Vaughan that he should continue to write in the paternal mode in which he began) to abandon his initial rhetorical strategy. This is another way in which the Revolution was represented obliquely. The first part of the *Autobiography* (the only part James and Vaughan had seen) was entirely written under the aegis of a certain rhetorical model that was legitimated by the authority of the father; and the first part of the text is more or less continuous, quite like the genealogy it was careful to trace. Franklin expressed the desire for "a Repetition of the same Life from its Beginning," and since such repetition was impossible, he said he would settle for a "*Recollec-*

tion of that Life," which, "to make [it] as durable as possible," he would commit to writing (p. 1307). Such a written representation would be "therefore fit to be imitated" by his "Posterity" (p. 1307) — that is, repeated by his descendants in perpetuity.

The rhetoric of direct paternal address, however, began to lose some of its force as Franklin, within a few pages, began (as we have seen) to disturb the pattern of genealogical continuity. He extricated himself from his father's authority by representing himself as the descendant of several other ancestors whose lives, he found, had prefigured his own, and he found patrons who offered him opportunities his father denied him. The act of writing his life allowed him, in short, to fashion for himself a genealogy in which his natural father was, as it were, shunted aside.

It was just such a deviation — a refusal of a certain origin, and a denial of that origin's authority — that the American Revolution performed. The antipatriarchal rhetoric that was an important element in revolutionary propaganda, and the emerging style of affectional parental behavior that was becoming more popular in actual families at the same time, have been well documented.[32] What we can learn from Franklin is that the authority formerly vested in the father, then denied by the Revolution, was thereafter invested in language; it was language, precisely, that enabled him, along with other Americans, to deny effectively the authority of the father, to make a break with the past, to institute a new order.

32. Fliegelman, *Prodigals and Pilgrims;* Peter Shaw, *American Patriots and the Rituals of Revolution* (Cambridge, Massachusetts: Harvard Univ. Press, 1981); Philip Greven, *The Protestant Temperament: Patterns of Child-Rearing, Religious Experience, and the Self in Early America* (1977; Chicago: Univ. of Chicago Press, 1988). Max Horkheimer contended that even "kindness" as opposed to "coercion" in a parent's behavior toward a child did not essentially mitigate the basic hierarchical structure of the family, and that it is this *structure* that produces authority-oriented personalities. See "Authority and the Family," in *Critical Theory: Selected Essays,* trans. Mathew J. O'Connel et al. (New York: Seabury Press, c. 1972), pp. 47–128. I should add that, in analyzing Franklin's particular family situation as the context of the formation of his character and attitudes, I do not at all mean to depreciate — in the way that Deleuze and Guattari have criticized in their *Anti-Oedipus: Capitalism and Schizophrenia,* trans. Robert Hurley et al (New York: Viking, 1977) — the political context of character formation. Rather, I hold, with Sartre (and Horkheimer) that it is inside a particular family that a child experiences the objective movements of politics: "The family in fact is constituted by and in the general movement of History, but is experienced, on the other hand, as an absolute in the depth and opaqueness of childhood": Jean-Paul Sartre, *Search for a Method,* trans. Hazel E. Barnes (New York: Alfred A. Knopf, 1967), p. 62.

And one enactment of this process in Franklin's *Autobiography* was his decision, recorded at the break between parts 1 and 2 of the text, to abandon the paternal rhetoric: he decided he would no longer write "with the simple Intention express'd in the Beginning, of gratifying the suppos'd Curiosity of my Son; and others of my Posterity." Franklin not only announced this deviation; he crossed out the words "simple" and "of gratifying the suppos'd Curiosity of my Son; and others of my Posterity" (p. 1372).[33] That is, not only did he deviate from his original intention; he began, also, to efface the very traces of the intention from which he was departing.

The text enacts in this way the eruption of the Revolution — the "Interruption" in the text, the deviation of part 2 from the intention governing part 1, represents indirectly the historical rupture that was the Revolution — but this indirection is nevertheless, obviously, somewhat obscure. The Revolution, we must still say, is for most readers effectively absent from the text.

I want, now, to consider in a slightly different way the meaning of interruption and deferral in the text of the *Autobiography*. The text is divided in many ways, on many levels. Franklin's predilection for dashes as punctuation (a feature of his writing that is unfortunately hidden by editors of modernized editions of the *Autobiography*) is a visible indication of the paratactic organization of the text. In addition, the outline from which he worked provided the skeleton, as it were, of this unsubordinated composition: "My writing. Mrs. Dogoods Letters — Differences arise between my Brother and me (his temper and mine) their Cause in general. His News Paper. The Prosecution he suffered. My Examination. Vote of Assembly. His Manner of evading it. Whereby I became free" (p. 1552, n. 1316.22). And so on. It is significant that this outline began with what I have claimed is the real subject of Franklin's narrative — his writing. And the very staccato form of the outline predicted the additive method of composition he then followed. This additivity is apparent on several levels — for instance, on the syntactic (Franklin's prose is Senecan) and on the architectonic

33. The cancellations are given in Franklin, *Writings,* p. 1557, n. 1372.30, and are evident in Lemay and Zall, *The Autobiography of Benjamin Franklin: A Genetic Text,* p. 72.

(each of the four sections is simply appended to what went before). His use of the ampersand draws attention to this additivity too. (Again, this feature of his prose is obscured by modernizing editors.) The insertion of supplementary texts—the note on the name Franklin, Uncle Benjamin's poem, a *Pennsylvania Gazette* editorial, the letters from James and Vaughan, the "golden verses" of Pythagoras, the wagon advertisement—gives a multiply grafted form to the text. One might also adduce, as further evidence (perhaps the most compelling) of the text's profound heterogeneity, or inner difference, Franklin's practice of folding in half, along a vertical axis, the paper on which he wrote: he drafted the text on one side of the crease that divided the sheet, and reserved the other half for the corrections, revisions, and additions he expected to make. Such a compositional practice advertises blatantly the inner division of his original intention: we might, for the sake of simplicity, label one side of the sheet "truth" and the other side "art." Such labels would not, of course, be strictly accurate, since even as he penned the first draft he was representing himself—that is, suppressing some facts, distorting others, probably inventing a few.[34] But in a qualified way, it is helpful heuristically to assume that when Franklin first put his account down on paper, he exercised his memory in a relatively haphazard fashion, and then, when he moved to the other side of the crease, he refined his memories with artistic purposes in mind. The configuration of the manuscript sheet itself, then, can be construed as a metaphor for the division of intent that also found expression in the formal disparities of the published text: like the gaps between the sections, the crease in the manuscript marks an interim, time elapsed between writing and rewriting.[35]

These formal features place Franklin's very identity in question, for it is Franklin's own repeated invocation of the figure of the *textual* self that enables us to say that in the *Autobiography* he has,

34. The misrepresentations in Franklin's account have been examined by Marc Egnal in "The Politics of Ambition: A New Look at Benjamin Franklin's Career," *Canadian Review of American Studies* 6 (1975): 151–64.

35. Derrida's study of the practice of spacing within literary texts—and his virtuosic enactment of such a practice—in "The Double Session" have suggested to me the importance of the materiality of Franklin's spacing. See *Dissemination,* trans. Barbara Johnson (Chicago: Univ. of Chicago Press, 1981), pp. 173–285.

as it were, rendered himself into textual fragments; in his heterogeneous text he displays his actual nontextual plurality. D. H. Lawrence quite legitimately took Franklin to be a convenient occasion for declaring, "I am many men" and asking, "Who are You? How many selves have you? And which of these selves do you want to be?"[36] The title given to the text by its editors—*Autobiography*—has given it a presumptive unity that disguises its actual multiplicity; Franklin's own title, *Memoirs,* ought perhaps to be preferred not only because it was Franklin's title but because it more adequately signifies the text's irreducible plurality. *Memoirs* also draws attention to the temporal lapses of which the text bears the traces. The four major fragments are, after all, divided from one another in the most flagrant way by the intervention of time; it is time itself that they bring into the text, as they record Franklin's delays and hesitations. Such hesitations, as I have said, recall Franklin's deferral of a decision to join the Revolution. They also refer obliquely to the difference in age separating him from his younger fellow patriots. But what they mimic most closely, I think, are the stammerings that Franklin was subject to as a speaker. What Osborne said of Franklin, after he had been so impressed by the latter's performance when reading Ralph's composition at their meeting, was by Franklin's own admission quite true: "In his common Conversation, he seems to have no Choice of Words; he hesitates and blunders" (p. 1342). Evidently Franklin suffered from what psychologists and speech pathologists call speech anxiety, which is manifested in an oral performance that is marred by hesitation phenomena and pathological reticence. Franklin was unable, when speaking before a group, to get his words out smoothly. As he said at another place in the *Autobiography*—significantly, right near another of the major breaks in the text, between parts 2 and 3—he acquired influence in public affairs only in spite of the real disadvantage presented by his severe inhibition as a speaker. Some kind of anxiety gripped him when he tried to speak in public: "For I was but a bad Speaker, never eloquent, subject to much Hesitation in my choice of Words,

---

36. D. H. Lawrence, *Studies in Classic American Literature* (1924; London: Heinemann, 1964), p. 9.

hardly correct in Language, and yet I generally carried my Points"
(p. 1393).

   Franklin's confession of his inadequacy as a verbal performer
came just before he enacted it textually by breaking off his writing
for a second time; what both the actual hesitation phenomena that
plagued Franklin as a speaker and the analogous textual phenomena indicate is what may be called non-self-identity in the act of
utterance. Basil Bernstein has constructed a set of categories that
may be usefully applied to Franklin, distinguishing between "restricted" and "elaborated" codes, which mean, roughly, the norms
of speech characteristic of, on the one hand, closed, homogeneous
social groups (restricted code), and on the other hand, linguistic
norms proper to larger, more impersonal social settings (elaborated code).[37] In the restricted code, much is taken for granted
among conversational partners, and therefore can be left unsaid,
since speakers within the group are assumed to share a common
stock of knowledge and to have interests in common. In the elaborated code, on the contrary, such group solidarity cannot be taken
for granted, and so meanings must be made explicit by speakers.
Bernstein has found that the more complex "verbal planning" —
choosing from the range of possible words, phrases, syntactical
structures, and so forth — required of a speaker who is using the
elaborated code results in a greater incidence of pauses or hesitations in the utterance, since more (and more complex) decisions
have to be made by such a speaker. This suggests that Franklin,
who was making a deliberate effort to enlarge his vocabulary, improve his style, and write in a manner (Addisonian) that was, by
definition, not restricted in its meanings but addressed to a cos-
mopolitan audience, would quite naturally have paused and hesitated frequently as he sought to learn and master the elaborated
code. Bernstein has found, in addition, that there is a correlation
between an individual's economic or social class and the availabil-
ity to him of the different codes. Franklin, as a working-class
youth moving into middle- and upper-class social circles, and trying deliberately to conform his speech habits to those considered

---

37. Basil Bernstein, *Class, Codes and Control*, Vol. 1, *Theoretical Studies Toward a
Sociology of Language* (London: Routledge & Kegan Paul, 1971), pp. 76–94.

proper in those circles, would have found the more complex verbal planning required by those new standards unfamiliar and difficult at first, and this difficulty would have been apparent in his anxious hesitations. These halting pauses, in which Franklin was literally at a loss for words, betrayed a fissure in the system of what Derrida has called "s'entendre parler," the presence-to-self of the individual in the moment of hearing-himself-speak.[38] The simultaneity of speaking and hearing-oneself-speak, and the physical proximity of speaker and auditor—their coalescence in one body—conspire to produce, according to Derrida, a secure sense of self-identity in the person in question. Hesitation phenomena and a lack of fluency have the effect of interposing a space of time within the act of utterance; they therefore place that sense of self-identity in jeopardy.

Something like this sense of non-self-identity is dramatized in the text of the *Autobiography:* we observe Franklin only, as it were, in his phases, never in his presumably integral being. And since what the *Autobiography* sought to achieve was a picture of Franklin as a representative American, in the auto-American-biographical tradition, the failure of that text to present a unitary figure was at the same time a failure to produce a unitary America. What it produced instead, however, was an unrevolutionary America, an America in which revolution is constantly deferred. In the space of the lapse that Franklin's hesitation created—in the gap between parts 1 and 2, for instance, where he represented the Revolution unwittingly by the very break that marked its absence—Franklin inserted the letters that posited an identity between himself and America, an identity that he could not, in good conscience, assert on his own behalf. That is, Franklin substituted in the place of the Revolution a model of identity between self and nation, and a method of deferral of pleasure that was exactly the opposite of the precipitating desire that helped bring on the Revolution. In effect, Franklin proposed that "frugality, diligence, and temperance," the famous work ethic of which he was an ardent proponent, would provide for Americans individually and America generally a more

38. Jacques Derrida, *Speech and Phenomena, and Other Essays on Husserl's Theory of Signs,* trans. David B. Allison (Evanston: Northwestern Univ. Press, 1973), p. 79.

secure foundation for the future than would the mode of action of the Revolution, which was one of sheer expenditure, precipitate action, and intemperate desire.

VII. Conversation and Conciliation

While engaged in his youth in the appropriation of others' eloquence, Franklin came upon "a Specimen of a Dispute in the Socratic Method" at the end of a grammar he was studying. He also found several examples of the same method in an edition of Xenophon's *Memorabilia* he possessed. "Charm'd" by the method, he adopted it, and practiced it thereafter with enthusiasm. As it happened, however, what Franklin adopted cannot be called a genuinely Socratic practice: he said he only falsely "put on the humble Enquirer & Doubter" (p. 1321). The so-called Socratic method he adopted was not a practice of genuine questioning, but a technique of pseudoquestioning which was directed not toward attainment of an unforeseen truth which would provide the basis for real human understanding, but rather toward the surreptitious enforcement upon others of an opinion he had already arrived at. He especially enjoyed using this method to force others into religious doubt. Having himself become "a real Doubter in many Points of our Religious Doctrine," he said,

> I found this Method safest for my self & very embarassing to those against whom I used it, therefore I took a Delight in it, practis'd it continually & grew very artful & expert in drawing People even of superior Knowledge into Concessions the Consequences of which they did not foresee, entangling them in Difficulties out of which they could not extricate themselves, and so obtaining Victories that neither my self nor my Cause always deserved. (p. 1321)

This was sophistry, not true Socratic dialogue: it was a method used "against" others in order to obtain "Victories." The others, perhaps, did not "foresee" the end of it, but Franklin certainly did; and he managed the conversation toward his predetermined end.

Franklin was unwilling, we may say, to allow the conversation to take its own course; he never forgot himself in the flow of talk, never surrendered himself to the mutuality that the medium of language could sustain. Even when, a few years later, he left his pseudo-Socratic method behind, "retaining only the Habit of expressing my self in Terms of modest Diffidence," he was essentially reserving the active manipulative role in conversation for himself. His habit now consisted in "never using when I advance any thing that may possibly be disputed, the Words, *Certainly, undoubtedly,* or any others that give the Air of Positiveness to an Opinion; but rather say, *I conceive,* or *I apprehend* a Thing to be so or so, *It appears to me,* or *I should think it so or so for such & such Reasons,* or *I imagine* it to be so, or *it is so* if *I am not mistaken*" (pp. 1321, 1321–22). The phrases in this repertoire of diffident poses, while they conveyed an appearance of uncertainty, did not affect the reality of Franklin's positive convictions and his desire for victory. Conversation was still a means to an end for him: "This Habit I believe has been of great Advantage to me, when I have had occasion to inculcate my Opinions & persuade Men into Measures that I have been from time to time engag'd in promoting" (p. 1322). The method of pretended uncertainty masking actual conviction would, indeed, become Franklin's habit. He would use it against his employer, the printer Samuel Keimer:

> We . . . had many Disputations. I us'd to work him so with my Socratic Method, and had trapann'd him so often by Questions apparently so distant from any Point we had in hand, and yet by degrees led to the Point, and brought him into Difficulties & Contradictions, that at last he grew ridiculously cautious, and would hardly answer me the most common Question, without asking first, *What do you intend to infer from that?* (p. 1339)

Despite having already announced that he gave up this practice, and having stated that he regretted ever having used it, Franklin yet took obvious delight in recounting the episode. His verbal aggression was, so to speak, the linguistic model of the general deception he practiced on Keimer: Franklin presented himself to his employer as a loyal subordinate, while in fact he was preparing to set up as Keimer's competitor. The advantage he took of Keimer was prefigured in the text quite clearly by another account of victimization: Franklin told how, at the time he was seeking a job, he was first taken to be introduced to Keimer by the father of the other printer in town (Andrew Bradford, from whom Franklin had first sought work, but unsuccessfully). The elder Bradford

> enter'd into a Conversation [with Keimer] on his present Undertaking & Prospects; while Bradford not discovering that he was the other Printer's Father; on Keimer's Saying he expected soon to get the greatest Part of the Business into his own Hands, drew him on by artful Questions and starting little Doubts, to explain all his Views, what Interest he rely'd on, & in what manner he intended to proceed. (pp. 1330–31)

Verbal parallels establish in the text a relation between the elder Bradford's duplicity towards Keimer and Franklin's: as the young man was "artful & expert in drawing People . . . into Concessions" (p. 1321), so too the older man "drew him [Keimer] on by artful Questions" (p. 1331). Franklin bestowed his moral disapproval not on himself but only on Bradford, however, observing "that one of them was a crafty old Sophister, and the other a mere Novice" (p. 1331). We might say the same thing about Franklin as he represented himself, or his selves, in the text: one of the selves was a crafty sophister who delighted in verbal dissimulation, while the other was a mere novice, an innocent victim of others' dissimulations.

Franklin's final habitual practice as a conversationalist — which was, according to his account, to divest himself of the "Positive assuming Manner that seldom fails to disgust, tends to create Opposition and to defeat every one of those Purposes for which Speech was given us, to wit, giving or receiving Information, or Pleasure" (p. 1322) — represented his final accession to the position of authority of his father, an assumption of what he described as his father's characteristic role in language. Josiah Franklin — who, as it happened, according to his son, "had a clear pleasing Voice" (p. 1314) — did not take an official role in public affairs, the need to support his family requiring him to stick to his trade. But because "his great Excellence lay in a sound Understanding, and solid Judgment in prudential Matters," he was "frequently visited by leading People, who consulted him for his Opinion on Affairs of the Town or of the Church he belong'd to & show'd a good deal of Respect for his Judgment and Advice" (p. 1315). His reputation for sound judgment led to his being "also much consulted by private Persons about their Affairs when any Difficulty occur'd, & frequently chosen an Arbitrator between contending Parties" (p. 1315). This talent for mediation aroused Franklin's envy: it would be his ambition, also, to perform this mediating function, to settle differences.[39] As he said in the *Autobiography,* he "made it a Rule to forbear all direct Contradiction to the Sentiments of others, and all positive Assertion of my own" (p. 1393). This was done in accordance with the policy of his Junto, the mutual aid and self-help group he formed with young men of his acquaintance, where all debates were to be conducted in a spirit of goodwill, "without Fondness for Dispute, or Desire of Victory," and where "all Expressions of Positiveness in Opinion, or of direct Contradiction, were after some time made contraband & prohibited under small pecuniary Penalties" (p. 1361). So Franklin adopted his father's practice of arbitration and compromise, made it his own, and extended it to the society around him. It was this habit, as he said, which enabled him to pursue his successful public career at a time when Philadelphia society was wracked by political, religious, ethnic, and class divisions. Franklin managed, in a kind of personal *Aufhebung,* to transcend those differences:

> I soon found the Advantage of this Change in my Manners. The Conversations I engag'd in went on more pleasantly. The modest way in which I propos'd my Opinions, procur'd them a readier Reception and less Contradiction; I had less mortification when I was

39. "Franklin was above all a negotiator, an expert bargainer inclined to reconcile conflicting parties on terms mutually beneficial," according to Richard L. Bushman. See "On the Uses of Psychology: Conflict and Conciliation in Benjamin Franklin," *History and Theory* 5 (1966): 237. Taking Franklin as a prototypical confidence man, Gary Lindberg holds that Franklin "sees and projects himself as an arbitrator, a means to facilitate compromise. He presides over the phenomena of convergence and interchange, showing how people can join to promote their mutual interest." See *The Confidence Man in American Literature* (New York: Oxford Univ. Press, 1982), p. 81.

found to be in the wrong, and I more easily prevail'd
with others to give up their Mistakes & join with me
when I happen'd to be in the right. And this Mode,
which I at first put on, with some violence to natural
Inclination, became at length so easy & so habitual to
me, that perhaps for these Fifty Years past no one has
ever heard a dogmatical Expression escape me. And to
this Habit (after my Character of Integrity) I think it
principally owing, that I had early so much Weight
with my Fellow Citizens, when I proposed new Institutions, or Alterations in the old; and so much Influence in public Councils when I became a Member.
(p. 1393)

We have already seen how Franklin's struggle to acquire skill as a
writer and speaker was, as he understood it, a struggle with the
authority of his father, who criticized his early efforts. His father
later, continued to criticize his writing: even though Franklin had,
by this time, established himself in Philadelphia independently
(the entire story of his apprenticeship in various printing offices
being simultaneously an allegory of the accession to language and
of the acquisition of financial independence), when he returned to
Boston with Governor Keith's letter recommending that his father
set him up in business, Josiah refused, having "advanc'd too much
already to my Brother James," as Franklin resentfully added. Josiah
neither credited his son's business ability nor his linguistic competence. He merely advised his son "to behave respectfully to the
People there [Philadelphia], endeavour to obtain the general Esteem, & avoid lampooning & libelling to which he thought I had
too much Inclination" (p. 1335).[40] Never mind that Franklin did,
in fact, have such an inclination — Josiah was no doubt recalling the

---

40. In his account of his first return to Boston after fleeing his apprenticeship,
Franklin was quite clearly imitating, but revising in several significant ways, the
biblical account of the prodigal son. His family killed no fatted calf, but they were
"very glad to see me and made me Welcome" (p. 1333), despite his having injured
them. But Franklin's account of his family and its inner dynamics shows that he
was closely acquainted with what might serve as its biblical model. We have seen
that Franklin's father had children by two wives, and that the resulting divided
filiation had consequences for the structure of authority in the family. The biblical
Benjamin was, coincidentally, also the youngest son of a father (Jacob) whose several wives bore him a large number of children whose separate filiations created

incident just before Franklin left Boston, when, while managing his
brother's newspaper, he "made bold to give our Rulers some Rubs
in it, which my Brother took very kindly, while others began to consider me in an unfavourable Light, as a young Genius that had a
Turn for Libelling & Satyr" (p. 1324) — it was his father's conde-
scending recommendation of submission to authority, coupled
with expressed worries as to his literary propensities, that quite naturally disappointed the son who had expected his father to be impressed by the independence and the patronage he had attained.

  Determined to acquire the authority that inhered in language —
if not with his father's aid, then in spite of his father's doubts —
determined, that is, to possess the authority that he observed his
father to enjoy as a result of his skillful linguistic practices, Frank-

---

dissension among them. Franklin's familiarity with the Genesis account is suffi-
ciently shown by the fact that he wrote a chapter of biblical parody, known as "A
Parable on Brotherly Love," which portrayed the jealousies among the sons of
Jacob (pp. 421–23). The biblical Benjamin's brother Joseph (the only other son
Rachel bore), like the American Benjamin's brother James (also of the same
mother), wanted to make his younger brother his servant (Genesis 44: 17); only
the American brother succeeded. One of the closest borrowings in Franklin's
"Parable" is in the fourteenth verse, where the magnanimous Judah agrees to share
his ax with his brother Reuben, after the other brothers (Simeon and Levi) have
refused to share theirs; at this point, according to Franklin, "Reuben fell on his
Neck, and kissed him with Tears" (p. 422), which the editors of the *Papers* gloss
(Franklin, *Papers*, 6: 127) as an adaptation of Genesis 33: 4 (where Jacob is greeted
by a tearful Esau), but which is actually better seen as a reference to another fourteenth verse, in chapter 45 of Genesis, where Joseph, discovering his identity to
his surprised brothers, "fell upon his brother Benjamin's neck, and wept; and Benjamin wept upon his neck." This happy reconciliation contrasts markedly with the
reception Franklin got from his brother James upon returning to Boston: James
was "offended . . . extreamly" when his younger brother showed up at the printing
house with "a genteel new Suit from Head to foot, a Watch, and my Pockets lin'd
with near Five Pounds Sterling in Silver" (pp. 1334, 1333), which he proceeded
to display to James's workmen. Silver thus served, for the American Benjamin, to
prevent any reconciliation with his brother, whereas for his biblical precursor the
discovery of a silver cup in his sack by Joseph's steward was the plot device that
returned all the brothers to Joseph's house, where their loyal refusal to allow Benjamin alone to be punished for the alleged theft so impressed Joseph that he revealed
his identity to them. When they departed from him, he gave Benjamin "three hundred pieces of silver" in addition to the new clothes the other brothers received
(Genesis 45: 22). Joseph, that is, atoned in some measure to his younger brother
for having been his father's favorite ("Israel loved Joseph more than all his children," Genesis 37: 3). It was Joseph's coat of many colors, sign of paternal preference, that aroused his brothers' enmity; it was the fact that Josiah Franklin had
advanced money to James, but would not do the same for Benjamin, that so galled
the younger brother. Franklin's statement that his father, when refusing his request
for money to set up as a printer, "said he had advanc'd too much already to my
brother James" (p. 1555, n. 1334.25), was later scored out, and the record of
resentment thereby suppressed.

lin abandoned his aggressive predilections and imitated the conciliatory approach of his father. That is to say, Franklin described his
Oedipal conflict as having been, essentially, a matter of language,
of his attempt to insert himself into the symbolic order of which
his father was master. His ultimate assumption of the mediating
role which his father played, and which was therefore associated
for Franklin with the exercise of paternal authority, implicitly
recommended to Americans that they, too, might imitate his
methods; that they ought to reconcile their differences rather than
exacerbate them. Franklin's aggressive verbal behavior in his youth
stands, in an allegorical fashion, for revolution—against paternal
authority, and therefore, transitively, against Great Britain. It
stands for the speech that emerges in opposition to what went
before, that denies what went before; "contradiction" in conversational exchanges is to "diffidence" what revolution is to social harmony. Franklin often implicitly equated revolution with aggressive speech, as when he wrote in 1773 to his sister Jane Mecom
that he "had us'd all the smooth Words [he] could muster," but
when he saw his conciliatory speech to have no effect, he determined to be "saucy."[41] The anxiety that is evident throughout the
text of the *Autobiography* with regard to the Revolution—the pattern of deferrals, the gap between parts 1 and 2 where the Revolution actually intervened—covertly represents what the overt
recommendation of the text is meant to eliminate. That overt recommendation is, in its simplest terms, the admonition to preserve, as a crucial social apparatus, the veneer of consensus that
such conversational "diffidence" created. In the years following
the Revolution, as Franklin knew, social coherence was seriously
at risk. The aggressive energies that the Revolution had released
were now, when deprived of an external object, all too likely to be
directed against objects internal to America. In the context of the
considerable reciprocal violence of late eighteenth-century
America—and this is the context in which Franklin's *Autobiography* acquires its greatest significance—the recuperation of paternal
authority in a conciliatory style of discourse amounted to a program which would institute, by means of language, an appearance
(if not the reality) of social unity.

41. Franklin, *Papers*, 20: 457.

CHAPTER THREE

"The Very Act of Utterance"
Law, Language, and Legitimation
in Brown's *Wieland*

I. The Novel in the 1790s

"If history furnishes one parallel fact," Charles Brockden Brown wrote in the "Advertisement" that prefaced his novel *Wieland* (1798), referring to his eponymous character's grotesque delusions, "it is a sufficient vindication of the Writer; but most readers will probably recollect an authentic case, remarkably similar to that of Wieland."[1] While Brown's immediate reference, according to recent scholarship, is certainly to a multiple murder committed in 1781 by one James Yates in Tomhanick, New York, under the delusion of a divine injunction to slay his wife and four children (a crime of which a magazine account appeared in 1796),[2] it is also more than likely that his novel's unusual plot had a more general reference. In the same "Advertisement," Brown expressed the hope that his novel would not "be classed with the ordinary or frivolous sources of amusement," as it might have been if it were merely a fictional reworking of a sensational crime story; he claimed that his intention was, rather, "the illustration of some important branches of the moral constitution of man" (p. 3). That is to say, he meant to represent something essential about man's social being, and, as I shall argue, he meant to represent something about the specific conditions of American social existence.

---

1. Charles Brockden Brown, *Wieland, or The Transformation: An American Tale*, ed. Sydney J. Krause et al., Bicentennial Edition, *The Novels and Related Works of Charles Brockden Brown*, vol. 1 (Kent, Ohio: Kent State Univ. Press, 1977), p. 3. Further page references to *Wieland* will be given parenthetically.
2. Alexander Cowie, "Historical Essay," in ibid., pp. 323–24.

What is interesting is that Brown found that a tale of mysterious voices, criminal delusions, and social mayhem was, in the last years of the American eighteenth century, a powerful (if somewhat obscure or even etiolated) allegory of moral and political experience. That he sent a copy of the novel to Thomas Jefferson is another sign of the same intention.[3]

This allegory operates not in terms of direct correspondences to public events of the day, although it approaches such immediate reference at certain points. Mostly it operates in terms of a deep correspondence between the conceptual grammar of the gothic plot and the predominant representations of history and politics given in the culture of postrevolutionary America. As I will be showing, certain issues of time, political legitimacy, social solidarity and cultural coherence that were conspicuously thematized in the public consciousness of the 1790s were transformed, in Brown's *Wieland,* into problems of plot discontinuity, genealogical and historical filiation, vocal confusion, and intersubjective communication and understanding. In Brown's case, as an effect of his abortive career in law and his continuing fascination with questions of legal order, the historicity of law, and the forms of knowledge institutionalized in legal institutions and practices, these issues (time, legitimacy, solidarity, and coherence) and their corresponding textual forms (discontinuity, filiation, voice, and intersubjectivity) take on in *Wieland* a kind of legal coloration. And this persistent legal reference turns out, in the event, to be reducible in crucial respects to questions of language and utterance.

Wieland is possibly the most profound reflection on the aporias of time, history, language, and knowledge that can be found in the literature of the early national period. As such, it is at the same time a reflection on the very conditions of existence of an unprecedented social experiment, a nation deprived of traditional sources of political legitimacy: the security and harmony of the United States depended, in Brown's view, on the risky exercise of something called "voice."

3. David Lee Clark, *Charles Brockden Brown: Pioneer Voice of America* (Durham, North Carolina: Duke Univ. Press, 1952), pp. 163–64.

"We do not extol it too highly when we attribute as much to the power of eloquence as to the sword, in bringing about the American revolution," Benjamin Rush claimed in 1798. "It is the first accomplishment in a republic, and often sets the whole machine of government in motion."[4] But if the force of spoken language was, as Rush contended, responsible for the Revolution, and responsible as well for the motions of government in the years of the early American republic, it also posed certain dangers to the republic. Speech retained much of its essentially insurrectionary power well into the postrevolutionary period, as many observers knew; as language had operated to dissolve one set of power relations, it could very well again operate to dissolve the fragile new republican arrangements. In fact, it may have seemed to Rush that the powers of language posed an even greater threat to political stability *after* the Revolution than they did prior to the political separation: since the legitimacy of the new political order was sustained, as I have said before, discursively—that is, by means of argument and persuasion, rather than by virtue of customary authority—the new political institutions were even more vulnerable to the assaults of words than were the old institutions, and those had proved destructible already.

This danger was at no time more intensely present to observers of American politics and society than in the final years of the eighteenth century, years that saw a dramatic amplification of public debate on crucial matters of national order. The mounting social and political disorder of 1798 and 1799 revived memories of the disruptive, destructive role speech had played a few decades earlier. Charles Brockden Brown, in much of his writing, examined and dramatized the question of speech in the republic, and in *Wieland*—which notoriously centers on the dangerous powers of the human voice—he carefully allegorized the American revolution as ·a story of language, speech, and utterance.

Wieland has received generous critical attention in recent years, and has been interpreted in several ways. Many interpretations take up the themes of perception and understanding that are so conspicuously important in the novel, and the allied issues of lin-

4. Rush, *Essays,* p. 16.

guistic representation.[5] Other readings concentrate on the relation
of the story to the historical and political contexts of revolution
and national formation.[6] Still other interpretations focus on the
novel as an expression of Brown's own psychological conflicts, in
particular those having to do with his abortive vocation as a lawyer.[7] I believe that the law, as an institution of fundamental importance in the early republic, does in fact figure significantly, if somewhat unusually, in *Wieland,* but not only as a question of the
author's personal vocational uncertainties. It figures also as the

5. On perception, see Beverly Voloshin, "*Wieland:* 'Accounting for Appearances,'" *New England Quarterly* 59 (1986): 341–57; James Russo, "'The Chimeras
of the Brain': Clara's Narrative in *Wieland,*" *Early American Literature* 16 (1981):
60–88; and Jay Fliegelman, *Prodigals and Pilgrims: The American Revolution Against
Patriarchal Authority, 1750–1800* (Cambridge: Cambridge Univ. Press, 1982), pp.
237–41. On knowledge, see Walter Hesford, "'Do You Know the Author?': The
Question of Authorship in *Wieland,*" *Early American Literature* 17 (1982/83):
239–48, and Michael Kreyling, "Construing Brown's *Wieland:* Ambiguity and Derridean 'Freeplay,'" *Studies in the Novel* 14 (1982): 43–54. On language, see Michael Davitt Bell, *The Development of American Romance: The Sacrifice of Relation*
(Chicago: Univ. of Chicago Press, 1980), pp. 46–61, and Mark Seltzer, "Saying
Makes It So: Language and Event in Brown's *Wieland,*" *Early American Literature*
13 (1978): 81–91.
6. See Emory Elliott, *Revolutionary Writers: Literature and Authority in the New
Republic, 1725–1810* (New York: Oxford Univ. Press, 1982), pp. 225–34, where
the uncertainties of *Wieland* are placed within the context of what Elliott calls, in
his first chapter, the "crisis of authority" in revolutionary America, a crisis which
prompted American writers, according to Elliott, "to search for some way to be
men of letters and moral leaders in the society" (p. 47). Edwin Fussell, in what is
perhaps the single most useful and knowing reading of *Wieland,* traces the ways in
which "in 1798 the American Revolution was still active—violently so—in
Brown's imagination." "*Wieland:* A Literary and Historical Reading," *Early American Literature* 18 (1983): 186, n. 9. Jane Tompkins maintains that *Wieland* is "a
political tract," one that "is directed toward solving the problems of post-
Revolutionary society" and that "presents a shocking and uncharacteristically negative view of what it meant to survive the War of Independence." *Sensational Designs: The Cultural Work of American Fiction, 1790–1860* (New York: Oxford Univ.
Press, 1985), p. 44. J. V. Ridgely states succinctly in the aptly titled "The Empty
World of *Wieland,*" in *Individual and Community: Variations on a Theme in American
Fiction,* ed. Kenneth H. Baldwin and David K. Kirby (Durham, North Carolina:
Duke Univ. Press, 1975), that "writing in a decade which followed upon the sun-
dering of America from the parent country, Brown himself was experiencing the
deprivation of a fostering social order, of those traditional institutions by which
the individual self attempts to gauge its proper role." In Ridgely's view, with which
I concur, Brown's implicit plea is "for greater awareness of otherness, for some
replacement for severed parental ties" (p. 16).
7. This aspect of Brown's involvement with the law, and the effect of that
involvement on his thought and art, has been fully explored in Robert Ferguson,
Law and Letters in American Culture (Cambridge, Massachusetts: Harvard Univ.
Press, 1984), pp. 138–42.

particular institutional context in which general issues of perception, knowledge, and linguistic representation became politically relevant in postrevolutionary America: the court of law was the scene in which such issues were historically present and concretely relevant. The court of law — in the new nation that had been explicitly founded as a society of laws — was the actual place in which otherwise abstract questions of epistemology and individual psychology became the very mundane questions of how facts can be known, how words can be trusted, and how judgments can be reliably entered. The court of law was, for Brown, the place where the very existence and security of the social realm were seen to require that facts *can* be known, words *can* be trusted, and judgments *can* be reliably entered. And because Brown's opinion, finally, is that knowledge is uncertain, language untrustworthy, and human judgment fatally prone to error, it follows that the social realm is desperately fragile, and especially so in a nation that has been founded on faith in reasoned discourse, rather than historical custom.

II. Ruptured Genealogy

The world represented in *Wieland* is a world in which, as Irving's Mustapha said, the United States "does every thing *viva voce,* or, by word of mouth."[8] The narrative is produced by nothing but acts of speech, a sequence of utterances. There are, of course, nonverbal events in *Wieland* (people sleep, travel, are killed, etc.), but these nonverbal events are often caused by, and always coordinated with, words spoken and words heard. Events are most often direct effects of utterances: as one critic has said, *Wieland* is a novel in which "saying makes it so."[9] Thus repeatedly a figure of speech is literalized in the actions of the characters, as when the senior *Wieland* first "complained, in a tremulous and terrified tone, that his brain was scorched to cinders" (p. 14), and soon thereafter is found to have, in fact, been "scorched and bruised" and his clothes "reduced to ashes" (p. 18) by the famous spontaneous combus-

---

8. Irving, *History, Tales and Sketches,* p. 144.
9. Seltzer, "Saying Makes It So," p. 81.

tion to which he is mysteriously subjected. As Mark Seltzer has observed, this pattern of the actualization of metaphorical expressions is repeated many times in the novel.[10] And the aporias that this pattern creates in the causal order of the narrative plot — for how can a figural expression, really, disown its metaphoricity and call into being its literal referent? — are the text's own model for its radical discontinuities. Everything happens because of voices and the words and noises carried by those voices, and therefore everything that happens seems uncaused and unexpected. Some of the crucial utterances of Carwin take the form of commands, for example, "Hold!" (p. 62), which is to say that they are utterances that intend to produce a material result. But intention is not the same as causation, and if a command is obeyed, it is not because the command itself produces the obedience. The attribution of occurrences to originating utterances, and the nonsense this makes of causal logic, is an enigma that refers covertly, in *Wieland,* to the circumstances of the new nation's creation, the utterance of America.

Since the convoluted and often obscure plot of *Wieland* is often misrepresented, and in any case needs to be kept in mind in order to attend to the argument I will be making, let me review it briefly. A brother and sister, Theodore and Clara Wieland, living on an estate outside Philadelphia with their friends and family, find their idyllic life disrupted by the arrival of a strange intruder named Carwin. The events of the novel take place, according to Brown's prefatory "Advertisement," "between the conclusion of the French and the beginning of the revolutionary war" (p. 3). That is, they take place in the years of prerevolutionary political agitation, when the history of the colonies is taking the turn that will lead to political independence. Brown's location of the fictional events in this hiatus between wars was carefully calculated for the resonance it would produce with the historical context of revolutionary upheaval.

The enigmatic Carwin turns out to be a "biloquist," a "doubletongued deceiver" (pp. 247, 244) whose preternatural faculty of projecting his voice and mimicking others' voices is exercised

10. Ibid., pp. 83–85.

harmfully in several ways. He first imitates the voice of Theodore Wieland's wife, Catharine, in situations where her husband can hear it, and this leads Theodore into various sorts of confusion (p. 32). He feigns the voices of murderers in Clara's closet as she lies in bed (pp. 55–58). He imitates Clara's voice at such times and places that Henry Pleyel, the family's close friend (and Catharine's brother), with whom Clara is infatuated, is led to believe that she is conducting an illicit love affair (pp. 132–35). Brown presents this family and its circle of friends as an epitome of American society, and the disorders of paranoia, resentment, and recrimination into which Carwin's intrusion and vocal deception throw them is meant to be understood as the equivalent, in this familial-national allegory, of the political catastrophe of the Revolution and the social and political uncertainties of its aftermath. The novel's final disasters — Theodore's murder of his wife and four children at the behest of what he believes is a divine commandment, and his attempted murder of his sister — may or may not be due to further vocal interventions by Carwin. The biloquist denies responsibility for that divine vocal imperative, even as he admits to having been the source of the other vocal deceptions. The novel in its entirety is presented as the retrospective narrative of Clara, who is trying, some time after the events she relates, to make sense, to herself and to the unnamed friends to whom she is writing, of the tragic circumstances that beset her and her relations and companions. She may not be a reliable narrator, as we are given clear indications that her understanding has been disordered by the confusing events she has lived through, and she has been, throughout most of the time of the novel, fascinated by and attracted to Carwin, who is uncouth in appearance but whose voice is seductively beautiful and unnaturally powerful.

Clara's narrative begins, as Franklin's *Autobiography* did, by detailing the prehistory of her family. Her paternal grandfather was the quintessential modern individual as that type was often represented in the eighteenth-century novel: a man for whom the identity prepared for him by the historical circumstances of his birth was rendered impossible, and who therefore found it necessary to refashion his life and make his own fate. He is of noble Saxon birth (I will return to the significance of this Saxon origin presently), but he makes the mistake of falling in love with the daughter of a merchant in Hamburg, and when he marries her he thereby consigns himself and his descendants to a bourgeois world where their individuality is no longer given but must be fabricated according to the norms of a culture of social and economic self-determination. This initial rupture of an order of things and with the causal chain it implies is, as becomes clear, only the first in a series of breaks in the chains of events. Soon after Clara's grandfather had "found it incumbent on him to search out some mode of independent subsistence" (p. 7) — which turns out to be the writing of plays, a professional choice (art) that reinforces the aura of alienation that the text grants to him — he dies, as does his wife, leaving their only child an orphan. This child will be Clara's father, who in his turn dies while his own children are young. But before this repetitive discontinuity is effected, several others intervene: the apprenticeship to which Wieland Sr. was consigned after his parents' death takes him away from Germany to England, where he converts to new and eccentric religious beliefs (occasioned by an accidental encounter with a book detailing the doctrines of the Camissards; p. 8). When his heterodox beliefs make it difficult to continue living in England, he moves to America, where, after fourteen years, he acquires sufficient wealth to cease laboring and devote himself thereafter to disseminating his religious beliefs. This he chooses to attempt among the "savage tribes" of America (p. 10). His twice-altered nationality, and new religion, his orphanhood and geographical removal, have a powerful cumulative effect: he leaves society altogether to live with the Indians, and when his efforts at conversion fail and he returns to Philadelphia and his family, he continues nevertheless to adhere to a completely private and idiosyncratic religion, for the exercise of which he constructs a personal temple on grounds near the Schuylkill River. It is not difficult to see that Wieland Sr. represents a reductio ad absurdum of antinomian religious enthusiasm as well as what might be called the limit case of the displacement of a decaying public sphere by private familial life.

It is as the children of this deracinated crank that Clara and Theodore enter the world. (Their mother also worships alone, having no fellow Moravians in the neighborhood.) Clara details this unusual background because she is always finding quasi-typological relations between past events and the experiences of her own life: she senses that in obscure ways this strange past determines present events. Her father's self-combustion, for instance, shows a "resemblance to recent events" that "revived them with new force in [her] memory, and made [her] more anxious to explain them" (p. 19). She has insisted on her first page "that the past is exempt from mutation" (p. 5), but in truth she is aware that the past is a discursive construct that isn't at all exempt from revision. It is precisely the deferred action of past events — their retrospective elucidation by present occurrences — that obsessively fascinates her. But, as she discovers, it is not easy to discern the actual causal relations that join past to present; it is usually only possible to create a *figural* relation ("resemblance"), and one of the basic implications of her narrative is that the past acts on the present not through concrete relations of material cause and effect but via the indirect, immaterial medium of figurations — prefigurations and realizations — which is to say, via linguistic representation.

If her father's unusual fate has a determining effect on the lives of his children, it is not through some form of immediate action. Rather it is through the variously mediating forms of discourse: through the written records of his fate, his children's interpretations of that record, and their repetition of the patterns they find in it. Although Clara says she intends her narrative to "exemplify the force of early impressions" (p. 5; her professed psychology is recognizably Lockean), she was not, as it happens, actually an eyewitness to the events that she nevertheless credits with making those "impressions." The factitiousness of her Lockeanism is crucial to this novel. The "impressions" she refers to were made by words: her father's own words in the autobiographical manuscript that Clara cherishes and peruses frequently, her uncle's words as he tells her again and again of her father's demise (and the uncle's narrative is largely a redaction of the father's own deathbed narration), and so forth. Clara later refers again to the "impressions that were then made upon [her]" at six years of age, and claims that they "can never be effaced," but her own account reveals that those "impressions" were made not at the age of six, but "as [she] advanced in age, and became more fully acquainted with these facts" and as her "uncle's testimony" became gradually fuller and more explicit. The "impressions" of "facts" are, in truth, functions of discursive *accounts* of those putative facts; they are, quite without exception, the products of reconstructive "inference" from those discursive representations (p. 19).

The rest of the novel repeats this model: from words, voices, and testimony, Clara draws inferences, and from them she posits "facts" and recalls "impressions." This model, in turn, suggests a way of understanding the problematic relation of a new nation to its history. The past, to the newly fabricated American nation, exerted its effects likewise: not through a material logic of cause and effect, but through the indirect and immaterial operations of discursive representation and consensual enactment. Such a problematic relation to the past is alluded to in Brown's bestowal upon the Wielands of a German and English prehistory, the details of which require further elaboration.

III. Saxon Constitution

The first sentence of Brown's working outline of *Wieland* reads: "Wieland was of saxon origin" (p. 427). And a later notation — "A voyage to Europe, to Saxony, to claim an estate" (p. 429) — is, like the first, one of the outline's prescriptions that is carefully realized in the novel. The reclamation of the Saxon estate is included in the plot as a *possibility,* but not, in the event, one that is acted upon by Wieland in the final form of the story. That he does *not* return to Saxony to restore his claim to an origin there is a matter of some significance in the ideological world of this novel. Wieland's grandfather was "a native of Saxony," and Pleyel feels a "partiality to the Saxon soil, from which he had likewise sprung" (pp. 6, 37). It is Pleyel, in fact, who while traveling in Europe discovered that war had eliminated all those whose claims to the Saxon patrimony were stronger, under the laws of primogeniture, than Theodore Wieland's would be, and who urges him, consequently, to return and institute legal proceedings to reclaim the "large domains in Lusatia" that belonged to the "noble Saxons" who were his ancestors (p. 37).

As an adjunct of the conceptual grammar that underlies *Wie-*

land — a grammar of cause and effect, temporality, language and history — these allusions to Saxon ancestry help link these concepts to the political mythology of the early American republic. As several historians have recently argued, republican political thought in the revolutionary period understood itself as the product of a complex genealogy that included among its most illustrious filiations the political systems of the ancient Greek and Roman commonwealths, a "Gothic" or "Saxon" golden age of liberty, and the ancient constitution of pre-Norman England.[11] And as J. G. A. Pocock points out (here with respect to Fortescue's *De Laudibus Legum Angliae* — the source text of Franklin's claims regarding his patronym, as discussed above), a set of nostalgic associations clusters around this purported genealogy: it represents the power of unwritten tradition, the authority of custom, and the mythic memory of a small agrarian form of society governed by immediate oral decision making among virtuous citizens.[12] The presumptive tradition linking American republicanism with the English constitution, which was, in turn, presumably derived (according to this theory) from the unconstrained deliberations of German warriors gathered in the forest, was a favorite authorizing fantasy among American statesmen.

As I said above (see chapter 2), this Saxon route to the past functioned, for Franklin, for instance, to divert the tracing-back of the genealogy of republican political forms from the track of immemorial English custom, and thereby to undermine the authority of the English constitution by making its derivation from another source apparent. So we find Jefferson, for one, writing in 1774 in his *Summary View of the Rights of British America* that landholding in America was organized according to "Saxon laws of possession, under which all lands were held in absolute right" rather than at the pleasure of the king.[13] And when Edmund

11. Bernard Bailyn, *The Ideological Origins of the American Revolution* (Cambridge, Massachusetts: The Belknap Press of Harvard Univ. Press, 1967), pp. 80–83; Gordon Wood, *The Creation of the American Republic, 1776–1787* (Chapel Hill: Univ. of North Carolina Press, 1969), pp. 31, 122, 227–28.

12. J. G. A. Pocock, *The Machiavellian Moment: Florentine Political Thought and the Atlantic Republican Tradition* (Princeton: Princeton Univ. Press, 1975), pp. 9–19.

13. Jefferson, *Writings*, p. 119.

Pendleton in 1776 suggested that the history of colonial Americans' obedience to the British monarch — their tacit acceptance of his view that all land belonged fundamentally to him, and was his to grant to his subjects or repossess at will — had *de facto* established feudalism in America, Jefferson replied that were it even so, it was "better now that we return at once into that happy system of our ancestors, the wisest & most perfect ever yet devised by the wit of man, as it stood before the 8th century"[14] — that is, in Anglo-Saxon England. Theodore Wieland's personal Saxon myth thus parallels quite closely revolutionary America's fantasy of a legal genealogy that would allow it to establish its separate legitimacy by leaping back, as it were, over the heads of British kings to a putative Saxon democracy.

Wieland's imagined return to such an origin is blocked, however, by the fact that a reaccession to such a foundation would need to go through a legal system that has since intervened to make such a resumption of archaic custom only accessible through modern statutory law. To reclaim his Saxon domains and all that they represent, "he must exchange present certainties for what was distant and contingent; for who knows not that the law is a system of expence, delay and uncertainty?" (p. 38). That is to say, Wieland feels his belatedness — the long historical derivation, deferral, and discontinuity that separate him from this presumed origin — as an insuperable dislocation. He might have in mind — or Brown might — such an argument as the lawyer and statesman James Wilson (whom I will be considering further in this chapter) made in his discussion of the foundations of the American legal-political order. Wilson was attracted to the theory (he also discusses its presentation by Fortescue) of the passage through German antiquity of the common law: he finds legal institutions being transmitted from Greece to Rome, from Rome to Saxony (possibly also directly from Greece to Saxony), from Saxony to Britain (and, again, also possibly directly from Rome to Britain), and from Britain to America.

But Wilson makes a crucial qualification in his description of such passages: he finds that at every stage of this transmission,

14. Ibid., p. 752.

the "obligatory force" of customs and laws "arises not from any consideration of that kind [mere origin], but from their free and voluntary reception into the kingdom."[15] Wilson thus deconstructs, as one might say, the privilege of immemorial custom, subjecting it at every point to what he elsewhere calls the "revolution principle" of popular sovereignty.[16] Only democratic consent invests law with its authority, no matter how closely the charismatic authority of ancient origin attaches to its specific forms. And, he concedes, "in truth, it is extremely difficult, if not altogether impracticable, to trace the common law of England to the era of its commencement, or to several springs, from which it has originally flowed."[17] Thus if the origin is lost in the recesses of time, or if the origin is multiple and dispersed anyway, and the claims it makes cannot be entailed all the way to the modern world but must be endorsed voluntarily at every transition — if legal authority depends absolutely on consent — then we are left, as it were, legal orphans.

Brown's fixation on Saxony is determined by this prevalent political myth and by its problematic relevance to American society. It is his anxiety concerning the apparent groundlessness of American political legitimacy that makes him at once wish for a connection to a determinate and authoritative Saxon origin, and at the same time despair of reclaiming it. Thus Theodore and Clara and the others have no possible recourse to an "ancient security" (p. 60), as Clara calls it, at least not a Saxon one. The function of the Saxon or Gothic myth in *Wieland* is precisely to raise such a possibility of restoration and then, ironically, to make its fictionality evident — just as Franklin's use of this myth in his "Edict of the King of Prussia" (which was written between the Seven Years' War and the Revolution, just when the action of Brown's novel takes place) served, finally, only to destroy the hope of such a genealogical legitimation of American national existence. It effectively undercut the legitimacy of British claims to American soil,

15. James Wilson, *The Works of the Honourable James Wilson, L.L.D.*, ed. Bird Wilson, 2 vols. (Philadelphia: At the Lorenzo Press, Printed for Bronson and Chauncey, 1804), vol. 2, p. 6.

16. Ibid., vol. 1, p. 21.

17. Ibid., vol. 2, p. 5.

but then left America to its own devices — its rhetorical and linguistic devices — to establish a new legitimacy. Thus the "ancient security" Clara refers to, when examined closely, turns out to be the security created *ex nihilo* by herself and her family and friends in their temple colloquies.

The fictiveness of their own family "Saxon constitution" is clear: its authority rested ultimately on their individual consent, not on an originary charm. This grounding in discursive consent is implied in Wieland's response to Pleyel's persistent urging of the project of ancestral reclamation: when Pleyel argues that Catharine and Clara will put aside their objections and submit to Theodore's will if he chooses to make the voyage to Germany, Wieland proclaims his respect for their family democracy. "You mistake. Their concurrence is indispensable. It is not my custom to exact sacrifices of this kind" (p. 43). The "custom" of this American family is precisely a noncustomary system of popular sovereignty. An ideal, orally instituted democracy exactly like the mythic community of virtuous Saxon citizens has been recreated in the suburbs of Philadelphia, and it represents not a restoration of imaginary filiation (which would have been possible only through statutory legal procedures with which such a customary society was incompatible), but an absolutely new creation. Its relations to the Saxon model are only fictive. This neo-Saxon community finds itself prone, however — as did the earlier Saxon democracy — to the intrinsic disorders of voice and time, and is ever prone to the alluring possibility of transcendent authority: deracinated, customless, traditionless individuals like Theodore Wieland, with only their private judgments to guide them in matters of social and political arrangement, are apt to seek to be delivered from their disenchanted world by a voice that seems to speak from an otherworldly authority.

IV. Ciceronian Elocution

The Saxon myth — the construal of political history in terms of an imaginary genealogy of constitutional and legal forms — finds a counterpart in one of the more intriguing details of *Wieland*. Some of the obsessive concentration with which Brown addressed the complex coherence of issues of language, speech act, law, and history can be gauged by attending to a textual anomaly that might easily be dismissed as minor or accidental, but seems to me to be too unusual to be inadvertent even if Brown does not make much of it. Clara tells us that her brother "was an indefatigible student" and that among the authors he was fond of reading "the chief object of his veneration was Cicero" (p. 24). This locates Theodore quite firmly within the political-moral ideology of the day, which endorsed civic virtue as it had been elaborated in classical literature and as that elaboration had been transmitted through English Whig political ideology. But Theodore's participation in such a nostalgic ideology is taken to rather unusual lengths: "He was never tired of conning and rehearsing [Cicero's] productions. To understand them was not sufficient. He was anxious to discover the gestures and cadences with which they ought to be delivered" (p. 24).

Theodore's attempt to hallucinate the voice of Cicero and mimic it may recall Franklin's similar practice of trying to reproduce and assume fully an alien discourse, as I have described that practice above (see chapter 2). It recalls also the fantasmatic relation that political leaders of the revolutionary era enjoyed to the heroes of classical antiquity. And it bears an obvious relation to the theme of ventriloquism: Theodore effectively wants to play Charlie McCarthy to Cicero's Edgar Bergen, to adopt not only the moral and political sense of his philosophy but the whole paralinguistic apparatus of Cicero's tone, gesture, cadence, and pronunciation as he is able to reconstruct it inferentially. Brown's presentation of the American revolutionaries' attempt to revive a classical theory of politics and rhetoric of virtue in the form of a ventriloquistic reassumption of vocal performance is surely parodistic: it implies that such a politics of nostalgia is an attempt to recreate what is inaccessible, and that such an ambition of recreation is absurd, artificial, and anachronistic.

Theodore's project of resumption has another aspect. "Not contented with this, he was diligent in settling and restoring the purity of the text. For this end, he collected all the editions and commentaries that could be procured, and employed months of severe study in exploring and comparing them. He never betrayed more satisfaction than when he made a discovery of this kind" (p. 24). One of Nietzsche's aphorisms has it that "only that which has no history is definable."[18] Theodore's efforts to restore a definitive text are attempts to collapse history, to retreat from time's vicissitudes to an original stability, represented here figurally by the model of a pure text that has been corrupted over the centuries. This wish for an original purity, for a text identical to itself, can only be realized by means of inference and conjecture, and can only fabricate an ideal unity from the concrete experience of collating discrepant present texts: nothing will ever make it certain that the restored text actually is identical to the lost original. Perhaps Theodore's attachment to "Moral necessity, and calvinistic inspiration" guides him in these endeavors; Pleyel, the "champion of intellectual liberty" whose "gaiety was almost boisterous" and who was "prone to view every object merely as supplying materials for mirth," was capable of ridiculing Wieland's efforts and even bluntly contesting "the divinity of Cicero" (p. 25). The carefully presented opposition of the temperaments and behaviors of Wieland and Pleyel functions here to suggest the most conspicuous ideological oppositions within the political culture of the new nation: on the one hand, the rather literal classical republicanism in alliance with a residual Puritanism, and on the other hand, the radical freethinking of the secular Enlightenment. Whether an intellectual collation and emendation comparable to Theodore's textual reconstruction could restore the pure original American text from these conflicting contemporary political texts could only seem doubtful in 1798 at the height of Federalist-Republican controversy.

A test of the possibility of such a mediation and melioration comes right along in *Wieland*. When the companions are enjoying the spring air in the temple one day (having converted its use from religious worship to secular colloquy, with a new idol—a bust of Cicero—presiding over the scene), Theodore and Pleyel are "bandying quotations and syllogisms."

> The point discussed was the merit of the oration for
> Cluentius, as descriptive, first, of the genius of the

18. Friedrich Nietzsche, *On the Genealogy of Morals, Ecce Homo*, trans. Walter Kaufmann et al. (New York: Vintage Books, 1969), p. 80.

speaker; and, secondly, of the manners of the times. Pleyel laboured to extenuate both these species of merit, and tasked his ingenuity, to shew that the orator had embraced a bad cause; or, at least, a doubtful one. He urged, that to rely on the exaggerations of an advocate, or to make the picture of a single family a model from which to sketch the condition of a nation, was absurd. (p. 30)

Robert Ferguson reminds us that Cicero was "every early American lawyer's favorite symbol of oratorical excellence and professional virtue."[19] The *Pro Cluentio,* however, has a peculiar status among Cicero's famous defenses: it records Cicero at his most brilliantly specious. The defense of Cluentius is a tour de force, in which Cicero successfully defended a remarkably weak case, by "throwing dust in the eyes of the jury," as he admitted himself.[20] Cicero described an extraordinarily tangled series of protogothic events (murder, poisoning, bribery, seduction), and did so in a nonsequential way that didn't clarify but only further obscured the relation of one event to another. Brown chose to make this oration, of all of Cicero's speeches, the object of Wieland's and Pleyel's disagreement; the analogies between the course of events described by Cicero and those described therein by Brown is apparent to any reader, as is the comparable disconnectedness of the narration. And the self-reflexive metacommentary on legal oratory (ad-vocacy) in Cicero's oration also bears evident relation to Brown's own concerns: Cicero reflects within this speech on the ethical status of his own discourse, the morality of advocacy. He concludes that the advocate has no need to believe in the truth of the argument he makes, and is free even to make an argument that, in its construction of the facts, controverts an argument he made in a previous trial which concerned the same events.[21] He is not committed, that is, to the view that there is one true world, one univocal set of facts. And although Cicero decries the cheap

19. Robert A. Ferguson, *Law and Letters in American Culture* (Cambridge, Massachusetts: Harvard Univ. Press, 1984), p. 142.

20. Cicero, *The Speeches: Pro Lege Manilia, Pro Caecina, Pro Cluentio, Pro Rabirio, Perduellionis,* trans. H. Grose Hodge, Loeb Classical Library (Cambridge, Massachusetts: Harvard Univ. Press, 1927), p. 212.

21. Ibid., pp. 371, 369–70.

lawyerly practice of appealing blatantly to prejudice, he repeatedly does so rather flagrantly, and in addition appeals to legal technicalities even after having promised not to do so. He talks around the issues constantly, strays from the point persistently, and in countless ways makes of his oration a catalogue of devices of rhetorical mystification and outright dishonesty. As an extravagantly self-contradictory text, it makes an apt object for disputes among its readers.

Theodore admires the oration. (It turns out to be a good model for his own oration at his trial for murder later on.) Pleyel, on the other hand, doesn't admire it: he especially resists Theodore's claim that the events narrated by Cicero can be taken to represent the conditions of Roman civilization at the time, and in particular that a single family can stand synecdochically for an entire nation. Again, it's hard not to think that Brown is giving indirect clues to the reader of his own novel, at once raising the possibility of a familial-national allegory and then casting doubt on it. What follows from this disagreement among the characters — a disagreement that incites, as it were, an undecidable question in the reader about the representative status of the Wielands *vis-à-vis* American society — is a series of narrative diversions and displacements that is characteristic of Brown's narrative method and that raises persistently the problematics of historical continuity, temporal linearity, and logical consequentiality that is everywhere at stake in this novel.

Theodore's and Pleyel's dispute about the representative status of Cluentius and his family goes unresolved because it is deflected by a new disagreement before any resolution is reached.

> The controversy was suddenly diverted into a new channel, by a misquotation. Pleyel accused his companion of saying "*polliceatur*" when he should have said "*polliceretur*." Nothing would decide the contest, but an appeal to the volume. My brother was returning to the house for this purpose, when a servant met him with a letter from Major Stuart. He immediately returned to read it in our company. (p. 30)

"Misquotation" again suggests the inevitable deflection or error inherent in a present resumption of the text of the past. And there is nothing accidental about the site of this purported misquotation—*polliceatur* or *polliceretur.* The Latin translates two forms of the verb "to promise," which is used in an ethically dubious fashion in at least three places in *Pro Cluentio* (pp. 294, 296, 394). Promising is an instance of what Austin called a performative utterance; it is, in fact, the classic case of a performative, an act of speech that does not so much *refer* to something as *do* something.[22] To speak a promise is to perform that promise. In Cicero's defense of Cluentius the word is used twice to refer to a false promise (Staienus promises money to certain judges for acquitting Oppianicus, without intending to pay it) and once when Cicero himself makes a promise to his listeners (to base a legal defense on statutory technicalities in future trials, even though—he claims falsely—he is not doing so in the present trial). The promise, as a representative performative utterance, does several things relevant to the themes of *Wieland:* it forms a contract, and hence is a verbal act fundamental to a legal order, and in doing so it forges a connection between present and future, entailing a future obligation and an expectation upon the parties to the promise. It thus effects a narrative order, actually establishing the temporal relation of intentionality that preforms a historical structure of narrative continuity. This is the kind of social contract that Burke endorsed: a relation of obligation between generations.[23] In contrast, the social contract of Rousseau was primarily a synchronic contract, an agreement among contemporaries. Burke insisted that the contractual relations that constituted a political order be extended over time, and that in fact social order depended upon the diachronic stability of such contractual relations. In direct opposition to such a traditionalist view, we might think of Jefferson's famous dictum that "the earth belongs . . . to the living," that past generations could not entail any obligations upon their descendants.[24] Only such a view—a fundamental delegitimation of received norms—could make possible the kind of reimagining of social re-

---

22. J. L. Austin, *How to Do Things with Words,* 2d ed., J. O. Urmson and Marina Sbisà, eds. (Cambridge, Massachusetts: Harvard Univ. Press, 1975), pp. 9–11 and passim.

23. Edmund Burke, *Reflections on the Revolution in France* (with Thomas Paine, *The Rights of Man*) (Garden City, New York: Anchor/Doubleday, 1973), pp. 108–111.

24. Jefferson, *Writings,* p. 959.

lations that Jefferson and other revolutionary leaders proposed. Pleyel, as the radical freethinker in this crowd, can be taken to stand in for Jefferson here, and Theodore — who seeks to resolve the dispute by an appeal to the text, by a return to an original authority — thereby becomes a stand-in for an indistinct Federalist point of view. Pleyel, the "champion of intellectual liberty," has a position on promises (on the verbally instituted relations of legal obligation that ensure a transtemporal stability to social arrangements and thereby make a continuous and intelligible history possible) that is similar to Jefferson's refusal of all that such promises imply. Theodore's contrasting position, if not quite Federalist, might remotely correspond to Madison's, who, in his reply to Jefferson's disavowal of received obligations, held that it was morally and practically necessary to assume a tacit contract between generations. If you held to Jefferson's position, Madison thought, you might finally disestablish all political legitimacy ("Would not a Government so often revised become too mutable to retain those prejudices in its favor which antiquity inspires, and which are perhaps a salutary aid to the most rational Government in the most enlightened age?"):[25] you required that consent be constantly reiterated by every member of a nation whenever any child was born. Pragmatically, in the face of such an impossibility, it was necessary to assume and institute a default position (as it were) in the system of consent, to hold that in the absence of any challenge to the legitimacy of the state, tacit consent had in fact been given ("I find no relief from these consequences, but in the received doctrine that a tacit assent may be given to established Constitutions and laws, and that this assent may be inferred, where no positive dissent appears").[26]

Now such a structure of tacit consent can readily be construed as a form of ventriloquism — a claim that someone has always already spoken for you, a myth of the alienation of one's "voice" in an always already preempting "general voice" — or, rather, an assumed alienation of one's "voice" in a text, a textualized *vox populi* that took the form in the new United States of the rhetorical

25. James Madison, *The Papers of James Madison,* ed. Charles F. Hobson et al. (Charlottesville: Univ. of Virginia Press, 1981), vol. 13, p. 19.
26. Ibid., p. 20.

we in its founding documents. Such a mythic general voice effectively makes any political disagreement, then, into a matter of misquotation, and requires that such disagreement be resolved by a resort to the original text.

In *Wieland* this textual recourse — Theodore's intended referral to his edition of *Pro Cluentio* — is diverted, however, and the reconciliation promised by it is deferred and never thereafter accomplished. Instead of the text of Cicero, Theodore returns to the group in the temple with a just-delivered letter from Major Stuart, which he reads to his friends. A rainstorm quickly ensues, and forces the group back into the house (Major Stuart's letter is carelessly left behind in the temple), where they soon enter upon another dispute about a description of a cataract in the recently read letter. Textual recourse is the proposed method for resolving this dispute, too: "To settle the dispute which thence arose, it was proposed to have recourse to the letter" (p. 31). And — it begins to be obvious that Brockden Brown's repetitions are *not* careless — this recourse to the text is *again* diverted. The series of interlocked recourses, which keeps tracing unsuccessfully back along a track of displacements — displacements that have taken us from the purported pure text of Cicero's oration through variant corrupt texts, to disputed quotation (displacement of a written text in oral citation of it), to suddenly interpolated letter, to disputed recollection of the letter's contents — this labyrinth of displacements and attempted returns is now further diverted by the first intervention of the biloquist. The intrusive voice of Carwin is thus the last in this local series of verbal dislocations. When Theodore leaves his friends to go to the temple and retrieve the Stuart letter, his performance of this retrieval is inhibited by what sounds to him like his wife's voice outdoors as he climbs the hill to the temple. This first action of the displaced, counterfeited voice that will figure so importantly in the novel inaugurates here a new series of vocal and verbal substitutions.

V. The Politics of Ventriloquism

In *Wieland* everything happens on account of voice. And what happens is that an orderly, peaceful society is destroyed by the weird exertions of a particularly strange voice. Carwin, the enigmatic biloquist whose arrival on the scene marks him clearly as the Proppian villain whose "role is to disturb the peace of a happy family,"[27] and the form of whose villainy is his uncanny ability to disguise his voice, project his voice, and appropriate the voices of others, thereby massively disrupts and deeply confuses the elementary structures of everyday experience in the suburbs of Philadelphia. Our everyday experience of the world is ordinarily constructed in the interaction of our various senses: we see, and feel, and hear, and the evidence presented to us through these distinct "avenue[s] to information" (p. 135), as they are called in the novel, is correlated and coordinated in the mind in such a way as to create a reasonably coherent, self-consistent phenomenal world. The different senses, though distinct, corroborate one another, just as the sensations and beliefs of different individuals corroborate one another, thereby enabling cooperation and understanding — enabling collective life. This is the ideal case. Sometimes, of course, the different senses of a single individual don't lock together quite perfectly, and sometimes the sense perceptions of different individuals conflict. One of the uncanny effects that especially fascinates Brown is when hearing and seeing are misaligned in one of his characters' experience, as when a voice is heard but no source for it is visible. This happens repeatedly in *Wieland,* so frequently that it comes as a surprise to Clara when she finally catches Carwin in "the very act of utterance" (p. 214) — when she *sees* Carwin utter the sounds as she hears them. It is precisely because she most often hears voices but doesn't see the mouth moving out of which the voices proceed, that she finds her mind, by her own report, "split into separate parts" (p. 140). It is not at all out of place, despite Brown's critical reputation as a stylistic bungler, to read the language of his phrases carefully, and in "the very act of utterance" we may find implied Brown's discovery that truth — verity — is an effect, finally, of utterance. The one true world which is a requisite condition for social life finds one of its necessary conditions in our ability to distinguish among voices,

27. V. Propp, *Morphology of the Folktale,* trans. Laurence Scott et al. (Austin: Univ. of Texas Press, 1968), p. 27.

assign voices to bodies, and locate voices in space and time. Carwin acts to make these elementary apprehensions and identifications difficult if not impossible, and this is the basis of his destruction of the peace of the happy Wieland family. The "anarchy" that besets the community derives finally from the dissonance engendered by Carwin's dislocations of auditory and vocal experience, and is therefore very aptly figured aurally as "discord" (p. 170).

Jacques Derrida has described the ways in which the inner experience of selfhood is determined by "hearing oneself speak."[28] This hearing oneself speak "is experienced as an absolutely pure auto-affection, occurring in a self-proximity that would in fact be the absolute reduction of space in general." This "auto-affection," he claims, "is no doubt the possibility for what is called *subjectivity.*"[29] And as no space intervenes to disintegrate this self-proximity, neither does any temporal hiatus disturb it: one hears oneself *as* one speaks, *at the same time as* one's voice reverberates in the cranium, and thus the absolute simultaneity coheres with the self-proximity to establish subjectivity as an experience of utter integrity or simple identity.

This much has been familiarized by the attention that has been given of late to Derrida's theory. What has been less noted has been his extension of these descriptions to the *inter*subjective realm of experience. "In colloquy," he continues,

> the propagation of signs does not *seem* to meet any obstacles because it brings together two *phenomenological* origins of pure auto-affection. To speak to someone is doubtless to hear oneself speak, to be heard by oneself; but, at the same time, if one is heard by another, to speak is to make him *repeat immediately* in himself the hearing-oneself-speak in the very form in which I effectuated it.[30]

This immediate repetition in the ear of the listener of the speaker's utterance is one component of the "very act of utterance" to which

28. Derrida, *Speech and Phenomena,* p. 79.
29. Ibid., p. 79.
30. Ibid., p. 80.

Clara drew our attention: the truth of the utterance seems to reside in, or be guaranteed by, the intersubjective phenomenological solidarity of hearing and speaking, the instantaneous reproduction in the consciousness of one subject of the expression proceeding from the other. This ordinary oral/aural phenomenon is foregrounded by Clara when she reports that "the voice still rung in my ears" (p. 93). If voice is inextricably experienced as personal identity — and such phrases in *Wieland* as "self-same voice" (p. 44) indicate that Brown found it so — then hearing-*another*-speak inevitably works to disintegrate personal identity just as hearing-oneself-speak functions to reinforce it. The very being of the speaker is, as it were, transported by sound waves into the body of the listener, where it effects a subtle confusion of subjectivities, a melding of consciousnesses. As Merleau-Ponty put it, "Whether speaking or listening, I project myself into the other person, I introduce him into my own self."[31] When the other's voice is heard and his mouth is seen, too, then the visually observed spatial discrepancy between separate bodies helps to limit this intersubjective confusion; but when the heard voice is disembodied, and its source is invisible, nothing prevents or inhibits this seeming interanimation of persons. The *only* place the voice exists, in that case, is apparently in the ear of the listener. The voices in *Wieland* are, in crucial instances, disembodied in this way, hence experienced only inside the head of the hearer, and the effect of this dislocation is, first, to drastically interrupt the integrity of the hearing subject and, second, substantially to collapse the space of social recognition.

What the foregoing excursion into the everyday phenomenology of speaking and hearing is meant to show is that ventriloquism is not an aberration within the forms of auditory experience; rather, it is a version of the ordinary condition of such experience, the deterritorialization of vocal expressions. Its principle is the very principle of communication, the imaginary transposition that takes place in intersubjective understanding. We

---

31. Maurice Merleau-Ponty, *The Prose of the World,* trans. John O'Neill (Evanston, Illinois: Northwestern Univ. Press, 1973), p. 19.

should recognize, at this juncture, that ventriloquism is only one aspect of Carwin's vocal performances. He is also a mimic: in addition to throwing his own voice, he imitates the voices of others. In most instances in *Wieland,* he throws the imitated voices of others, thereby performing two operations at once: projection and mimicry. Although in practice he joins these two operations, we should bear in mind the distinction between them, for in both cases he is performing verbal acts that are, as I say, versions of ordinary vocal activity, not absolute aberrations. When, for instance, I hear someone speak—automatically repeat in myself, in Derrida's terms, the speech I hear at the very moment of hearing it—am I not appropriating that person's vocal identity in a way more like than unlike the mimic's vocal appropriation, and am I not displacing it as well, more like than unlike the ventriloquist's dislocation? And, conversely, when I speak for another's hearing, and effectuate within that person, by acting on his eardrum, an immediate repetition of my voice, am I not invading that person's self-proximate subjectivity, placing my voice, as it were, inside his head via his ear? "He is able to speak where he is not," Clara says of Carwin (p. 218). Who among us does not? To speak and to be heard is necessarily to speak where one is not. And when Clara says, "I stand aside, as it were, from myself" (p. 222), she is only describing, albeit in a way that makes it seem strange, the taken-for-granted fundamental condition of social speech, that is, speech that is heard.

In its largest implications, Brown's attention to the disintegration of subjectivity and the confusion of subjectivities entailed by the very nature of speaking and hearing is an observation of the dangerous instabilities that afflict the phenomenological order of speaking and hearing on which all societies depend, and on which, as we have seen (chapter 1) the new American nation particularly depended. Carwin effectively demolishes (and, by implication, Brown deconstructs) the foundation of communicative order to which his characters and their collective life are beholden. "Something whispered that the happiness we at present enjoyed was set on mutable foundations" (p. 54). The story of *Wieland* is given, in its essential form, in that sentence: a whisper, a fragile exhalation, the slightest of utterances, proceeding from an indeterminate origin ("Something"), undermines in the most powerful fashion the security of the social world.

* * *

Aside from these consequences for the world of experience and for the social order it underwrites, ventriloquism in *Wieland* suggests a variety of other correlates. These confirm the dependence I have described between vocal phenomena and social experience. There is the fact that the language we speak is not ours simply but rather a public institution. This is not merely the socializing function Benveniste has most eloquently identified as intrinsic to language: "It is, indeed, in and through language that the individual and society define one another. . . . Society is not possible except through language; nor is the individual. The awakening of consciousness in the child always coincides with the learning of language, which gradually introduces him as an individual into society."[32] Nor is it the mediating function identified (again by Benveniste) as the interrelation of a transindividual code (which precedes in time and supersedes in present existence the individual speaker) and individual expression (which seems to emerge from an autonomous individual, a seeming autonomy that is paradoxically made possible by its dependence upon the impersonal linguistic system). But it is analogous to the latter relation. Everyone feels his or her voice to be uniquely his or her own, and in fact the complex pattern of phonic habit, timbre, rhythm, volume, and so on, that creates the idiosyncratic quality of an individual's voice is so distinctive that it can take the place of fingerprints in identifying specific persons. (In a curious figure of speech, this unique vocal quality is sometimes called vocal "signature" or "voiceprint.") But the uniqueness of this complex quality, while it obviously depends in large part on certain physiological features — the morphology of one's teeth, mouth, throat, larynx, and so forth — also depends on the phonic system of a given natural language, as well as the customary pronunciation of, for instance, a family,

---

32. Benveniste, *Problems,* p. 23.

geographical region, or social class. That is, the very individuality of a voice depends necessarily on socially and historically given structures. The mimicability of a voice is proof enough of this fact. In the idiom of recent critical theory, in a variety of ways language speaks us, even as we speak it.

Brown himself is a ventriloquist: he is the writer who creates the illusion of the voices of his characters. He is the origin, for instance, of Clara's narrative voice, and, by extension, of the other voices Clara's narrative reproduces. As the authorial ventriloquist, who both imitates the voices of others and projects those voices in another place (the text) and in another medium (writing) Brown is in an obvious way comparable to Carwin. At the same time, Brown is not absolutely the origin of these voices-within-voices: he, too, is spoken by other voices. His performance is in large part an effect of a variety of socially and historically given linguistic forms, for example the sentimental novel, the gothic novel, the didactic novel. He is a product of a long history of the evolution of literary forms which he hears, as it were, and reutters. He is also, at a time of growing linguistic nationalism — the search for American idioms and standards — and at a time of linguistic modernization within the trans-Atlantic, English-speaking community, a speaker of an archaic, stilted, highly formal literary English. And without implicitly endorsing a rigid hierarchy of spoken and written language, it is nevertheless possible to argue that as a writer he is literalizing a projected voice, throwing his voice into a written and printed text, and mimicking by means of a graphic technology a vocable and audible phenomenon. The sequence is perfectly reversible: the writing, in turn, when realized in the consciousness of a reader, effectively projects its voice, and mimics a vocable and audible experience in the reader's mind.

If the literary performance thus involves various forms of ventriloquism, so too does politics in late eighteenth-century America. There is, for instance, the highly contested issue of political representation as it concerned Brown and his contemporaries: in classical republican theory, it was said that the nation needed to be small enough so that all citizens could gather, as it was often put, within the sound of one another's voices to confer and deliberate on public questions. The American republic was too large to admit of such collective vocal presence, and so had to resort to schemes of representation—to designated voices representing other voices, legislative representatives speaking for their constituents. What is such speaking-for but a kind of ventriloquism? (The undecidability of agency is effectively what makes representation viable: Are the constituents making their delegate speak for them, or is the delegate making his constituents accept his speech as their own?) The speech of lawyers (ad-vocacy) representing clients in courts of law was another form of ventriloquism, another version of one voice in place of another. This aspect of legal practice—its displacement of vocal presence—was probably one of the features of the legal order that Brown disliked, as one of the themes of antilegal rhetoric in the period was precisely the professionalization that established, as anti-legal crusaders and editorialists often said, a fundamental bad faith in the very place of ritual social consolidation.

The catalogue of allusions which is implied by Brown's fascination with voice could be extended. One obvious homology is with the Protestant representation of personal religious judgment as an "inner voice." Brown's was a Quaker family, and when Pennsylvania went to war the state effectively spoke for the pacifist Quaker population that could not, on principle, add its voice to the clamor of revolution. It has been argued that one of the circumstances that made the Revolution possible was "America's predominantly 'aural' culture": "speech was even more important than print in mobilizing a revolutionary mentality."[33] The argument is that in many respects, the colonies in the mid-eighteenth century were a fundamentally premodern society, in which face-to-face communications were the leading mode of social interaction. The Great Awakening, with its organization of masses of citizens into formless crowds united only by their concentration upon the thrilling sound of a famous voice like Whitefield's, only reinforced the oral-aural nature of the socius. Voices like Whitefield's prepared people to hear and be moved by voices like James Otis's and Patrick Henry's. Whatever the valuation of a

33. Harry S. Stout, *The New England Soul: Preaching and Religious Culture in Colonial New England* (New York: Oxford Univ. Press, 1986), p. 283.

"print mentality" in the aftermath of the Revolution, when the reconstruction of social discipline required a symbol and a technology that lent its qualities of diffusion and stability to the postwar aspiration to social generality, the *disruptive* aspiration of the agitation for revolution depended, on the contrary, on the thrill and provocation of oral utterance.[34]

Carwin's expropriation of other's voices and his dislocation of vocal presence may thus be taken, I have suggested, to represent metonymically a variety of familiar forms of vocal displacement as these were conspicuous in postrevolutionary America. What Brown knew of ventriloquism he is assumed to have gained from several printed sources he cites in his text: articles in the *Weekly Magazine* (to which he was a contributor) in 1796, an encyclopedia published in Philadelphia in 1798, a book called *Le Ventriloque* by de la Chappelle. These sources have been canvassed by the editors of the Brown edition, and the encyclopedia article has been quoted extensively in the introduction to a reprinting of *Wieland*.[35] Brown probably needed no such sources, however: the phenomenon plainly fascinated him, and his use of it in his fiction owes next to nothing to the specific information given in these sources. What is more to the point, for instance, is not the encyclopedia's article on ventriloquism, but its article on voice. "Voice, in matters of election, denotes a vote or suffrage."[36] This is the crucial association for Brown; this is the figural use of "voice" most prominent in the discourse of the time. This figure is implicit, for instance, in discussions of political representation in terms of voice, as I mentioned above. In the literature of the period, Brown would have found again and again that "voice" was a figure for political participation — not suffrage alone, but the exercise of citizenship generally. To "have a voice" in public decision making, to "have a say" in political deliberations — these idioms are still customary today, and they were familiar to Brown. The "voice of the people," the "public voice," and "general voice" are,

<hr>

34. See chapter 1, n. 84
35. Brown, *Wieland*, pp. 325–27; Fred Lewis Pattee, "Introduction," in *Wieland or The Transformation, Together with Memoirs of Carwin the Biloquist, A Fragment* (New York: Hafner Publishing Company, 1958), pp. xxxi–xxxiv.
36. *Encyclopedia; or, a Dictionary of Arts, Sciences, and Miscellaneous Literature* . . . (Philadelphia: Printed by Thomas Dobson, . . . 1798), vol. 18, p. 685.

by extension, figures of collectivity and solidarity, as the "voice of faction" is a figure of dissent. To imagine a community as a blending of voices, to represent it figurally as a fusing together of separate voices, is not far from the confusion of voices effected by Carwin. It is a figure, however, that has a certain literality to it: solidarity in America, as we have seen, is in fact a result of talk, an effect of vocal interaction and discursive legitimation. That the voices of Carwin should destroy the happiness of a community while bearing such extensive relations to the necessary processes of social and political community-building was Brown's way of pointing to the dangers intrinsic to America's forms of political association.

VI. Post-Revolutionary Nostalgia

"The law," Clara Wieland says, "is a system of expense, delay, and uncertainty" (p. 38). She is discussing her brother's decision not to travel to Germany to press his claim on the ancestral estate that Pleyel has discovered Theodore Wieland has inherited. Theodore declines to pursue the prospect of this addition to his wealth, for to do so would be to "exchange present certainties for what was distant and contingent" (p. 38). As the events of *Wieland* are set in Pennsylvania "between the conclusion of the French and the beginning of the revolutionary war" (p. 3), when the sense of an impending crisis was in the air, and the question of exchanging the certainties of the present colonial situation for the imagined improvements of national independence was conspicuously posed, Theodore and Clara Wieland's rhetoric of certainty and contingency bears a subtle reference to larger questions than those of their personal fortunes. It is particularly worthy of remark that the Wielands' prospective *change* takes the form of a *return* or *restitution,* and that this ironic structure matches quite well the "conservative" nature of the American Revolution. And their derogation of legal process as a reliable means of prosecuting such improvements of fortune has a larger historical and political reference as well. But before engaging these references, I want to ask why it is that Brown should exhibit, through his characters, an intense nostalgia for pre-revolutionary harmony and contentment, and a distrust of the political gamble that, while it had successfully gained independence by the time of his writing, did so at the cost of epistemological and moral security.

Brown, especially in *Wieland,* I shall argue, expresses a sense of loss and regret with respect to the Revolution, a sense he shared with Franklin, Crèvecoeur, and other near-contemporaries. Crèvecoeur's twelfth letter, "Distresses of a Frontier Man," most explicitly describes this sense of regret, and his text features such uncanny resemblances to that of Brown that it is tempting to think that Brown read and absorbed *Letters from an American Farmer.* Crèvecoeur's narrator famously expatiates upon the "pleasing uniformity of decent competence [that] appears throughout our habitations," and proclaims that "we are the most perfect society now existing in the world."[37] His presentation of the ideology of rural virtue, centered in the independence of yeoman freeholding, is definitive; it is this ideology to which Brown appeals in his description of the tranquillity, happiness, and serene virtue that marked the lives of Clara, Theodore, and their friends on the banks of the Schuylkill. It is the same culturally sanctioned nostalgia to which Mercy Otis Warren appealed in her history of the American Revolution when she described America as "a land previously blessed with peace, liberty, simplicity, and virtue," and then heightened the appeal of this picture of pre-revolutionary bliss by contrasting it with a figurative representation of the Revolution as "the dismemberment of the colonies."[38]

Clara's and Theodore's father exploded into flames when Clara was six years old (Brown's own age at the moment of a crucial *punctum* in his personal experience of revolutionary upheaval, when the British forces under General Howe defeated Washington's troops at Brandywine and Germantown, and then occupied Philadelphia), and their mother soon died of a disease which ensued from the shock of her husband's spontaneous combustion. "The impressions that were then made upon me, can never be

37. J. Hector St. John de Crèvecoeur, *Letters from an American Farmer and Sketches of Eighteenth-Century America,* ed. Albert E. Stone (New York: Penguin Books, 1981), p. 67.

38. Mercy Otis Warren, *History of the Rise, Progress and Termination of the American Revolution,* 3 vols. (Boston, 1805), vol. 1, p. iii.

effaced" (p. 19), Clara says (and one thinks of the impressions that the devastation of war must have made upon six-year-old Charles Brockden Brown), but she also says that their "lives were molested by few of those cares that are incident to childhood" (p. 20), and that "the felicity of that period was marred by no gloomy anticipations. The future, like the present, was serene. Time was supposed to have only new delights in store" (p. 21).

Clara herself might well have said, "We are the most perfect society now existing in the world," as Crèvecoeur did say.[39] He, too, claims that the perfection of equality and happiness he enjoys is not "transitory," but discovers, like Clara Wieland, that after all life was as uncertain and contingent in America as it had been in the imperfect old world.[40] The calm and security of his pre-revolutionary existence is destroyed by the onset of war:

> Once happiness was our portion; now it is gone from us, and I am afraid not to be enjoyed again by the present generation! Whichever way I look, nothing but the most frightful precipices present themselves to my view, in which hundreds of my friends and acquaintances have already perished; of all animals that live on the surface of this planet, what is man when no longer connected with society, or when he finds himself surrounded by a convulsed and a half-dissolved one?[41]

Crèvecoeur's figured "precipice" anticipates the symbolic pit into which Clara Wieland nearly falls, as her brother beckons to her across the gulf in a nightmare of hers. This abyss seems to represent some unspecified but powerfully ambiguous disaster that will convulse or dissolve the peaceful relations among the Wielands and their friends. It has been suggested that the pit represents the anxiety and guilt that attend the unusual "closeness of the married brother and the unmarried sister," and that Carwin, when he catches her arm and calls out to her to "Hold! hold!" (p. 62) has in fact "saved Clara from an incestuous relation with her brother."[42]

---

39. Crèvecoeur, *Letters,* p. 67.
40. Ibid., p. 67.
41. Ibid., pp. 200–201.
42. David Brion Davis, *Homicide in American Fiction, 1798–1860: A Study in Social Values* (Ithaca, New York: Cornell Univ. Press, 1957), p. 90. Cf. also William

While this is a plausible interpretation, it seems to me necessary to note that the danger of incest, if it figures here, does so in a particular way. It does so not as a sin against nature or religious morality, but as an offense against the social order. As recent scholarship has shown, the familial rhetoric of the American Revolution—its call for autonomy, for separation from the British parent—contained a metaphor that equated the family with the state. The family, as an institution, and the marriage regulations that constitute it, are the basis of political order; thus incest is antisocial. (Remember, Brown himself raised this question with respect to Cicero's *Pro Cluentio.*) Brown's association of prerevolutionary political harmony with the Wieland family's affectionate relations is allied with one of the large cultural metaphors of his day, and his suggestion of possible incestuous desires must be understood in relation to that metaphor. As such, it functions in a more general way as a representation of the threatening possibilities that may attend such a dislocation of the basic rules of social formation, that is, epistemological and linguistic undoing. The abyss into which a dreaming Clara nearly tumbles is the abyss that underlies the putative ground of a common world of things, and the system of accepted meanings for words that people use to refer to those things. Clara's loss of cognitive certainty is central to Brown's dramatization of political upheaval: "You will believe," she says, "that calamity has subverted my reason, and that I am amusing you with the chimeras of my brain, instead of facts that have really happened" (p. 65). Her perplexity and confusion recall Crèvecoeur's farmer's dismayed disorientation:

> So much is everything now subverted among us that the very word *misery*, with which we were hardly acquainted before, no longer conveys the same ideas, or, rather, tired with feeling for the miseries of others, every one feels now for himself alone. When I consider myself as connected in all these characters, as bound

---

Hill Brown, *The Power of Sympathy, or, The Triumph of Nature*, ed. William S. Kable (1798; Columbus, Ohio: Ohio State Univ. Press, 1970), p. 62, where Hariot writes to Myra of Ophelia's seduction by her cousin Martin: "She was like one who had been deluded by an *ignis fatuus* to the brink of a precipice, and there abandoned to his reflection to contemplate the horrours of the sea beneath him, into which he was about to plunge."

by so many cords, all uniting in my heart, I am seized
with a fever of the mind, I am transported beyond that
degree of calmness which is necessary to delineate our
thoughts. I feel as if my reason wanted to leave me.[43]

Crèvecoeur's themes here, and their collocation, will be familiar
to readers of *Wieland*. Political upheaval involves the dislocation
of the knowing subject's relation to facts; words lose their conventional meanings as the bonds of social interdependence are loosed.
In his *Alcuin* Brown had been explicit about the conventionality
of words: "Men are at liberty to annex to words what meaning
they think proper. What should hinder you, if you so please, from
saying that snow is of the deepest black? Words are arbitrary," Mrs.
Carter pronounces.[44]

This apprehension of semantic undoing is one that Crèvecoeur
believes has already become reality: in time of revolution, amidst
the "useless reasonings" of "jarring contradictory parties," the
common ground of relations between words and meanings has
collapsed — "What one party calls meritorious, the other denomi-
nates flagitious. These opinions vary, contract, or expand, like the
events of the war on which they are founded."[45] Certainty is lost;
"nothing but the plausible and the probable are offered to our
contemplation. . . . Sophistry, the bane of freemen, launches forth
in all her deceiving attire!"[46] It is with despair that Crèvecoeur
refers to "fictitious reason,"[47] as though the adjective were the inevitable attendant of the noun; and this failure of reason has everything to do with "this unfortunate revolution."[48]

Any reader of *Wieland* will, as I say, recognize in Crèvecoeur
the mood of "epistemological terror and moral confusion," to borrow Jay Fliegelman's apt characterization, that dominates Brown's
book. Fliegelman calls *Wieland* "the dark flip side of Franklin's *Autobiography*," on account of Brown's reversal of Franklin's opportu-

43. Crèvecoeur, *Letters*, p. 201.
44. Charles Brockden Brown, *Alcuin: A Dialogue*, ed. Lee R. Edwards (New
York: Grossman Publishers, 1971), p. 71.
45. Crèvecoeur, *Letters*, p. 205.
46. Ibid., p. 204.
47. Ibid., p. 209.
48. Ibid., p. 204.

nistic sense that a world of mutable appearances is a conveniently plastic context for ambitious self-presentation; in *Wieland* "the same post-sensationalist world is invoked, but in all its terror rather than its freedom."[49] Fliegelman continues:

> The book's subtitle, *The Transformation*, refers not only to the transformation of Wieland but to a broad historical transformation, the shift from a world that assumed stable forms and fixed relations between appearance and reality and between man and society to a world sensitive to shifting values, deceptive appearances, mixed motives and, most significantly, the tyranny of language over things, rhetoric over logic. A secure world has been made insecure and that, Brown announces, is the price of its having become "free." By placing his novel in the decade before the American Revolution, Brown suggests, by implication, that the great conflict for American independence, rather than merely being a result of that larger "transformation," decisively hastened it.[50]

I would state it more baldly: Brown represents a world not simply "sensitive" to the flux of experience, but devastated by it; and the Revolution, in his view, did not merely "hasten" this devastation, but decisively precipitated it. Brown, like Crèvecoeur's James, might say, "I am conscious that I was happy before this unfortunate revolution. I feel that I am no longer so; therefore I regret the change."[51]

One might speculate on the effect revolutionary upheaval would have had on the psyche of a child in Philadelphia. Brown was born in 1771, and his infancy coincided with the dislocations of the war; his nostalgia for what he imagined as a utopia of pre-revolutionary quietude may be the fictional translation of a personal sense of lost childhood security. His Quaker family adhered to the cause of independence, however perfunctorily, but like

---

49. Fliegelman, *Prodigals and Pilgrims*, p. 240.
50. Ibid., p. 240.
51. Crèvecoeur, *Letters*, p. 204.

other Friends they practiced pacifism amidst the violence of war. At age eleven, Brown entered the Friends Public School, where he was instructed by Robert Proud, a professed Tory. Emory Elliott remarks that Proud "*had* been an opponent of the Revolutionary War,"[52] but in 1782 the war was not, of course, yet ended, and Proud's opinions had a present-tense reference. Whether Proud had any decisive influence on his student's mind or not, we can safely assume that Brown, reaching his intellectual maturity in the years following the Peace of Paris, witnessing the multifarious disorders of the postrevolutionary period, studying the processes of social reconstitution and political institution-making, and, especially, attempting to find a vocation in the law — in the ideals of formalist legality and rational consensus building in which the new nation had invested much of its faith — would have been well situated to evaluate critically the adequacy of reasoned discourse as a foundation for government, and to reach a judgment as to the success or failure of the Revolution's achievements. And if we read *Wieland* as such a critical evaluation of American political foundations, as I believe we can, then the judgment he renders is at least a dismayed and probably a disturbed one. For in the world *Wieland* depicts, formal reason and discursive legitimation are baffled at every turn, and the claims of a reactionary political order grounded in historical precedent are heard with a sympathetic ear.

VII. Law and Liberalism

Brown's unhappy apprenticeship to the lawyer Alexander Wilcocks extended from 1787 to 1793. His aversion to the law as a profession is well known, and the sources of that aversion have been studied, most fully by Robert Ferguson, whose account of the "configuration of law and letters" in the early republic provides an explanation of the way the legal order functioned in the literature of the period as a figure of "ideological coherence."[53] Brown's family pressed him into a legal career against his wishes; he preferred the solitary pursuit of literary creation to the worldly pur-

---

52. Elliott, *Revolutionary Writers*, p. 219, emphasis added.
53. Ferguson, *Law and Letters*, pp. 8, 10.

suit of wealth and status in what was the preeminent respectable career of his time. Information on the immediate causes of his abandonment of a legal career is not plentiful, and scholars have found it necessary to advert to the "Series of Original Letters" Brown published in *The Weekly Magazine* in 1798, wherein a young man called Henry D. carries on an epistolary exchange with his sister in which he debates, among other things, the suitability of a legal career for himself. The letters themselves are dated 1794, the year after Brown's rejection of a legal career, and their autobiographical content is obvious; they can, in fact, be read as a displaced *apologia*. As such, it is noticeable that in addition to Henry D.'s temperamental aversion to the routines of legal practice, there emerge in the letters some hints, however elusive, of what may be taken as Brown's serious critique of the premises upon which the legal order rests. In interpreting these hints, it is necessary to extrapolate from them the larger contours of what I take to be Brown's considered rejection of these premises, and *Wieland,* with its dense thicket of allusions to legal principles and practices, will assist in this extrapolation.

Henry D., the melancholy law student, is conscious at first of feeling that because "destiny has given [him] a *liberal* profession,"[54] he holds the other young men with whom he lives (a tailor, a clerk, and an usher in a school) in contempt. His sister Mary (his correspondent) presently admonishes him to consider whether a tailor is not as useful to society as a lawyer, and therefore entitled to as much respect; and whether an usher may not serve to communicate knowledge at least as well as a lawyer — "whose business it is, instead of enlightening, to perplex and bewilder the human understanding" (p. 107). Mary goes on to state that a lawyer is one "who makes a trade of weaving together subtleties and sophisms calculated to mislead the consciousness of justice implanted in the mind of every rational being" (p. 107). Henry, disturbed by Mary's derogation of his profession, is moved to defend it, in spite of his own misgivings: "The qualifications and exercises which it requires from its pupils are wholly intellectual. It is a sci-

---

54. Charles Brockden Brown, *The Rhapsodist and Other Uncollected Writings,* ed. Harry R. Warfel (New York: Scholars' Facsimiles and Reprints, 1943), p. 103. Further page references will be given parenthetically.

ence, and the investigation of truth is always delightful to ingenu-
ous minds. It was the regulator of the claims and conduct of men
in society" (p. 108). But his defense soon collapses, as he finally
agrees with his sister's insinuation that, as he phrases it, "my business is merely to weave quibbles into a net by which I may
entangle justice" (p. 109). Henry does not truly believe that the
law is a science, despite his earlier claim:

> A fortnight's reading can give me no information as to
> the merits or demerits of the *trade*. It shews me, in a
> slight degree, of what materials the *science* is com-
> posed. They are sufficiently refractory and rugged.
> Wrapt up in barbarous jargon, a spurious and motley
> compound of obsolete French and Latinized English.
> My poor head has been honoured by you, with the
> epithet of metaphysical; but as skilful a dissecter as I
> am of complex ideas, and as nice a weigher of abstruse
> distinctions, I fear I shall never untie legal knots or dis-
> envolve from this maze my already bewildered under-
> standing. (p. 109)

That bewilderment should be the result of legal reasoning is, to
say the least, an ironic consequence; the protocols of legal thought
are meant, to be sure, to produce perspicuous certainty. But just
as Brown's language here begins to put in question the law's status
as a "science" (and its status as a "liberal profession" rather than a
"trade"), so he begins to question the efficacy of those rational
protocols. And his questioning here coincides with the similar fail-
ures of reason in *Wieland,* where bewilderment later figures so
conspicuously. And in *Wieland,* too, it does so in explicit relation
to the forms of legal thought: all the legal procedures and principles that are invoked in the novel are unavailing in the face of the
violent crime around which the plot revolves. Theodore Wieland's
brutal murder of his children and his wife is, after all, the fact
which, brought before the "bar" of reason, implacably defies
understanding.

To return for a moment to the "Series of Original Letters":
Mary replies in turn to her brother's dismayed agreement with her
critique, and now she reverses herself just as he did, by offering a

new justification of the legal profession, one that gets to the heart of Brown's quarrel with legal reason. Here she seems to be speaking Brown's mind quite directly:

> Absolutely speaking, nothing is more true than that justice is due from every human being to his fellows; and that it ought to be spontaneously rendered. That this opinion should universally regulate the actions of mankind would argue the most perfect state of society and its prevalence would, in most cases, supersede the necessity of permanent institutions for the protection of life, liberty, or property. (p. 111)

Such a utopian state of society, we may recall, was what Clara and Theodore Wieland's perfectionist father sought to institute, and what he found to be impossible of achievement amidst the imperfections of actually existing society. In the senior Wieland's case, such perfectionism was, finally, antisocial; against Mary D. and the Wieland father, Brown's implicit argument is that perfect justice is simply not spontaneously renderable in human society, where people's interests often collide and cannot all be completely satisfied. But it is possible to detect in Brown a belief in a somewhat fuller (if still incomplete) community of interests, a belief that attaches itself to an image of what is sometimes called "traditional" or "customary" society. And it is precisely in this kind of society—one characterized by what Tönnies called *Gemeinschaft*—that a complex legal order is unknown and superfluous. As the legal philosopher Roberto Mangabeira Unger has noted, the emergence of bureaucratic law—the elaboration of an autonomous legal order consisting of "a separate body of legal norms, a system of specialized legal institutions, a well-defined tradition of legal doctrine, and a legal profession with its own relatively unique outlook, interests, and ideals"[55]—follows historically upon the disintegration of traditional community norms, the decay of common standards of conduct and established forms of social life to which people give their spontaneous (or at least habitual and uncritical) alle-

---

55. Roberto Mangabeira Unger, *Law in Modern Society: Toward a Criticism of Social Theory* (New York: The Free Press, 1976), p. 54.

giance. With the evolution from customary to liberal society, implicit and unquestioned standards give way to explicit rules which must be discursively and publicly justified, rather than just taken for granted. What once could be left unsaid now must be articulated. When Unger says that the positive law mentality emerged along with "the discovery that order could and indeed had to be devised rather than just accepted ready-made,"[56] we know that he is referring to just such a discovery and emergence as the American Revolution reflected and enacted.

> From the standpoint of consciousness, the disintegration of community means the development of a situation in which one feels increasingly able to question the rightness of accepted practices as well as to violate them. Only then do explicit and formulated rules become possible and necessary. Positive law remains superfluous as long as there is a closely held communion of reciprocal expectations, based on a shared view of right and wrong. In this setting the normative order will not surface as formulated rules; indeed, it may remain almost entirely below the threshold of explicit statement and conscious understanding.[57]

It is this kind of transition to which Mary D. refers, and which she deplores. People no longer "spontaneously" render justice to their fellow men; if only they did, "the exertions of every individual would tend to secure these enjoyments and to promote every accession to the great mass of wisdom and happiness" (p. 111). But since people do not do so, for whatever reason, a legal order and the lawyers who serve it are required. "I deem it *wrong* that laws should be multifarious or unintelligible: Nevertheless I perceive they are so. The conduct of individuals is regulated by institutions whose written language is, to a large majority, without a meaning. It is therefore unquestionably *right* that some one should be capable of interpreting it to them" (p. 112). And it is

56. Ibid., p. 130.
57. Ibid., pp. 61–62.

better that this interpreter be "a sage rather than an idiot; that he should be a man of principle rather than a knave" (pp. 112–13). Mary concludes, therefore, that because her brother Henry is intelligent, honest, and eloquent, "for you . . . the profession of the law is eligible" (p. 113).

We should here consider, as Unger has done, the premises on which the modern legal order rests—premises that he calls the "liberal doctrine."[58] This doctrine comprises premises of epistemology, language, history, and psychology. It holds that "there is only one world of facts and only one form of understanding, fundamentally alike in everyone. A man may know more or less about the world, but whenever two men know something truly what they know is the same thing."[59] This world is completely described by language, which consists of words to which conventional meanings have been assigned, and which is therefore uniformly intelligible to all people, regardless of whether they share the same values and desires or not.[60] More likely than not they do *not* implicitly share the same values and desires; but they do share the faculty of reason, which operates with a shared language in respect of a common world of facts; and reason allows them to override private desires in the interest of the "demands of collaboration that mark social life."[61] Thus they can formulate rules to ensure this necessary collaboration, and these rules can be applied formalistically and impersonally to adjudicate the conflicts that arise when one person's desire conflicts with that of another person. Because "there is no natural community of common ends," rules and their coercive enforcement are required; "a legal order is entailed by the very concept of a society of men with conflicting values."[62] This kind of society—pluralistic, inorganic, modern—is a historical phenomenon produced as a result of the epochal discovery that the normative order is susceptible to fabrication and amendment, and is not simply given in the nature of things. In

58. Roberto Mangabeira Unger, *Knowledge and Politics,* (New York: The Free Press, 1975), p. 3.
59. Ibid., p. 40.
60. Ibid., pp. 101, 32.
61. Ibid., p. 68.
62. Ibid., pp. 75, 72.

a formulation that is congenial to Brown's allegory, Habermas calls this world-historical transition the "linguistification of the sacred."[63]

This conception of legal order was one that Charles Brockden Brown found untenable. In *Wieland* nearly all of these premises are forcefully negated, and I believe that this negation reflects Brown's serious, incisive, and destructive analysis of the early republic's faith in legal order; it is this analysis that led most likely to his considered rejection of a career that would have required him to act on premises he could not accept. *Wieland* is densely packed with legal phrases, terms, ideas, and images, and this compaction of legal reference within the text is a calculated effect of Brown's careful attempt to dramatize the untenability of the premises of the legal mentality. Such words as *witness, testimony, attester, evidence, corroboration, proof, advocate, charges, accusation, summoned, arraigned, confess, plead, trial, judge, bar, magistrate, criminal, tribunal, verdict, vindication, convicted, punish, sentence, condemn, innocence, guilt, defence, treason, justice, equity, injustice* — such words are conspicuous on every page of *Wieland,* and their prominence is the measure of Brown's engagement with the questions regarding the validity of the procedures of legal reasoning that I mentioned earlier. The ubiquitous presence in the text of the vocabulary of law creates a subliminal sense that the action of the story is permeated by a legalistic aura. It is the measure also of Brown's doubts regarding the efficacy of legal institutions for preserving social order, and of his skepticism toward the disenchanted worldview which the legal order endorsed.

Theodor Adorno, writing in *Against Epistemology,* criticizes Husserlian phenomenology on grounds remarkably similar to those on which, I have been arguing, Brockden Brown criticizes the foundational epistemological assumptions of his society. By framing questions of knowledge and certainty in terms of courtroom procedures, and by soaking his prose in the language of legal process, Brown charges his society with doing what Adorno

---

63. Jürgen Habermas, *The Theory of Communicative Action,* trans. Thomas McCarthy, 2 vols. (Boston: Beacon Press, 1984), vol. 2, pp. 77ff.

claims Husserl does: "unwittingly constru[ing] epistemology analogously to a legal contest."[64] Such a construal implicitly promises that contradictions between individual beliefs can be resolved in a moment of authoritative judgment when a consensual consciousness attains an absolutely noncontradictory view of the world as a state of affairs that is unvarying and independent of the human minds seeking to know it. A jury's attempt to determine facts that are in dispute is, obviously, the nearest thing to an actual social performance of such a consensual cognitive act. Juries have been known to fail to agree on the facts, however. And a jury's determination of the facts has been known to be influenced by the powerful pleading of an advocate's voice. These are problems that Brown confronted repeatedly in many of his works, for instance in *Memoirs of Stephen Calvert,* where, at one point, as Calvert narrates, "A score of eye-witnesses communicated each a different tale, and a different description of my person."[65] Calvert reasons from such discrepancies that "though many different representations will be given of every incident, yet it *may* always be, that one among the number shall be true."[66] The uncertainty indicated by the conditional verb ("may") is the point on which so many of Brown's plots pivot. *Wieland* is propelled by the anxieties produced by the discrepancies between what the different characters' senses tell them is happening, by their pursuit of corroboration for their accounts of things, and by the desperation induced by their separate intimations that there will be no final resolution of these inconsistencies.

Brown's implicit claim may, I believe, be compared to Adorno's: "The reality in which men live . . . is human and even absolutely extra-human nature is mediated through consciousness. Men cannot break through that. They live in social being, not in nature."[67] And in *Wieland,* as we have seen, the structure of social experience

---

64. Theodor W. Adorno, *Against Epistemology: A Metacritique; Studies in Husserl and the Phenomenological Antinomies,* trans. Willis Domingo (Cambridge, Massachusetts: The MIT Press, 1983), p. 26.

65. Charles Brockden Brown, *Memoirs of Stephen Calvert,* ed. Hans Borchers (Frankfurt am Main: Peter Lang, 1978), p. 50.

66. Ibid., p. 53, emphasis added.

67. Adorno, *Against Epistemology,* p. 28.

is determined largely by relations of speaking and hearing. Before proceeding to a final examination of the social and political allegory of *Wieland,* however, it is necessary to explicate further the legal ideology against which Brown is contending.

VIII. Legal Epistemology

Brown entered the law offices of Alexander Wilcocks in 1787, at the age of sixteen; he remained there until the summer of 1793, when he abandoned the profession. 1787 was the year of the Federal Convention that wrote the Constitution — no doubt it was a heady time for a young man to be entering the legal profession, a moment in which it would have been difficult to be cynical about the ability of legal reasoning to ground a political order on normative rationality. In 1793 Washington and Adams were reelected president and vice president, and the new government gained an added measure of stability; at the same time, the monarchy was abolished in France, and the Reign of Terror was instituted. A discontented young man might very well choose to believe that reason, exercising a corrosive effect on established institutions, might, if unchecked by any reverence for tradition and authority, result in the collapse of political order and social peace.

It is possible that in 1790 Brown attended the lectures on law given in the College of Philadelphia by James Wilson, the statesman and jurist, in which Wilson attempted to construct a grand intellectual synthesis designed to provide a philosophical foundation for the legal order of the new republic. Wilson had been born in Scotland in 1742 and came to Philadelphia in 1765; he read law under John Dickinson, the author of the *Letters from a Farmer in Pennsylvania* (1767–68), one of the first significant protests against the Parliamentary tax policies that precipitated the Revolution. Wilson himself soon entered the pamphlet warfare with an essay that denied the authority of Parliament over colonies that had no representation in that body, and hence no means of giving consent to its laws. As a delegate to the Continental Congress, a signer of the Declaration of Independence, a member of the Constitutional Convention (where his contributions were second only to those of Madison), and a justice of the first Supreme Court,

Wilson was admirably situated to make an argument for the legitimacy of the newly fabricated American legal order. In his 1790 inaugural lecture as first professor of law in the College of Philadelphia—an address to which President Washington, Vice President Adams, and other national leaders were drawn, in addition, one can assume, to such interested individuals as local law students—Wilson laid it down that "a revolution principle certainly is, and certainly should be taught as a principle of the constitution of the United States, and of every State in the Union."[68] This "revolution principle" was the same one he had argued for in his pamphlet of 1768; at a time when it was uncertain whether a "revolution principle" could serve as the foundation of a stable social order, Wilson insisted that it definitely could.

> This revolution principle—that, the sovereign power residing in the people, they may change their constitution and government whenever they please—is not a principle of discord, rancour, or war: it is a principle of melioration, contentment, and peace. It is a principle not recommended merely by a flattering theory: it is a principle recommended by happy experience. To the testimony of Pennsylvania—to the testimony of the United States I appeal for the truth of what I say.[69]

Wilson's appeal to experience was, to say the least, rhetorical in nature. Experience in Pennsylvania especially, and in the United States generally, supported his claims virtually not at all; this "revolution principle" was hotly contested in the years of the debate on the Constitution, and Wilson's claims for it were expressions of faith rather than an account of "happy experience." His subsequent lectures were devoted to complex arguments in support of this faith. He surveyed the fields of epistemology, linguistics, psychology and history, assembling his accumulated findings into a magnificent intellectual edifice that very closely resembles the "liberal doctrine" delineated by Unger and discussed above. It provides a useful summary of the intellectual background to Brown's

68. Wilson, *Works,* vol. 1, pp. 20–21.
69. Ibid., p. 21.

disillusionment, for it is Wilson's faith in law and reason that
Brown so conspicuously lacked, and it is, in essence, Wilson's argument that *Wieland* deconstructs.

Wilson's Lecture XIII, "Of the Nature and Philosophy of Evidence," is, in a sense, the linch-pin of his whole system, for it is
here that Wilson provides the epistemological doctrines on which
the practices of the courtroom depend, and it is on this section of
Wilson's tome that *Wieland* reads like a critical commentary. Early
in her narrative, after the first of many situations in which the
"testimony" of one person's senses conflicts with the "testimony"
of another's — in this instance, Theodore has heard his wife's voice
warning him away from danger in the hilltop temple near their
home, when she is ostensibly present in the house with the others
at the time her voice is heard outdoors — Clara remarks that her
brother's apparent delusions "argued a diseased condition of his
frame, which might show itself hereafter in more dangerous
symptoms." Of course her premonitions turn out to be correct;
but she goes on here to outline her theory of the mind's operations. "The will is the tool of the understanding, which must fashion its conclusions on the notions of sense. If the senses be depraved, it is impossible to calculate the evils that may flow from
the consequent deductions of the understanding" (p. 45). This
statement is, as Jay Fliegelman has noted, "vintage Locke." It is
not, however, "the novel's primary assumption," as Fliegelman
also says;[70] it is, rather, *Clara's* assumption, one that the novel, as
Brown has designed it, undercuts. And as it is the assumption of
the world in which Clara lives, and, in particular, the assumption
on which the legal order rests, Brown's purpose seems to be to
undercut that premise as well. For Wieland's mind is not diseased;
his senses are not deranged. What gets him into trouble is that he
trusts his senses uncritically, and assumes that what the senses report is, in fact, an adequate reflection of what actually exists in
the world. For he *has* in fact heard a voice that is, to his senses,
indistinguishable from that of his wife; but even perfectly func-
tioning sense organs like his own can be fooled. The character in
Wieland whose senses do *not* function very well is Clara; her mind

70. Fliegelman, *Prodigals and Pilgrims,* p. 237.

does not operate passively, as Locke would have it, registering sensations as they come to it, but actively, as the tool of her will. As James R. Russo has extensively argued, Clara "flits back and forth between imagination and reality throughout the novel,"[71] and is therefore the unreliable narrator *par excellence*. Constantly "tormented by phantoms of [her] own creation" (p. 83), the effects (as Russo argues) of her unrelieved state of sexual excitation, it is Clara whose understanding is depraved, whose misapprehensions lead to her making deductions that result in various ill consequences. Clara sees what she wants to see, hears what she wants to hear; then she assembles from these putative sense-impressions a narrative construction that strengthens her belief in what she wants to believe. Brown thus insinuates a terrible doubt of the reliability of sense-impressions into the phrase of which he will make repeated use throughout the novel: "The testimony of the senses." In this familiar but complex figure of speech the supposed immediacy of sense-impressions is already compromised by the term "testimony," which implies a verbal redaction—a linguistic mediation—of the supposedly simple sense experience. James Wilson specified, in the first entry in his ranked list of fourteen more or less credible sources of evidence, that evidence "arises from the external senses: and by each of these, distinct information is conveyed to the mind."[72] By placing sense experience in the privileged first place in his list of sources of evidence, he implies that it is foundational, and in elaborating on this fundamental source, he admits that while there is no cogent reason to trust the senses—no way of proving that they are reliable sources of knowledge—such a reason or proof is unnecessary, since human nature determines that we ineluctably believe in the evidence the senses provide. Wilson has earlier made it quite clear that he takes the reliability of sense experience as self-evident:

> Many philosophers allege that our mind does not perceive external objects themselves; that it perceives only *ideas* of them; and that those ideas are actually in the mind. When it has been intimated to them, that, if this

71. Russo, "'The Chimeras of the Brain,'" p. 60.
72. Wilson, *Works*, vol. 2, p. 75.

be the case; if we perceive not external objects themselves, but only ideas; the necessary consequence must
be, that we cannot be certain that any thing, except
those ideas, exists; the consequence has been admitted
in its fullest force.[73]

Against such epistemological idealism, Wilson enters the following objection:

Suffice it, at present, to observe, that the existence of
the objects of our external senses, in the way and manner in which we perceive that existence, is a branch of
intuitive knowledge, and a matter of absolute certainty; that the constitution of our nature determines
us to believe in our senses; and that a contrary determination would finally lead to the total subversion of
all human knowledge. For this belief we cannot, we
pretend not to assign an argument; it is a simple and
original, and therefore an inexplicable act of the mind.
It can neither be described nor defined.[74]

Wieland might be described as the fictional working out of what
Wilson here admits to be the "necessary consequence" of rejecting
what he insists is a "simple and original" principle of the human
mind; for if sense impressions are unreliable, then it follows that
a deep and dangerous chasm divides the human mind from the
world of objects it vainly seeks to apprehend. For Wilson to call
sensory apprehension an "act" of the mind already, however,
places the simplicity and certainty of such apprehension in doubt;
even consenting to discuss the question, for that matter, as much
as concedes that the issue is one that no "intuitive" or "self-
evident" principle automatically settles, else the question would
not even arise. To *argue* from self-evidence is inherently self-
contradictory; and it is this contradiction that, in *Wieland*, unrav-
els the edifice of epistemological certitude that Wilson so pa-
tiently constructs.

73. Ibid., vol. 1, p. 238.
74. Ibid., vol. 1, p. 239.

IX. Counter-Revolution

Wieland is a deeply political text. In it Brown examines the grounds of political order, and, in particular, the grounds of the new American political order. And while it is possible to detect certain references to the political conditions of the late eighteenth century, which are represented in an allegorical fashion in the events of the plot, it is more important — and, finally, reflects better on Brown's artistic achievement — to consider his novel not as a close commentary on political events of the postrevolutionary period, but as a discouraged reflection on the tenability of the claim that a viable political order could be guaranteed by discursive reason without the aid of the unspoken loyalty and reverence that supported the legitimacy of previous states. It is important, in reading *Wieland,* to avoid the kind of error into which, for instance, Jane Tompkins falls in her reading of the novel. Tompkins begins by noting that when Brown first published the novel, he sent a copy to Thomas Jefferson, who was at that time vice president of the United States. This gesture invites interpretation, but to suggest (as Tompkins does) that it indicates that Brown saw *Wieland* as "an attempt to influence public policy," and that it "was not designed as a well-made novel, but as a political tract,"[75] is to flatten out the texture of the novel and to attribute to Brown a more prosaic and uncomplicated intention than the strangeness of the novel suggests. Tompkins at once gives Brown too much credit as a simple political propagandist and not enough credit as an artist imaginatively engaged with the most profound implications of the massive social dislocations and political innovations through which he lived and about which he worried. To call *Wieland* a "tract," even in an effort to establish through hyperbole the novel's claim to political seriousness against those readers who read it in purely psychological, or formal, or generic terms, is to reduce its bizarre complexity unnecessarily. For if ever a novel's odd and indeterminate meanings were the effects of a surplus of determining conditions *Wieland* is that novel.

Besides, Brown wrote any number of political tracts, and while

75. Tompkins, *Sensational Designs,* pp. 43, 44.

they provide interesting suggestions about the politics of *Wieland,*
they do so by demonstrating how the nuanced epistemological
politics implicit in the novel could later be paraphrased by the author himself in a crudely reductive fashion. Brown's later political
pamphlets make the sophistication of *Wieland* appear vivid by
contrast. Charles Cole has pointed out that Brown, in the interim
between his abortive legal career and his novel-writing period, was
something of a radical.[76] *Alcuin,* his 1797 pamphlet dialogue on
the subject of women's political rights, for instance, presents arguments to the effect that the Constitution is "unjust and absurd" in
certain points, for example, in its exclusion of women, minors, the
propertyless, and blacks from the privileges of political participation.[77] Brown's political inclinations altered fairly rapidly, however, after *Alcuin.* From an admirer of William Godwin and Mary
Wollstonecraft in 1797, he became a vociferous anti-Jeffersonian
in the early 1800s. It seems likely that the experience of writing
Wieland had some role in this transformation, and we might do
well to consider that the *Transformation* of the novel's subtitle had
an unwitting personal reference. In any case, the moment of *Wieland,* and of Brown's gift of a copy of the novel to Jefferson, was
a moment of confused political transition, for Brown and for the
nation, and its equivocal message is an expression of that confusion. To write a gothic romance in the land of Enlightenment is
already a reactionary move; to send it to the leading American
philosophe is practically an insult. Brown's motives were obscure,
and possibly disingenuous; what is certain is that they were nothing like a clear-sighted wish to "influence public policy."

Brown's later political pamphleteering may shed a retrospective
light on the equivocations of *Wieland.* He wrote his six novels
in fewer years: their publication dates are from 1798 to 1801.
Subsequently, during the remaining years of his life, Brown (who
died in 1810) edited magazines and tried to intervene in the political life of the nation with a series of four pamphlets:

1. *An Address to the Government of the United States, on the Cession
of Louisiana to the French* (Philadelphia, 1803).

2. *Monroe's Embassy, or, The Conduct of the Government, in Rela-*

---

76. Charles C. Cole, Jr., "Brockden Brown and the Jefferson Administration,"
Pennsylvania Magazine of History and Biography 72 (1948): 253–63.
77. Brown, *Alcuin,* p. 29

tion to Our Claims to the Navigation of the Mississippi (Philadelphia, 1805).

3. *The British Treaty of Commerce and Navigation, concluded December 31, 1806* (Philadelphia, 1807).[78]

4. *An Address to the Congress of the United States, on the Utility and Justice of Restrictions Upon Foreign Commerce* (Philadelphia, 1809).

There are numerous analogies and affiliations traceable between Brown's pamphlet literature and his fictional writing, and I will attempt to describe some of them. The first pamphlet is a rhetorically intricate attempt to instill in Americans a paranoid fear of French duplicity. Brown, the anonymous author, begins by stating that "he means to draw his arguments from the mouth of an enemy," this source being a French "counsellor of state" whose written advice to Napoleon on dealings with America is said to have been anonymously published in a very few copies, and to have come fortunately into the author's hands.[79] The French document is, of course, spurious; but it is not presented within the pamphlet as a literary device but as a fact. Brown's decision to "draw his arguments from the mouth of another" immediately alerts us to some obvious connections between this pamphlet and his novel of a few years before: Brown is counterfeiting the voice of a dangerous plotter just as Carwin had done. The bogus document runs for forty-three pages, and it is full of aspersions on American national character, suggestions for manipulating the alleged weaknesses of that character, and strategies for exploiting the opportunities presented by American gullibility and helplessness. And although Brown's authorial pose is that of an alarmed discoverer of a document in which the diabolical plans of France are boldly revealed, he is, after all, at the same time the creator of the diabolical French counsellor whose words, he hopes, will alarm other Americans as well. As Brown created Carwin the biloquist, so here he creates this French schemer. But Brown himself is the biloquist now.

In the purported memorandum of advice, the counsellor urges

78. There is some disagreement among scholars as to the authenticity of the attribution of this pamphlet to Brown. The passages I quote from it below seem to me to support the attribution.

79. Charles Brockden Brown, *An Address to the Government of the United States, on the Cession of Louisiana to the French, a new edition, Revised, Corrected and Improved* (Philadelphia: Published by John Conrad, & Co., et al., 1803), pp. 3, 4.

Napoleon to seize the opportunity to people the American continent. Spain had secretly ceded the Louisiana territory to France,
and Napoleon's adviser urges him to occupy it swiftly before the
United States can resist; under the impotent leadership of Jefferson, he says, the United States government will stupidly allow
France to establish itself on the western frontier. In describing the
pathetic defenselessness of the American republic, Brown's own
views plainly dictate the Frenchman's arguments, and his dismayed evaluation of the state of the nation is presented in only
barely disguised terms:

> Was there ever a people who exhibited so motley a
> character; who have vested a more limited and precari-
> ous authority, in their rulers; who have multiplied so
> much the numbers of those that govern; who have dis-
> persed themselves over so wide a space; and have been
> led by this local dispersion, to create so many clashing
> jurisdictions and jarring interests, as the States of
> America?
>   They call themselves *free*, yet a fifth of their number
> are slaves. That proportion of the whole people are
> ground by a yoke more dreadful and debasing than
> the predial servitude of Poland and Russia. They call
> themselves *one*, yet all languages are native to their citi-
> zens. . . . Already there are near twenty states, each of
> which is governed by a law of its own; which have
> formed a common union, on voluntary and mutable
> principles; and a general constitution, whose end is to
> secure their utmost efficacy to popular passions, and
> to prevent the scattered members from coalescing into
> one symmetrical and useful body. They are a people of
> yesterday. Their institutions have just received birth.
> Hence their characters and views are void of all stabil-
> ity. Their prejudices are all discordant. Their govern-
> ment is destitute of that veneration which an ancient
> date, and of that distinctness and certainty in its opera-
> tions and departments which long experience, confers.
> Their people are the slaves of hostile interests; blown

in all directions by froward passions; divided by invet-
erate factions; and the dupes and partizans of all the
elder nations by turns.[80]

This "patchwork republic,"[81] as the Frenchman derisively calls it,
can offer no resistance to French encroachment. The Americans'
only strength is in their numbers; but numbers will be of no avail,
for a reason that the French counsellor expresses figuratively—
and the figure he chooses (the figure that Brown chooses for him)
will again recall *Wieland:* "Their numbers! *That,* when the parts
are discordant, is only fuel more easily kindled, and producing a
more extensive and unquenchable flame."[82] Later in this inflam-
matory tract, Brown again adverts to a kindling metaphor, this
time in his own voice: he claims that the numbers of black slaves
"are indeed a train of powder, so situated as to make it not impossible for the French in Louisiana, to set fire to it."[83]

The same ventriloquistic device is employed by Brown in his
next pamphlet (published later in 1803), only this time the voice
Brown counterfeits is Jefferson's. He libels Jefferson as an un-
worldly thinker who uses his mind to rationalize the instincts of a
coward: "an head of subtlety, defending the suggestions of a timo-
rous heart."[84] For seven pages Brown's exposition presents a fac-
simile of the words of Jefferson, who makes obviously specious
arguments for a policy that is the effect of simple fear.[85] Jefferson's
policy of negotiation and concession in the face of French belliger-
ence is held by Brown to be not a careful method of statesmanship
but at best naive, and at worst a form of appeasement. And after
presenting the supposed voice of Jefferson, Brown goes on to
mimic another voice, that of a merchant who, impatient of Jeffersonian diplomacy, demands reparation for the economic losses he
has incurred as a result of France's exclusion of his trade from the

80. Ibid., pp. 37–38.
81. Ibid., p. 38.
82. Ibid., p. 38.
83. Ibid., p. 48.
84. Charles Brockden Brown, *Monroe's Embassy, or, The Conduct of the Government, in Relation to Our Claims to the Navigation of the Mississippi* . . . (Philadelphia:
Published by John Conrad, & Co., 1803), p. 13.
85. Ibid., pp. 14–20.

navigation of the Mississippi. Where Brown had, in his first pamphlet, given as one item of the crafty French counsellor's abuse of America the claim that America was "a nation of pedlars and shopkeepers," for whom "money engrosses all their passions and pursuits,"[86] in the second pamphlet he allows such a peddler to abuse Jefferson on behalf of money-making interests.

Brown's attacks on Jefferson in 1803 were as nothing, however, compared to the venomous condescension with which he described the president in 1808, in a pamphlet which castigated the government for its weak response to the British attack on the U.S. frigate Chesapeake. Against Jefferson's attempt to avoid warfare by instituting trade restrictions and negotiating with the British, Brown urged, with pretended reluctance, a declaration of war. His jingoism is informed by an ugly Hobbesian view of international relations, in which might makes right, and no principles must interfere with the pursuit of competitive advantage in trade and commerce. Brown describes the "great defects" that prevent Jefferson from taking such a disenchanted view of things; in spite of his otherwise "considerable share of genius," Jefferson is inhibited from waging war manfully, as he ought to do:

> Like others who have fallen into the idle habit of questioning established truth, his faculty of weighing evidence is impaired. Hence such an astonishing degree of credulity, that he could not only believe the French were free while suffering oppression the most cruel and bloody that ever poor wretches groaned under, but (finding it printed in a French book) he believed, and gravely told the Congress, there is a great mountain of salt in Louisiana. Mr. Jefferson has also the misfortune to be a schemer, perpetually occupied with some strange out-of-the-way project. If this were confined to speculation, it would be a harmless foible; but he tries to carry his projects into effect. . . . He labours also under such defect of mental vision, that he seldom sees objects in their natural state and true position: just

86. Brown, *An Address to the Government,* p. 39.

as when we look through a fog, many things near us are not perceived, and those we see appear larger and nearer than they really are.

We have said Mr. Jefferson is not deep in any science. He is more deficient in that of politics than in any other; and indeed it is impossible he should ever become a statesman; because a clear, distinct, and comprehensive view of objects, with a ready conception of their bearings on each other, is a needful prerequisite. A second prerequisite is so to weigh evidence, presumption and probability, as properly to give or withhold our faith: in short, to believe what we ought, and no more. A third is never to indulge notions which have not experience to recommend them: for though it be possible that after the many years which history numbers, and the many thousand events it records, something new in the science of ethics may be discovered, it is not likely; and if it were, the maxim of physicians should be adopted, to make experiments on bodies of little value, and not on the body politic.[87]

The depth of Brown's accumulated resentment is evident here, as is the utter completeness of his reversion to a language of faith in the clarity of reason and its ability to judge evidence accurately and arrive at conclusions securely. There is no problem here with reason; there is only a problem with Jefferson's reason. The president's mind is defective; a sound mind could presumably do better. And yet no sooner has Brown relied upon a criterion of sound reason to make an invidious judgment on Jefferson's mind, than he once again resumes his fundamental distrust of reason. Not only was Jefferson's reason unsound, but even if it had been sound, he would have been wrong to trust it rather than custom and usage.

If any gentleman assume as a principle that mankind can be governed by reason; and insist, notwithstand-

---

87. Charles Brockden Brown, *The British Treaty*, . . . (America: printed, unknown where, or by whom sold; London: reprinted for John Joseph Stockdale, 1808), p. xiii.

ing the evidence of all history, ancient and modern,
sacred and profane, that we may prudently rely on reason for the defence of nations, we would advise him
to commence a course of experiments with his own
family, and see how far reason will go there.[88]

Might Brown have been remembering here an experiment he
made in a fictional representation of a family that mistakenly tried
to govern itself by unaided canons of reason, and was led to ruin
by the first manipulator to exploit their credulous respect for the
testimony of the senses, and their trust in the reasonings founded
on that testimony?

In his fourth and final political pamphlet, Brown argues against
Jefferson's notoriously ineffectual Embargo policy. While doing
so, he makes general observations on American history and on
the motives of nations generally. He insists that (contrary to the
argument in his last pamphlet) nations do not ever act on the basis
of a rational calculation of interest, but rather are impelled by irrational motives of pride, wounded vanity, and fear. It is impossible
to evaluate the Embargo on rational grounds, he concludes;
whether Great Britain or America is harmed by it the most is undecidable. Plausible arguments appear on both sides of the question. And it is equally impossible to understand, in retrospect,
whether the American Revolution was, finally, advantageous or
disadvantageous for either Great Britain or the United States.

> Why did Great Britain carry on a seven years war with
> her American colonies? Why did America make such a
> desperate and ruinous resistance? Was either side im-
> pelled by considerations flowing from the value of life,
> personal liberty or property. No. These considerations
> were trampled under foot. The impulse was a move-
> ment of the imagination, which annexed a value, on
> one side, to the idea of political control over certain
> regions in North America, and on the other, to exemp-
> tion from that control. No matter how faint the con-
> nection had been between them, how modified the au-

88. Ibid., p. xiii.

thority claimed or exerted might be; to abolish it on the one hand, and maintain it on the other, a whole generation was willing to perish: To incur every evil to which property, liberty and life can be exposed. This spirit is undecayed. The bulk of every nation must be ever swayed by it. All calculations, therefore, built upon the value of individual life, liberty, or property with a view of influencing the conduct of states to each other, are idle and useless.[89]

Brown then defensively states that in considering the Embargo, he will show little reverence for the public and maritime laws that are taken to govern trade issues, and that he expects lawyers to censure him for this disregard. Against the accusations such readers may fling at him he cannot protect himself: "At their bar I must stand mute. I can urge no plea why sentence of *combustion* [!] should not be passed upon me."[90]

Brown treats the arguments pro and con with respect to the Embargo as variations on the themes of revolutionary rhetoric, and he has as little patience with any attempt to ground one position or the other on rational legal grounds in 1809 as he does with respect to 1776. "It is a pity that statesmen think it necessary to justify their conduct by any principle, but that right which the course of sublunary things give to the *strong* over the *weak*."[91] Better to admit honestly that the conduct of foreign nations "flows from a single principle; the promotion of their own advantage: and is regulated by a single circumstance; their power to promote it," and equally that "our conduct has no other foundation."[92] Thus he is deaf to the language of revolution that is being revived to excite anti-British sentiment once again: "How much have we heard of tribute: How earnestly been called upon to recollect the spirit of the revolution: To reject the fetters of colonial servitude! When I hear these calls, I start upon my feet, in terror: Good

89. Charles Brockden Brown, *An Address to the Congress of the United States, on the Utility and Justice of Restrictions Upon Foreign Commerce . . .* (Philadelphia: Published by C. & A. Conrad & Co., 1809), p. iv.
90. Ibid., p. vi.
91. Ibid., p. 51.
92. Ibid., p. 66.

Heavens! Tribute! Colonial bondage! Is it possible that things
have come to that pass once more!"[93] Brown's impatience with
such overheated rhetoric leads him to decry the "talkative, loud,
noisy, vociferous" character of American political discourse, which
is occupied with "terms" and not "things," which will object strenuously to "the *name* of tribute" but will accept "the *thing* itself"
readily enough.[94] In place of a politics that deals in verbal representations and rational pretensions, and attempts to pitch the tent
of legitimacy on those shifting sands, Brown would substitute a
politics that recognizes the necessity of a respect for traditional
authority as the only bulwark against the uncertainties and distortions that can afflict reasoned discourse. Stated baldly, Brown's
politics may seem like those of a simple reactionary. It is in *Wieland* that his persuasions, dramatized and allegorized, reveal him
to be a complex counter-revolutionary writer.

93. Ibid., p. 67.
94. Ibid., pp. 80, 64, 70.

CHAPTER FOUR

"Tongues of People Altercating with One Another" Language, Text, and Society in Brackenridge's *Modern Chivalry*

I. The Polyglot World

THE NOVEL, ACCORDING to Mikhail Bakhtin, is distinguished from other literary genres stylistically by its "multi-languaged consciousness," and from the epic in particular by its "maximal contact with the present (with contemporary reality) in all its open-endedness."[1] These formal characteristics are organically linked to the historical situation of the rise of the novel as a dominant literary form, "a very specific rupture in the history of European civilization: its emergence from a socially isolated and culturally deaf semipatriarchal society, and its entrance into international and interlingual contacts and relationships."

> The new cultural and creative consciousness lives in an actively polyglot world. The world becomes polyglot, once and for all and irreversibly. The period of national languages, coexisting but closed and deaf to each other, comes to an end. Languages throw light on each other: one language can, after all, see itself only in the light of another language.[2]

This epoch in European history was, of course, also the epoch of the European discovery of the American continent, and the en-

---

1. Mikhail Bakhtin, *The Dialogic Imagination: Four Essays,* ed. Michael Holquist, trans. Caryl Emerson and Michael Holquist (Austin: Univ. of Texas Press, 1981), p. 11.
2. Ibid., pp. 11, 12.

counter of European civilization with the native cultures and languages of America. This encounter had a decisive impact on European consciousness, an impact felt most intimately in problems of
translation and understanding that necessarily arose in the course
of such contact.[3] The parochial self-possession of European attitudes toward language, aptly figured by Bakhtin as deafness, was
crucially disturbed by this new linguistic contact. And if the passage to an "actively polyglot" world was irreversible, that did not
prevent modern nations from trying to reverse the process by a
host of devices. One such device was the erection of a national
language standard. As Bakhtin says, along with the encounter
with linguistic plurality came the end of the "naive and stubborn
coexistence of 'languages' within a given national language . . .
there is no more peaceful co-existence between territorial dialects,
social and professional dialects and jargons, literary language,
generic languages within literary language, epochs in language,
and so forth."[4] Correlatively with the relativization of European
languages in relation to one another and to newly encountered
languages around the world, came a rectification and standardization within the national languages.

In the United States, these processes were drastically com-
pressed temporally: born into the modern polyglot world, this nation of emigrants immediately sought to establish a monolingual
standard to aid in its attempted national self-constitution. Hugh
Henry Brackenridge's *Modern Chivalry* is probably the best textual
witness we have to the contradictions and ironies of this simultaneous exogenous pluralization and endogenous standardization:
it not only thematizes this simultaneity but performs it in its own
language too. It is the American dialogic novel par excellence, full
of a multitude of nonstandard languages of various kinds, and at
the same time it is ostensibly devoted to the programmatic fabrica-

3. Eric Cheyfitz, *The Poetics of Imperialism: Translation and Colonization from* The
Tempest *to* Tarzan (New York: Oxford Univ. Press, 1991); Steven Greenblatt,
Marvelous Possessions: The Wonder of the New World (Chicago: Univ. of Chicago
Press, 1991); Tzvetan Todorov, *The Conquest of America: The Question of the Other,*
trans. Richard Howard (New York: Harper & Row, 1984).
4. Bakhtin, *The Dialogic Imagination,* p. 12. See also Joshua A. Fishman, *Lan-
guage and Nationalism: Two Integrative Essays* (Rowley, Massachusetts: Newbury
House, 1972).

tion of a single linguistic standard. It is overtly a universalizing linguistic project, and covertly (or actually) a pluralizing project. In this respect its form is a mirror of American social and political history.

Its thematization and realization of this linguistic irony may be studied in both a synchronic and a diachronic fashion. In *Modern Chivalry* language functions as a social semiotic; that is, the language system, with its pattern of hierarchically and laterally interrelated subsystems, stands in a metonymic relation to the social system with its corresponding pattern of subsystems. In the words of M. A. K. Halliday, "language *actively symbolizes* the social system, representing . . . in its patterns of variation the variation that characterizes human cultures."[5] This structural correspondence is attended by a historical correspondence: the evolution of language systems corresponds to the similar evolution of social systems, the alterations of one reflecting and being reflected by the alterations of the other, in a mutually creative process of maintenance and modification. In *Modern Chivalry,* a text that deliberately foregrounds matters of language as well as matters of history, both of these dimensions may be observed and described.

The novel's intrinsic relation to certain linguistic phenomena is the counterpart to its relation to certain sociohistorical phenomena. Bakhtin alluded to some of these in his reference to the emergence of European civilization from a "semipatriarchal" to a more indeterminate condition. Recently Michael McKeon has specified this transition in greater detail, tracing the relationship of the appearance and dominance of the novel to the "destabilization of social categories" in the early modern period.[6] The general process of the delegitimation of a social order founded on the assignment to individuals of prescribed social statuses, and the simultaneous valorization of personal virtue as the legitimate foundation of social reputation together created a widespread mutability of social identities and uncertainty regarding proper social behaviors. McKeon claims that the novel acquired its value as a literary form

5. M. A. K. Halliday, *Language as Social Semiotic: The Social Interpretation of Language and Meaning* (Baltimore: University Park Press, 1978), p. 3.
6. Michael McKeon, *The Origins of the English Novel, 1600–1740* (Baltimore: Johns Hopkins Univ. Press, 1987), p. 131.

because its narrative capabilities were peculiarly suited to address this mutability and uncertainty: prose fiction could negotiate and mediate the crisis of social norms by telling stories of individuals who lived the experience of such crisis. The *Bildungsroman* in particular, as Franco Moretti has shown (albeit with respect to another century), was dedicated to the depiction of successful negotiations of personal crises fostered by the decay of a prescriptive social order.[7]

Brackenridge's *Modern Chivalry* may be located squarely within the field of these problematics: it is at once about the uncertainties of a peculiarly fluid social formation — a new and expansive democratic nation that yet retains from its colonial past some important features of an abandoned prescriptive social ideology — and about the crucial function of language as a social institution in such an open historical situation. It addresses these issues explicitly, and it also addresses them implicitly by means of its own textual forms.[8]

II. Magnum Opus

"It is for this reason, that I have undertaken this work."[9] With these words in his "Introduction," Hugh Henry Brackenridge announces *Modern Chivalry* as a text entirely premeditated, one that he vouches will be seen to derive monolithically from a single literary intention.[10] I will say what his "reason" is in a moment, but I want to observe, first, what is obvious: that this unique, specific intention is attributed, auto-referentially, to the author whose "I" utters the sentence. That is, an imaginary speech situation is

7. Franco Moretti, *The Way of the World: The Bildungsroman in European Culture* (London: Verso, 1987).

8. On many points my reading coincides with that of Cathy N. Davidson, who provides a wider survey of picaresque fiction in the early republic, along with an incisive reading of *Modern Chivalry*. See Cathy N. Davidson, *Revolution and the Word: The Rise of the Novel in America* (New York: Oxford Univ. Press, 1986), ch. 7.

9. Hugh Henry Brackenridge, *Modern Chivalry*, ed. Claude M. Newlin (New York: Hafner Publishing Company, 1962), p. 3. Further page references will be given parenthetically in the text.

10. I allude to the norm of formal and intentional integrity which Pierre Macherey criticizes when he writes that a "literary work, then, is never entirely premeditated; or rather, it is, but at several levels at once, without deriving monolithically from a unique and simple conception." *A Theory of Literary Production,* trans. Geoffrey Wall (London: Routledge & Kegan Paul, 1978), p. 41.

implied, one in which author and reader are virtually present to one another as sender and receiver. This is not an unusual literary effect, of course, but must be recognized at the start if we are to see the blatant persistence with which *Modern Chivalry* disrupts its own enabling model of communication. A drama of disintegration of this simple model of literary communication immediately ensues; this drama has, in fact, already begun. The collocation of deictics ("this," "I," "this") seeks to establish a strong referential effect to the domain of enunciation, but needless to say, the reader, with the printed page before his eyes and no human author visible in the vicinity, finds this indicated domain less than coherent. (By the way, it may be noticed that this invisibility of the sender of the message resembles the experience of hearing the seemingly senderless voice produced by a ventriloquist.) And in the prose of this sentence of Brackenridge's, the impersonal grammatical construction of "It is" has already started to undermine the imaginary proximity of intention, author, and utterance, and their imaginary mutual co-presence with the implied reader.

Brackenridge's text itself concedes the incoherence of this fictive scene of face-to-face communication when, at the end of the third Volume of Part I (1793), reflecting upon his foregoing narrative and projecting its continuation, he laments the fact that the utterance he has produced in Pittsburgh (where he lives and writes) has not elicited any enunciated response from the literary capital, Philadelphia:

> I have only farther to say at present, that I wish I could get this work to make a little more noise. Will nobody attack it and prove that it is insipid, libellous, treasonable, immoral, or irreligious? If they will not do this, let them do something else, praise it, call it excellent, say it contains wit, erudition, genius, and the Lord knows what! Will no body speak? What? Ho! are ye all asleep in the hold there down at Philadelphia? Will none of you abuse, praise, reprobate, or comm[e]nd this performance? (p. 250)

The complaint implies a distinctly dialogic model of literary communication, one according to which *Modern Chivalry* must summon a response or fail in its intentions. It implies an intertextuality, in which the literary utterance is not integral, closed, and complete, but open to the situation in which it is placed.

Such contradictory textual effects — an intentional monologic structure in contention with a pretended vocal dialogic context, and a subtle impersonality undercutting this dialogism in turn — may be merely ineluctable properties of language. Be that as it may, their production here, where Brackenridge makes his most explicit beginning claims for the governance of his writing by a performed intention, makes them the most compellingly intimate instances of effects that will, in the course of the writing of *Modern Chivalry*, take larger and more sensational forms. For this is a text which, with great ingenuity, undermines its own monological model at almost every turn. It finally is a text that is not so much intended as determined, an artifact of language whose formal features and thematic concerns are repeatedly inflected by historical and contextual determinations whose traces are always being betrayed in the writing.

It will be my purpose first to describe, in some detail, the most conspicuous formal features of this text, and to observe the way these surface forms advertise their own relations to the conditions and events that impinged upon their fabrication. *Modern Chivalry* notably exhibits its ongoing relation to historical circumstances, both by explicit reference and by various covert mimeticisms: it was written and published in seven volumes, which were ultimately gathered into two parts, and published over the course of twenty-four years. The case could even be made, if the initial abortive verse text, *The Modern Chevalier* — written 1788–89 — is taken into account, that the genesis of *Modern Chivalry* extends over twenty-*eight* years. In the "Postscript" to the first volume, the narrator writes that he "had first begun this work in verse" and has a volume "two parts in three as large as Butler's Hudibras" written; having extracted the present prose narrative from the earlier verse form, he now thinks of issuing the metrical version also, to "let the people take their choice" (p. 76). The competing verse and prose versions may be said to stand in a dialogic relation to one another, and they uncannily recall Franklin's experiments in such formal transpositions from prose to verse and back, which had been similarly directed toward evolving a literary style.

The somewhat irregular architectonics of the book may be use-fully schematized, with some rough indications of their correla-tions with historical circumstances (as evidenced by the sequence of early national American presidential administrations):

PART I
Volume I (1792)
Volume II (1792) } Washington
Volume III (1793)

Volume IV (1797) } Adams

PART II
[Volume I] (1804)
Volume II (1805) } Jefferson

Volume IV [*sic*] (1815) } Madison

Each Volume is divided into several Books, within each of which the Chapters are numbered separately. This organizational struc-ture is marked by several asymmetries. In length, the ratio of Part I to Part II is roughly 2:3, although the relatively shorter first Part has four Volumes, while the second Part has only three. A mere five years separates the publication dates of the first and last vol-umes of Part I, while an interval of eleven years separate the first and last volumes of Part II. And because the textual bridge (so to speak) over the five-year span of Part I is supported by four struc-tural members (i.e., Volumes), while the eleven-year span of Part II is bridged by only three sections, the narrative construction of Part II is, in its grossest terms, weaker (more attenuated) than that of Part I. This greater attenuation of Part II is perhaps in some measure mitigated by the fact that the individual Volumes are in themselves longer than the Volumes of Part I (by a ratio of 2:1 on the average). Such quantifying measures as these seem necessary to estimate the largest formal effects of a book that by reputation may qualify as the paradigmatic instance of what Mitchell Breit-wieser, referring to the academic word-of-mouth on eighteenth-century American writing, has called "by-the-ton orals reading."[11]

11. Mitchell Breitwieser, "Commentary: Afterthoughts," special issue on Eighteenth-Century American Cultural Studies, *American Literary History* 5, 3 (Fall 1993): 591.

The total effect of the work is of pieces of writing that grow progressively more prolix, but also take longer to compose and to appear in print, and are stitched together more loosely as time goes on.

This gross effect is accompanied by another, subtler effect: throughout *Modern Chivalry*, narrative chapters are interspersed with essayistic chapters (which are usually, but not always, numbered in sequence with the narrative chapters), and these essay-chapters stand out, unlike the narrative chapters, because they have individual titles. The titles mostly represent variations on several patterns: "Containing Reflections," "Containing Observations," "Containing Remarks," "Containing Explanations," "Observations." Occasionally these "Reflections," "Observations," and so forth, are adjectivally modified as "Some," "General," or "Preliminary." Volumes I and III in Part I have chapters of "Introduction," as does Book II of Part II, Volume I. In Part I, both Volumes I and II have a "Postscript," Volume III has both an "Appendix" and a "Conclusion," and Volume IV begins with "A Chapter to be Referred to the Third Volume at the Conclusion." In Part II, each of Volumes I and II has a "Conclusion," and Volumes II and IV have several anomalous chapters each: "Containing a Dissertation, in the Manner of St. Evremont" and "In the Manner of Montaigne" in Volume II, and "Fragments" and "A Key to the Preceding" in Volume IV. Thus sequential regularity and narrative continuity compete in *Modern Chivalry* with various effects of textual rupture produced by these formal anomalies.

As a means of making some of the largest architectonic features of this tome apparent, some further quantitative calculations may be useful. The ratio of narrative chapters to chapters of prose exposition grows larger as the book grows longer. In Part I, the essayistic chapters per Volume (calculated according to number of chapters) range from 15 to 40 percent of the whole and average 29 percent, while in Part II the range of variation in this ratio is narrower (from 18 to 27 percent) and the average is smaller (24 percent). Brackenridge comments on this pattern himself: "It may be observed, that as I advance in my book, I make fewer chapters, by way of commentary, and occupy myself chiefly with the narrative. It is the characteristic of old age, and may be decorous towards the conclusion of the work" (p. 278). Again, this enlargement of the ratio of narrative chapters to essay chapters is partly offset by the countervailing effect of an increase of the average page length of essay chapters in relation to the length of narrative chapters: in Part I, the chapters average 3.9 pages (essay chapters slightly below average at 3.7, even with the unusually lengthy 36-page "Introduction" to Volume III factored in), while in Part II they average 4.4 pages (essay chapters above average at 5.1 pages, even though the longest one is just 18 pages). The anomaly of the third Volume of Part II being called Volume IV is due to the fact that a large addition to the previous Volume (Chapter VI through the "Conclusion" of Book IV of Volume II) was made when the whole novel was republished in 1815 at the time of the first publication of the final Volume.

The purpose of all this superficial description of the mechanical form of the organization of this work of writing is to emphasize, in the most empirical manner possible, the way the utter asymmetry and near randomness of its constituent forms coexists with some striking overall patterns of formal development. In a century of digressive novels exhibiting programmatically hybridized forms (Fielding's "comic epic poem in prose," *Joseph Andrews,* is exemplary), *Modern Chivalry* nearly carries the program to its absurd limit. It is perhaps as close as one could get to the "loose and baggy monster" of Henry James's famous indictment,[12] and its plethoric disorder goes unmatched in American literature until Melville, in *Moby-Dick,* attempts a "classification of the constituents of a chaos."[13] The name of Brackenridge's protagonist, Captain John Farrago, indicates the novel's aspiration to utter heterogeneity (if the "very name" of his servant Teague O'Regan "imports what he was" [p. 6], Farrago's name imports what the *book* is), and its equally exaggerated commitment to inclusivity is signaled by its claim to be "an opus magnum, which comprehends law, physic, and divinity." So comprehensive does it mean to be,

12. Henry James, "Preface to *The Tragic Muse,*" in *Literary Criticism: French Writers, Other European Writers, The Prefaces to the New York Edition* (New York: The Library of America, 1984), p. 1107.

13. Herman Melville, *Redburn, White-Jacket, Moby-Dick,* (New York: The Library of America, 1983), p. 933.

that "were all the books in the world lost, this alone would preserve a germ of every art. Music, painting, poetry, &c." (p. 727).
This claim is made, symptomatically, near the end; at the beginning, the narrator's belief was instead that "it is not in nature to
have all things in one," that "a Jack of all Trades, is proverbial of a
bungler," and that he would therefore write a book that would
confine itself to being "simple, and one thing only" (pp. 3, 4).

The trajectory of the writing is quite plainly exhibited by the
juxtaposition of those contradictory beginning and ending claims:
from "one thing only" to "all things in one": out of the one, many.
And when, near the end, the narrator explicitly concedes that his
single intention has devolved into an utterly plural one, he finds
nevertheless that, paradoxically, he has arrived somehow at the
same total effect. That is, an infinite *totality* curiously resembles a
unity. The immediate occasion of this reassessment of the unity/
plurality issue is his "dissertation" (in Part II, Volume IV, Book II,
Chapter I) "on the origin of the languages of Europe, and incidentally upon other subjects" (p. 727). It is admittedly a digression,
and one from which further digressions proceed, and this formal
comedy of repetitive and multiple distractions bears an obvious
relation to the ostensible subject matter of the original digression.
This subject is the derivation of the modern languages from their
putative origins. This digression, the narrator says, "may seem
incongruous with the nature of this work; did it not occur to a
diligent observer, that there can be nothing incongruous, or inconsistent, with a book which embraces all subjects, and is an encyclopedia of the sciences" (p. 727). That is, it is the very incon-
gruity of the digression that makes it congruent with such a
persistently digressive and promiscuously inclusive book. Where
nothing is excluded — where the formal principle is one of indis-
criminate inclusion — nothing conflicts with that principle.

Difference, in short, is not necessarily contradiction. This, I will
claim, is the carefully earned theoretical recognition toward which
this elaborately fragmented work of writing materially evolves.
And it is no accident that the occasion of its utterance is a casually
digressive "consideration of the language of nations" (p. 723) in
which the fundamental assumptions of historical philology are
comically inverted. "Pinkerton" is cited as "the greatest philologist

of modern times, at least that I am acquainted with" (history has arranged that the surname has become, inadvertently, a good joke: the philologist as detective), and his authority is invoked to assert "that the Greek is derived from the German; and that the German is the original Persian" (p. 721). This metaleptic reversal/dislocation of a linguistic-genealogical series makes the point that somehow in America such orders of precedence (like orders of social hierarchy, and like the logic of noncontradiction) no longer hold. The point is made elsewhere in the same chapter somewhat differently, when the narrator remarks that "it is but extremely little we know of the earth we live upon," but that this is perhaps not to be regretted, as to know more would be, sadly, only "to increase our knowledge of bloody battles; or, of individual misery." In the interest of obviating a history of conflict that only engenders more conflict, he asks, "Would it not rather be desirable that the whole remembrance of past events was struck out of our minds, and that we had to begin a new series? What happens every day now, is so like what happened before, that the sameness is wearisome" (p. 726). The boring sameness and identity of history, in this account, is ironically a repetitive history of differences and conflict. The cure for this eternal sameness of unreconcilable difference is the instatement of a violent rupture — a dramatic new beginning, a "new series" — that would divide an imagined non-violent future of utter nondifference from its opposite past. Benjamin Rush's proposed instruction in "the art of forgetting" (see chapter 1 above) would perhaps be instrumental here.

Released from such historical entailments, from the endless repetition of the same differences, humanity might create something radically different. Within the structure of this sketch of a projected fundamental historical rupture, however, the content of the form reverses the terms. The "sameness" of the past is the endless "bloody battles" among the dissimilar, while the different, indeterminate proposed future is one of seeking after the elemental and self-identical: "Instead of consuming so much time in acquiring a knowledge of history, we might employ ourselves in searching the mountains for simples [i.e., elements], or digging for minerals" (p. 726). From the repetitive sameness of an endless war of differences, to a radically different collective search for the nonalloyed:

from history to nature. This imaginary narrative of human transformation exactly parallels the course of the writing of *Modern
Chivalry* itself, which goes from a simple initial intention (undermined by a complex performance) to an eventual resignation to
complexity and contradiction (which, by virtue of its unlimited
and undefined heterogeneity produces, ironically, a kind of noncontradictory totality).

If the gradual formal dispersal of the book somehow achieves
an effect of total congruity, the sheer length of *Modern Chivalry*
(808 pages in the modern reprint), however, raises an insuperable
barrier to readerly recomposition of a narrative totality: *Modern
Chivalry's* length (and temporal dissemination) resists indefatigably any critical wish to recuperate it as an integral object. All the
paratextual apparatus of introductions and conclusions, of organization into Volumes, Books, and Chapters — its systematic asymmetry, as it were — has the effect of making it seem to the reader
just what it unavoidably is: a nearly anarchic textual field.

If we think of its initial readers, who presumably read it volume
by volume as it was issued in installments over twenty-four years,
we will also recognize that its reading was, by design or by accident, inevitably an experience of dissemination of meaning. It's
difficult to believe, for instance, that, given these conditions of
publication and reading, the "Chapter to be Referred to the Third
Volume at the Conclusion" (p. 253) that was situated at the beginning of Volume IV in 1797 (and therefore sought metaleptically
to connect itself to the preceding volume) wasn't in fact a joke of
Brackenridge's about the very difficulty of the readerly reconstruction of narrative continuity that this text so carefully disrupts. The
giant hiatus in the supposed manuscript ("Here is a great gap"
[p. 329]) between Parts I and II, and other analogous textual details, contribute to this general effect of the staging of discontinuity. Such deformations, explicitly signaled like this one or not, also
multiply toward the end of the book, as for instance in Chapter
IV of the last Book of the last Volume of the last Part: "There
would seem here to be an hiatus in the manuscript, or the sheets
misplaced. The editor cannot connect the narrative" (p. 735).
Even we, who have the whole thing together in our hands simultaneously (unlike the book's initial readers) will find such an effort

of totalizing recomposition unrewarding (and the few critical attempts to find a method in this unmethodical text seem, as one would expect, perfectly vain). As the textual devices for inducing such metaleptic and proleptic reordering and disordering multiply in the work, the effort of such readerly reconstruction is at once incited and inhibited. The logic of supplementarity that recent critical theory has found to govern even the most integrally crafted texts is here given license to thereby proliferate and attenuate meaning till it is nearly vaporous. One consequence is that when, late in the novel, its "great moral" is explicitly stated — "the evil of men seeking office for which they are not qualified" (p. 611) — the preceding textual performance seems absurdly incommensurable with such a minimal didactic proposition.

Brackenridge's massive novel, with these literary effects of fragmentation and deferral operating, is made to cover, as it were, the era of constitutional innovation and the first six presidential terms of United States history (four presidential administrations). The time of the narrative action is nearly contemporary with the time of writing and publication, there being usually a lag of only a year or two between the two temporal series of story and discourse. Even when, at the end of Volume I in the second Part, the narrator makes one of his most concrete references to the actual historical time of composition, in order to account for an anticipated temporal lapse between writing and publication, the lapse oddly does not appear to take place.

> These concluding pages I had written, and had printed off, to this point of the game, if I may so express myself, this 19th of Nov. 1804; and had intended to publish; but it struck me that it might give offence to the legislature, and it might be as well to let it rest until next spring after they had risen; and if any thing should give umbrage; though I cannot possibly see what, they might have a summer to think of it before they met again, and so could do nothing hastily. (p. 462)

He asks the "printer boys" for their advice, and they disagree among themselves. So he concludes to wait. "Six or nine months hence, it may be safer to let it come forth" (p. 462). Nevertheless, Brackenridge seems to have relented; the Volume was published in 1804, and another whole volume was out in 1805, while yet another volume was even then already in composition. He was writing to the moment, and while he contemplated introducing a minimal interval between writing and events, he failed to do so. Such an interval, on his account, would have given "offense" or "umbrage" to the legislature — i.e., would have caused certain effects in the realm of politics — and might have caused the legislature to "do" something in response. Brackenridge thus announces his wish to block such results, to remove his text to a determinate distance from political events. That he does not seem to have done so, finally, by implication places politics within the range of his text's performative ambitions. Thus the very history of institution-building, national identity-formation, and cultural integration is subjected to the textual logic of disintegration, differentiation, and deconstruction. And this in spite of a declared intention of offering to the new nation a formal model of (textual, dictional, grammatical, stylistic, idiomatic and orthographic) perfection and unity.

III. Fixing the Language

The "reason" why Brackenridge undertook the writing of *Modern Chivalry,* he says, was to "give an example of good language in his composition, which might serve as a model to future speakers and writers," in the belief that "it would do more to fix the orthography, choice of words, idiom of phrase, and structure of sentence, than all the Dictionaries and Institutes that have been ever made" (p. 3). He alludes to the long history of attempts "to fix the English language," and mentions Swift as an example of an English writer who proposed such linguistic stabilization. Obviously Samuel Johnson would be another such stabilizer, and in the United States Noah Webster was the most active proponent of promulgating such norms. Brackenridge's stated ambition, then (even if, as is likely, he meant it ironically) affiliates *Modern Chivalry* with a variety of contemporary efforts to institute linguistic standards. These efforts had a particular importance in the United States, for at least two main reasons: first, the English language, because it was shared with Great Britain, seemed to some observers to compromise or at least inhibit progress toward political and cultural independence; and second, as an immigrant nation it included many different linguistic communities among its population, and this linguistic pluralism seemed to present another difficulty to cultural nationalists. In short, national independence and national unity both seemed to be dependent upon linguistic matters, and to be placed at risk therefore by the commonality of language between the United States and Great Britain, and the multiplicity of tongues in America.

I have outlined above the range of responses that this linguistic predicament incited in the Federal period, from Webster's dictionaries and spellers to proposals for a new national language, and from proposed language institutes to a widespread debate over just what literary style would be truly American.[14] Nationality, as it had been experienced by almost anyone who had come to the colonies or to the new nation, had been understood and experienced as an effect of linguistic homogeneity. To the present day, language planning has been often a component of political formation in new and postcolonial states.[15] As the first "new nation," the United States was also the first site of such planning, although not much of it was ever carried out, as the continuing agitation for monolingual education and legislation for making English the official language evidences.

Brackenridge wrote in English, and seems never to have contested the eligibility of English for his purposes. But he did, plainly, recognize as a legitimate issue the question of literary style as an instrument of national identification, and while his declaration that *Modern Chivalry* is *only* about literary style is plainly

14. Richard Ruland has anthologized prescriptive statements concerning American literary style in *The Native Muse: Theories of American Literature from Bradford to Whitman* (New York: E. P. Dutton & Company, 1976), and *A Storied Land: Theories of American Literature from Whitman to Edmund Wilson* (New York: E. P. Dutton & Company, 1976). See also Howard Mumford Jones, "American Prose Style: 1700–1770," *Huntington Library Bulletin* 6 (November 1934): 115–51.

15. Joshua Fishman, "Language Modernization and Planning in Comparison with Other Types of National Modernization and Planning," *Language in Society* 2 (1973): 23–43.

ironic, he also begins by writing a prose that in many respects conforms to the kinds of prescriptions that were being widely offered as rules for American literary style. He begins by writing a plain, "attic" prose, one in which clarity rather than ornament is taken as a virtue: a zero-degree style that attempts to support, by its very normality, the narrator's pretensions to represent an ideally moderate standard of intellectual and political judgment.

Without belaboring this point, I should note that this normality extends to all features of Brackenridge's narrative language: to its ordinary diction, grammatical correctness, standard (albeit occasionally inconsistent) spelling, and so forth. Only a few pages of such writing effectively conditions the reader to grant such normative language its self-asserted privilege and then to discriminate all deviant linguistic effects as marginal, stigmatized, and inferior in relation to the privileged norm. Brackenridge frequently reiterates his normative intention, and even ingeniously inserts into volume III of his text (not unlike Franklin's inclusion of the Abel James and Benjamin Vaughan letters in his *Autobiography*) a purported review of volumes I and II which endorses his intentions and testifies to his successful enactment of them: "Confining ourselves therefore to the stile of this performance, we observe, that it has what is the first characteristic of excellence; viz. Simplicity. This consists in the choice of the plainest and most familiar words, and in the arrangement of the words in their natural order" (p. 163). This supposed reviewer for "Young's magazine" judges that a writer should always use "the phrase that anyone would use," and the words "which they themselves would use in conversation," and asks rhetorically, "Ought not language to be precisely the same whether spoken or written[?]" These are the prescriptions Brackenridge accepts: he prefers "that which is common, and comes first upon the tongue, in easy and familiar conversation" (p. 163).[16] And his reviewer is right: the general effect of Brackenridge's writing is that of language which is common, familiar, plain, conversational: the ordinary language of "anyone."

16. See Janel Mueller, *The Native Tongue and the Word: Developments in English Prose Style, 1380–1580* (Chicago: Univ. of Chicago Press, 1984), which traces the history of the conversational standard for English prose style.

Because this *is* the general effect of his writing, when nonstandard linguistic forms begin to appear in *Modern Chivalry,* their irregularity is immediately salient. They seem patently uncommon, strange, fancy, or vulgar. And such nonstandard forms do appear, in plenty. There are, most conspicuously, the various dialects (represented graphically by phonetic transcription of some acuity): predominantly Irish and Scots dialects, in each of which several characters are made to speak, most notably Captain Farrago's two comic servants Teague O'Regan and Duncan Ferguson. For the first few chapters, Teague's speech is rendered indirectly (e.g., "Teague acknowledged that he had changed his mind" [p. 17]), and the reader is told by the captain that "he is but a simple Irishman, and of a low education; his language being that spoken by the aborigines of his country . . . if he speaks a little English, it is with the brogue on his tongue" (p. 24). The brogue is not directly represented, however, until well into the first volume; just as the Captain is often advising Teague to "keep a good tongue in [his] mouth" (p. 39), so too does Brackenridge confine Teague to the realm of reported speech, all the while allowing the captain to comment critically on Teague's brogue. Finally, however, when Teague gets caught invading the bed of a maidservant at an inn, by a young clergyman also lodging there, his defense is rendered, in his own direct speech:

> By shaint Patrick, said he, I was aslape in my own bed, as sound as the shates that were about me, when I heard the sound of this young crature's voice crying out like a shape in a pasture; and when after I had heard, aslape as I was, and come here, I found this praste, who was so wholy, and praching all night, upon the top of the bed, with his arms round this young crature's neck; and if I had not given him a twitch by the nose, and bid him ly over, dear honey, he would have ravished her virginity, and murdered her, save her soul, and the paple of the house not the wiser for it. (pp. 30–31)

This graphic simulacrum of an audible effect is vivid if somewhat uneven (Brackenridge gets progressively better at this over the course of the novel). And Brackenridge's illegitimate use of *misspellings* to create a prejudicial sense of Teague's verbal (in)competence, where such misspellings do not, in fact, indicate a nonstandard pronunciation (e.g., "wholy," a perfect homophone of "holy") is particularly ineffective. Since the purpose of such graphic irregularity is precisely to evoke the sound of a vocal dialect ("evocalization" in Garrett Stewart's account),[17] to use ink to evoke air, the absence of an endophonous effect of this pointless graphic erratum is curious; it makes of writing a mere *metaphor* of speech, severing grapheme from phoneme. A few pages later, after again reverting to indirect discourse to represent Teague's speeches, Brackenridge seems to admit the greater effectiveness of direct, dialect speech when the captain convinces Teague to confess his own guilt with respect to the servant girl and spare the minister's reputation from undeserved calumny: "But suppose we give the speech in his own dialect. Master prastes, said he, I persave you are all prastes of the gosple, and can prach as asily as I can take a chaw of tobacco. Now de trut of de story is dis . . . " (p. 34). Again, "gosple" tries to incriminate Teague in nonstandard speech by an irregular spelling that in fact is a perfect homophone of the standard spelling. Such may be the kind of casual error that is almost inevitable when a writer attempts to communicate an audible effect by means of graphic signifiers. Or, as I said above, it may be a calculated effect, intended to focus the reader's sight upon the printed page and disrupt the automatic endophony that dialect is meant to induce in the reader.

One of the effects created by dialect in a novel is, of course, precisely to produce a hallucination of voice amid the soundless writing of the narrative prose. Just as Franklin's typographical mannerisms in such writings as the "Edict of the King of Prussia" sought to create an imaginary *aural* effect (see chapter 1), so the nonstandard spellings of written dialect are calculated to create a *vocal* effect. The phonetic character of such dialect representations accounts for this effect, as the binarism *dialect writing/standard writing* operates metonymically to represent the binarism *voice/*

---

17. Garrett Stewart, *Reading Voices: Literature and the Phonotext* (Berkeley: Univ. of California Press, 1990), p. 6.

writing. ("I stop here to observe," the narrator will later write, "that the opening the mouth when an exertion of the mind or body is required, is a habit very common with uninformed men, and not at all peculiar to Teague: you will observe, that men who have not been long, or at least much in the habit of writing, when they put pen to paper, open the mouth, and protrude the tongue, moving it as the pen turns to the right hand or to the left; or draws the stroke long or short" [p. 207]). It may be that dialect speech or nonstandard speech of some kind must necessarily be represented in a novel, where it will create this effect of an imaginary vocal presence, in order conversely to make the standard writing produce the effect Brackenridge said he wanted it to convey, when in his introduction he claimed that his model of writing style would not only provide a model for writers but for "speakers" too (p. 3).

The legitimation given to the linguistic standard in this way is constantly reinforced by the periodic eruption of dialects and other illegitimate forms. Duncan's Scots brogue is of particular interest since Brackenridge was himself born in Kintyre, Scotland, in 1748, and moved to America when he was five years old. While he probably lost, at that age, whatever brogue he brought with him, his parents probably didn't, and that would have been enough to guarantee that he would be conscious of his family's audible difference in their new community. True to his usual inclination toward complicating his linguistic themes self-reflexively, Brackenridge first represents Duncan's speech in the course of a conversation that is about a form of language: names. "Duncan asking the Captain of what denomination he was," Farrago replies: "I am denominated Captain . . . but my name is John Farrago, though I have had other epithets occasionally given me by the people amongst whom I have happened to sojourn," and he cites a few of these labels: "the modern Don Quixotte," "the Knight of the single Horse," "the Owner of the red-headed Bog-trotter," "the Master of the raw Scotchman" (pp. 256–57). Farrago's mistake is to take the word *denomination* in another sense than that intended by Duncan, to mistake the name of *name*. "Captain, said Duncan, it canna be, but ye ken right weel what I mean. It is na the denomination o' your temporal capacity, that I wad be at; but of your religion, and to what perswasion ye belong; whether o' the Covenant, or of the Seceders, or the high kirk o' Scotland" (p. 257). Farrago's misunderstanding of Duncan's meaning has several dimensions: he is rather too literal, taking *denomination* in a quasi-etymological sense, but he also reveals his own tendency toward an ornate diction (the Captain might very well use a fancy word like *denomination* where anyone else would use *name*). This misunderstanding highlights the actual historical correlations between linguistic identities and both ethnic and religious identities in the new United States. The Captain seems to be ethnically neutral, but in terms of economic class and status identity he is high where Duncan, Teague, and others are low. There is also the comical French pronunciation of the dancing master, Monsieur Douperie, whose pretension to elegance and disgust with Teague's vulgarity are expressed contradictorily in a ludicrous pidgin that violates several kinds of linguistic propriety while its precious diction, like the Captain's, salutes another. And in Douperie's flattery of the Captain he reveals another inconsistency: "Monsieur Capitaine, said he, ver great sensible of de honneur, que vous me faites, de attitude of dourself be so ver natural, dat prove de high degree que vous acquis in de art dat I tashe; and trow un grand lustre, on de talents dat I possede" (p. 206). The effect of great "art," in this comic figure's account, is to be "natural." The effect of *Modern Chivalry's* art was ostensibly to be the recording and promotion of a natural, conversational style of speech: by placing a version of his own ostensible program in the mouth of this fool, Brackenridge renders his own commitment to it somewhat doubtful.

A similar comic structure of violent misalignment between form and content is present in Brackenridge's presentation of the Guinea black man Cuff, who finds an unusual stone "in the mud of the Wye river" (p. 114) which his master then sends to the Philosophical Society, whereupon Cuff is admitted to membership. Eventually Cuff is solicited to "pronounce the annual oration," and, at his master's suggestion (who knew that an oration had once been delivered to the Society that claimed all Africans had once been white), he makes the converse argument that "men were all once black" (p. 115):

Now, shentima, I say, dat de first man was de black a
man, and de first woman de black a woman; and get
two tree children; de rain vasha dese, and de snow
pleach, and de coula com brown, yella, coppa coula,
and, at de last, quite fite; and de hair long; an da fal
out vid van anoda; and van cash by de nose, an pull;
so de nose come long, sharp nose. (p. 116)[18]

The dramatic situation, a scene of public oration, adds a new imperative to the usual instigation to endophony always attending
written dialect. After the oration is given, "the society could do
no less than appoint a committee to wait on Mr. Cuff, and request
a copy of his oration, that it might be published" (p. 116). This
leaves us to wonder if it is the published version of the oration
that *Modern Chivalry* is here quoting, and whether the phonetic
transcription of Cuff's black dialect is his own, or the philosophical society's, or the narrator's, and thus where in this series of
graphic and typographic representations of nonstandard speech
the norm is to be located.

Among the other nonstandard linguistic forms that interrupt
the normality of Brackenridge's prose are the various specialized
idioms that also create separate linguistically instituted communities within the nation. There is, for example, the slang of horse-
racing (pp. 6–9), the "hard words" and "jargon" of medical discourse, with its latinate features (pp. 9–10), and the "strange
phrases" of legal mumbo-jumbo (pp. 146–47). The peculiar mode
of address of the Quakers is another obvious verbal style recognized
in *Modern Chivalry* for its effect of identifying a subcommunity (p.
134). Further instances could be cited. The point is, Brackenridge
depicts a multilingual American society, one that as a consequence
of its division into separate and often noncommunicating speech
communities is at risk of disintegration. His own effort to provide
a linguistic standard in the text is obviously posed as a solution to

18. Apparently Brackenridge records in these passages "what must be early
Plantation Creole characteristics," according to J. L. Dillard, *Black English: Its History and Usage in the United States* (Vintage Books, 1973), p. 92; see also pp. 126,
190–91.

this problem, but in the course of writing he betrays his own intention. He is more interested in the contact and contest of languages and discourses than in the effort to reconcile them.

IV. Revolutionary Rhetorical Hybridity

The dominant discourse of political agitation in revolutionary America was a distinctly hybrid language, compounded mainly of republican and biblical strains, and Brackenridge was a notable adept of this discursive duplicity. His service as a chaplain in Washington's army in 1776–78 provided him his chief opportunities for the skillful exercise of this particular rhetorical talent, but it continued to have effects on his literary performances, even in *Modern Chivalry,* and these effects were among the features of the novel that entrenched it within the larger public discourses of the early national period. Thus it will be necessary to provide a moderately detailed descriptive foreground before enlarging upon this assertion. This double rhetorical system was strongly marked by its combination of two powerful idioms, that of Protestant millennialism and that of classical republicanism.[19] As Nathan O. Hatch has shown, modern scholarship has inexplicably turned its attention alternately to one or the other of these two major components of the American revolutionary discursive formation, examining either the features derived from what is variously characterized as Country, Commonwealth, opposition, Real Whig, or classical republican political thought;[20] or, alternately, features drawn from the biblical, apocalyptic, Protestant, millennial tradition of historical interpretation.[21]

19. Of course there were other idioms that functioned together with and/or in competition with the millennial and republican discourses. See Isaac Kramnick, "The 'Great National Discussion': The Discourse of Politics in 1787," *William and Mary Quarterly,* 3d ser., 45 (1988): 3–32, for a survey of the major rhetorical systems (he cites "the languages of republicanism, of Lockean liberalism, of work-ethic Protestantism, and of state-centered theories of power and sovereignty" [p. 4]). Garry Wills has made a case for "the contractarian theory of the Scottish Enlightenment" in *Inventing America: Jefferson's Declaration of Independence* (Garden City, New York: Doubleday & Company, 1978), p. 368.

20. Nathan O. Hatch, *The Sacred Cause of Liberty: Republican Thought and the Millennium in Revolutionary New England* (New Haven: Yale Univ. Press, 1977), p. 4. Robert Shalhope has canvassed the scholarly literature on republicanism in "Toward a Republican Synthesis: The Emergence of an Understanding of Republi-

There is now a body of scholarship that seeks not to argue for one or the other of these discourses, but rather to describe their "convergence" or "overlap[ping],"[22] "conflation,"[23] "amalgam [ation]" or "blend[ing],"[24] or "interaction."[25] These critical terms all point up the difficulty of representing the process of rhetorical interanimation, resorting as they do to spatial metaphors to describe the phenomenon. Other scholars have composed phrases, some of them near oxymorons, and mostly consisting of a noun with a qualifying adjective, to designate this hybrid aspect of the rhetoric and the structure of imagination it labels: "apocalyptic Machiavellism,"[26] "civil millennialism,"[27] "civil religion,"[28] "Calvinist Whigs" and "political religion,"[29] and "revolutionary millennialism,"[30] for example. These might all find their original in Samuel Adams' image of America as "the *Christian* Sparta."[31] In these phrases, there is always an implicit judgment as to the priority of

canism in American Historiography," *William and Mary Quarterly,* 3d ser., 29 (1972): 49–80, and "Republicanism and Early American Historiography," *William and Mary Quarterly,* 3d ser., 39 (1982): 334–56. Recently the "republican synthesis" has been challenged on several accounts: see Isaac Kramnick, "Republican Revisionism Revisited," *American Historical Review* 87 (1982): 629–64.

21. Ruth Bloch, *Visionary Republic: Millennial Themes in American Thought, 1756–1800* (Cambridge: Cambridge Univ. Press, 1985); Sacvan Bercovitch, "How the Puritans Won the American Revolution," *The Massachusetts Review* 17 (1976): 597–630; Larzer Ziff, "Revolutionary Rhetoric and Puritanism," *Early American Literature* 13 (1978): 45–49; Stephen J. Stein, "An Apocalyptic Rationale for the American Revolution," *Early American Literature* 9 (1975): 211–25; Emory Elliott, "The Puritan Roots of American Whig Rhetoric," in Emory Elliott, ed., *Puritan Influences in American Literature* (Urbana, Illinois: Univ. of Illinois Press, 1979), pp. 107–27; Alan S. Heimert, *Religion and the American Mind: From the Great Awakening to the Revolution* (Cambridge, Massachusetts: Harvard Univ. Press, 1966).

22. Bloch, *Visionary Republic,* pp. 4, 45.

23. Bailyn, "Religion and Revolution: Three Biographical Studies," *Perspectives in American History* 4 (1970): 136.

24. Hatch, *Sacred Cause,* pp. 22, 59.

25. Donald Weber, *Rhetoric and History in Revolutionary New England* (New York: Oxford Univ. Press, 1988), p. 8.

26. J. G. A. Pocock, *The Machiavellian Moment: Florentine Political Thought and the Atlantic Republican Tradition* (Princeton: Princeton Univ. Press, 1975), p. 513.

27. Hatch, *Sacred Cause,* p. 23.

28. Catherine L. Albanese, *Sons of the Fathers: The Civil Religion of the American Revolution* (Philadelphia: Temple Univ. Press, 1976).

29. Cushing Strout, *The New Heavens and New Earth: Political Religion in America* (New York: Harper & Row, 1974), p. 50 and passim.

30. Bloch, *Visionary Republic,* p. 75.

31. Qtd. in Gordon Wood, *The Creation of the American Republic, 1776–1787* (Chapel Hill: Univ. of North Carolina Press, 1969) p. 118.

the secular political component or the sacred element: the modifier is demoted to a contributing factor, while the noun is granted the status of the essential element. Thus we find Bailyn, for instance, admitting that assumptions of Puritan "covenant theology" were "channeled into the main stream of eighteenth-century political and social thinking by a generation of enlightened preachers,"[32] but also that "religion . . . had no singular influence on the Revolutionary movement. . . . The effective determinants of revolution were political" and religion had at best the role of "significant reinforcement to the Revolutionary movement."[33] Edmund Morgan, in a much-cited essay, argues that the values of the Puritan ethic "were pre-eminent" in American revolutionary ideology,[34] but Pocock finds that this Puritan ethic appears to be "lightly disguised classicism."[35] Pocock admits that "the apocalyptic dimension" is present in revolutionary rhetoric, but says it "is hardly dominant there. Americans of that generation saw themselves as freemen in arms, manifesting a patriot virtue, rather than as covenanted saints."[36] Conversely, Bercovitch holds that the patriot clergy sanctioned "the union of sacred history, local progress, and spiritual self-fulfillment, and so established the terms in which Yankee Americans could usurp the types of scripture for national ends," but that when this usurpation occurred "sacred history provided the controlling metaphors."[37]

I could go on citing participants in this scholarly debate who hold briefs for the predominance of one component of the double rhetoric or the other.[38] What should be apparent, however, is that

32. Bernard Bailyn, *The Ideological Origins of the American Revolution* (Cambridge, Massachusetts: The Belknap Press of Harvard Univ. Press, 1967), p. 32.

33. Bernard Bailyn, "Religion and Revolution," p. 85.

34. Edmund S. Morgan, "The Puritan Ethic and the American Revolution," *William and Mary Quarterly*, 3d. ser., 24 (1967): 18.

35. J. G. A. Pocock, "Virtue and Commerce in the Eighteenth Century," *Journal of Interdisciplinary History* 3 (1972): 132.

36. Pocock, *The Machiavellian Moment*, p. 513.

37. Sacvan Bercovitch, "The Typology of America's Mission," *American Quarterly* 30 (1978): 147, 151.

38. An interesting, rather eccentric analysis of this double rhetoric is given by Trent Schroyer in a pair of articles: "Cultural Surplus in America," *New German Critique* 26 (1982): 81–117, and "Corruption of Freedom in America," in John Forester, ed., *Critical Theory and Public Life* (Cambridge, Massachusetts: The MIT Press, 1985), pp. 283–315.

any generalization about the totality of revolutionary discourse that asserts such a priority for one element or the other is pointless; the scholarly debate is factitious. In any particular utterance, one or the other discourse may be dominant, of course; and possibly an exhaustive word-count and analysis would determine the mathematical ratio of biblical-to-republican terms in the total published propaganda. This would leave the much more massive and unrecoverable body of everyday speech out of the count, however, and would tell us nothing about the relative effectivity of each rhetoric upon the minds of various groups of people. About this, there can only be informed speculation. Bailyn, for instance, while minimizing the effectivity of biblical tropes, concedes that Puritan ideas "offered a context for everyday events nothing less than cosmic in its dimensions," but restricts the relevance of this context to "those who continued to understand the world, as the original Puritans had, in theological terms."[39] Emory Elliott, conversely, notes that even "that unlikely Puritan, Thomas Jefferson, proposed the use of the American Puritan heritage to political advantage" since "religious feeling flowed like an underground river through the colonies from New England to Georgia and might be brought to the surface with the appropriate codes and symbols."[40]

Ruth Bloch has pertinently observed that "millennialism and civic republicanism gained ascendency together in revolutionary England": radical whig ideology had its roots in the English Revolution and Commonwealth of the 1640s and 1650s, which "were also years of millennial expectation," and many of the theorists of republicanism read and admired by American patriots "were religious Dissenters" whose polemics were "infused" with millennial themes.[41] With equal pertinence, Bloch has observed that despite the historical inextricability of the political and religious themes, they were, in certain important respects, at odds with one another. While there were many key terms that functioned interchangeably in prominent positions in the two rhetorical domains, and these crucial semantic bivalences made the col-

---

39. Bailyn, *The Ideological Origins,* p. 32.
40. Emory Elliott, "The Dove and the Serpent: The Clergy in the American Revolution," *American Quarterly* 31 (1979): 187, 188.
41. Bloch, *Visionary Republic,* p. 4.

lapse of these rhetorics into one another relatively easy, this smooth semantic fusion disguised some fundamental conceptual incoherences. "The very words 'corruption,' 'virtue,' and 'vice,' which so infused radical whig rhetoric, were laden with religious connotations. Even the qualities thought to be inherent in the civic virtue of the body politic — self-sufficiency, industriousness, frugality, public responsibility — were cornerstones of the Puritan ethic."[42] Another key term, *liberty,* also figured conspicuously in both registers.[43] It is likely that, given these shared terms, speakers who were familiar with these idioms did not consciously discriminate between the religious and republican contents of these words when they used them, and that their listeners either did not discriminate semantically between the possible references of the words, or were free to hear, as it were, what they wanted to hear, depending on their orientation toward one idiom or the other. The very vagueness and undecidability of the hybrid rhetoric therefore made it a magnificent instrument for the formation of political consensus: it could command the assent of listeners whose understandings were not compatible, but behind the veneer of consensus, they need not have discovered their disagreements.

The effective congruence of these idioms, however, was somewhat factitious: while formally compatible, some of their most important implications were at odds. The most important of these incompatibilities for our present purposes was their distinct figurations of time and history. The discrepancy between the chronotopic schemes assumed by the apocalyptic and republican idioms is carried over into *Modern Chivalry.* Classical republicanism figured time as cyclical, while millennialism figured it as a linear progression.[44] And while it may be possible in theory to construct a complex figure that manages to fuse the linear and cyclical patterns, it is difficult to imagine that such an elaborate figuration had any widespread public authority. It seems likelier that this was

42. Ibid., p. 4.
43. Ibid., pp. 44–46.
44. Ibid., p. 4–6. See also Stow Persons, "The Cyclical Theory of History in Eighteenth-Century America," *American Quarterly* 6 (1954): 147–63; and Michael Lienesch, *New Order of the Ages: Time, the Constitution, and the Making of Modern American Political Thought* (Princeton: Princeton Univ. Press, 1988).

one of the basically fractural features of the double rhetoric of the American Revolution, one of the inner inconsistencies that gave it its explosive power. For the contradictory nature of such a rhetoric should not be seen as disabling it; on the contrary, it underwrote whatever energy and effect the rhetoric had, precisely because of the tension built into it. The violent conflation of the two idioms with their partially discrepant implications guaranteed an inner instability to the rhetoric that gave it considerable power to establish a kind of liminal experience in its hearers, one that by virtue of its vertiginous fluctuations deconstructed the listeners' common-sense understandings of experience, and thereby made subjective reorientations possible.

The cyclical pattern ascribed to time by republicanism had, of course, a rising arc, and that arc could be assimilated conceptually to the progressive vector of the millennial chronotopic scheme; likewise, the linear millennial scheme was not a simple, constant pattern, but one that included occasional passages of declension or backsliding, and those moments could be assimilated conceptually to the falling arc of corruption that republican time included. Thus a configuration of cyclical and progressive time schemes could be imagined,[45] but it would be always at the risk of disintegrating whenever one of the two components of the republican cycle did not coincide with the appropriate passage of the millennial vector. Hence, despite local occasional congruences, the cyclical and linear figurations are ultimately contradictory, and this contradictoriness is a profound source of the revolutionary rhetoric's disruptive energy.

V. Language and Events

Brackenridge's revolutionary sermons, given to soldiers in Washington's army, provide an important point of access to the very

45. Bercovitch describes the way George Bancroft, in his *History of the United States*, hitches the classical cyclical figuration to a biblical linear figuration, with the result that "unlike the repetitive cycles of the wheel of fortune, each revolution is linked to the others in an ascending spiral." Sacvan Bercovitch, "Puritanism in a Revolutionary World," *Lex et Scientia: The International Journal of Law and Science* 14 (1978): 233.

specific and concrete site of language's power to affect events. If the United States was ever literally "spoken into being," it was here, where words incited immediate military actions to secure political independence. In one sermon Brackenridge addressed self-reflexively the very topic of this rhetorical incitement. Preserved in his *Gazette Publications* as a "Fragment of a sermon delivered to a section of the American army, after the Declaration of Independence at Morristown New-Jersey, in 1776," it begins with questions of language:

> There are two ways, in which a man may contribute to the defence of his country: by the tongue to speak, or by the hand to act. To rouse with words and animate with voice is the province of the Orator. To execute with promptitude, and resolution is that of the soldier. These mutually subserve and assist each other. Shall a sheep-skin beat upon; or shall the air reverberating from the cavity of a fife brace the nerves, swell the mind, and rouse to action; and shall not the human voice coming to the heart, with thought as well as sound, produce a still stronger effect.[46]

Brackenridge comes perilously close here to attributing to oratory a materially causative power: the reverberating air carries a physical impulse into the listener's ear where it rouses, braces, animates, and swells a response. He cites the examples of "the tongue of the female oratoress, Deborah," whose words aroused Baruch "to attempt the deliverance of his country";[47] Tyrtaeus, whose "discourses . . . roused the Spartans to the noblest ardor, and though not a soldier or general himself, he gave soul and animation to those that were. An irresistable enthusiasm, was kindled by his words";[48] and Demosthenes, whose "power of speech" was so great that it "produced a delirium of the brain, a madness, an impetuosity of valor."[49] He attributes to Ossian a "magic voice" that

46. Hugh Henry Brackenridge, *Gazette Publications* (Carlisle, Pennsylvania: Printed by Alexander & Phillips, 1806), p. 265.
47. Ibid., p. 265.
48. Ibid., p. 266.
49. Ibid., p. 266.

would have ensured that even "a man of the gown" such as himself "must have caught the madness and rushed to war."[50] Concluding his reflections on the role of oratory in revolutionary activity, he again ascribes to speech (figurally) an effective force that is as good as directly materially productive, saying: "Those therefore may be useful, who though not martial themselves, may rouse that temper in others. The air that fills the sail is itself but light, and can sustain but little weight; nevertheless it wafts fleets across the ocean, and gives an utterance to all the thunders of the engagement."[51] If I am correct, an essential part of this effectivity is produced by the explosively incoherent nature of the civil-millennial rhetoric. The *Six Political Discourses Founded on the Scripture,* published in 1778 just as Brackenridge left the ministry, are textbook examples of the genre of the revolutionary sermon. Strangely, in the preface to the publication, Brackenridge seems uncertain about the makeup of the rhetoric: "Let not the word *scripture,* in the title page, prevent that general attention to these discourses which they might otherwise receive." He worries that the advertised religious content of the sermons will alienate readers, and insists "that these discourses are what they pretend to be, *of a nature chiefly Political.*"[52] Yet the title pretends that, while they are "political" discourses, they are "founded" on scripture: the Bible is given as their foundation, while their political nature is represented as an adjectival modification. And, in fact, they turn out to be in their form conventionally sermonic (opening with a biblical text and proceeding to interpret and apply that text to contemporary events) and to be saturated with the most intensive kind of biblical-figural exposition.

It may be that this indecision as to the nature of the texts reflects the fact that they were *spoken* to ordinary soldiers, for whom the apocalyptic assumptions were most persuasive, but *read* subsequently by a more literate, enlightened, secular urban population, for whom Brackenridge needed to devalue the biblical tropology.

50. Ibid., p. 267.
51. Ibid., p. 267.
52. Hugh Henry Brackenridge, *Six Political Discourses Founded on the Scripture* (Lancaster, Pennsylvania: Printed by Francis Bailey, [1778]), p. 2. Further page references will be given parenthetically.

If he did assume that the sermons when spoken would have a concrete effect on events, then that effect must be credited to the actual
content of the sermons—their profoundly millennial assumptions—as much as to their political references. In these six sermons,
Brackenridge chose to improve a set of scriptural verses that have
obvious millennial implications. The first three were taken from
Jude's exhortations to God's true followers to beware the ungodly
who, "in the last time," shall mock God and be punished for it, and
the last three from the twelfth and thirteenth chapters of the Revelation, where a dragon cast down from heaven becomes "that old serpent, called the Devil" (Rev. 12:19), who animates other mon-
strous beasts with a purpose of deceiving mankind:

> I. Woe unto them, for they have gone in the way of
> Cain. Jude i, 11.
> II. —And ran greedily after the error of Balaam, for
> reward. Jude i, 11.
> III. —And perished in the gainsaying of Core.
> Jude i, 11.
> IV. And there was war in heaven. Rev. xii, 7.
> V. And there was given unto him a mouth, speaking
> great things and blasphemies. Rev. xiii, 5
> VI. Having great wrath, because he knoweth that he
> hath but a short time. Rev. xii, 12. (p. 4)

Brackenridge's improvements of these texts take the form of relating them to political and military events in America. In the first
sermon, "The Bloody Vestiges of Tyranny," it is "the fierce, cruel,
unrelenting, and bloody king of Britain" who has "gone in the
way of Cain" (p. 5). In the second sermon, "The Nature and the
Artifice of Toryism," it is American loyalists who, covetous of government preferment, have run "greedily after the error of Balaam,
for reward" (p. 27). In "The Fate of Tyranny and Toryism," the
third sermon, the "gainsaying of Core" is said to be a spirit of
"obstinacy" or "contradiction" which has led some Americans to
resist the authority of the American Articles of Confederation
(p. 35). Core's obstinacy was, of course, expressed in his refusal to
recognize the legitimacy of the hereditary succession of Moses and
Aaron to the priestly and civil offices, and hence was "an opposition to the will of God" (p. 33); since in America "the consent of

the governed, is that which gives to any one, a right to empire and authority," resistance to popular sovereignty is equivalent to Core's gainsaying (p. 35). Thus the "choice and approbation of the people comes in the room of the divine appointment, or, in other words, is expressive of it. This may be the foundation of that very common maxim — The voice of the people, is the voice of God" (p. 35). The fourth sermon makes in its title the outright claim for "The Agency of Heaven, in the Cause of Liberty," and accumulates evidence to demonstrate that the success of the patriot cause must be credited not merely to human exertion but to God's superintending providence (p. 49). The British lieutenant-general, John Burgoyne, is described in the fifth sermon — "The Blasphemy of Gasconade, and Self-Dependence in a Certain General" — as one whose pretentious proclamations and declamations reveal a prideful oratorical excess that can be compared only to the "mouth, speaking great things and blasphemies" of Revelation 13:5 (p. 62). And the sixth and final sermon, "The Great Wrath of the Tyrant, and the Cause of It," again draws a comparison between George III and the devil, claiming that the lately augmenting anger of "the tyrant of Great-Britain" is a sign that "he knoweth that he hath but a short time" (p. 79). The most explicitly millennial of the sermons, it returns to the subject of the first sermon (the British king), and thereby closes a thematic circle, but also summons a vision of a utopian future for an American nation that has cast off the "reign of the tyrant" that is also "the reign of Satan" (p. 87).

These sermons are densely packed with figural conflations of biblical and classical topics, and quite unabashed translations of American military events into the terms of apocalyptic-republican rhetoric. They are also packed with references to speaking and hearing, the sounds of human voices and the effects those voices have. The fifth sermon is particularly interesting in this regard, since in it Brackenridge addresses the question of the contrast between Burgoyne's rhetoric (its nature and sources) and the rhetoric of American patriotism, and this sermon in its *own* rhetoric performs a separation of the two. Brackenridge insists that "we are all usually one half of what we are, by imitation" — that is, that our linguistic expression is formed by studying models and assimilating their forms and themes — and that it is therefore possible to judge a speaker on the basis of his selection of such models (p. 66).

Playing literary critic to Burgoyne's swelling language, he credits Burgoyne's description of the Battle of Bunker Hill with surpassing even the violent effects that standard poetic license allows to millennial portrayals:

> He [Burgoyne] made his first appearance on the continent, in a sky-rocket, and fire-work description of the day of Charles-Town, and the Bunkerhill engagement. Pyramids of flame, and the roar of cannon, musketry and mortars, sounded and blazed throughout the paragraphs. I have seen poems on the *last* conflagration that were nothing to it. The heart of every Whig was made to tremble, for certainly a man that thought and spoke so loftily, must be capable of doing very lofty actions. (p. 63)

Continuing to mock Burgoyne's verbal breast-beating, Brackenridge prepares an elaborate simile, likening Burgoyne's intensifying but as yet unexercised "fierce indignation" to "an earthquake . . . pent up in the bowels of the earth" (p. 63). Finally released in "the last campaign" — the incursion from Canada down the Hudson Valley in 1777 — this mighty valor "burst forth, all at once, in the sound of a proclamation" (p. 63). Brackenridge compares Burgoyne's proclamation to the "great vaunt of words" attributed to Goliath when confronted with David; just as the giant was, "as all bullies are, a coward at bottom," one whose boasting "was intended to intimidate, and, if possible, prevent the young soldier from coming on the ground at all," so Burgoyne's words were empty pretensions. As he mentions in a footnote, Brackenridge adapts some language from Burgoyne's play, "The Blockade of Boston," to compose this proclamation which he now puts in the British general's mouth:

> O ye saints and rebels of New-England, wherefore are ye come out against me with pitch-forks, and with pruning hooks? Am I a dog that you think to drive me into Lake Champlain, with staves and with broken bayonets? But if so, leave your prayers, and your fastings, and come along, that I may scalp your heads, and

toma-hac your carcases. *I have but to give stretch to the Indian forces under my command, and they amount to thousands.* (pp. 64–65)

Continuing the Burgoyne-Goliath comparison, Brackenridge asserts, "The one proclamation is very much a copy of the other; yet I am not certain that the British general had this monument of jewish history in view, because I am not certain that Burgoyne reads the scripture" (p. 65). Burgoyne's irreverent derogation of the New Englanders as "saints and rebels," and his dismissal of their "prayers" and "fastings," sufficiently expose him for an irreligious braggart, who is again comparable to Goliath who had "*cursed him* [David] *by his gods*" (p. 64). This leads Brackenridge to infer that Burgoyne's actual oratorical models were not biblical but pagan: Achilles' proclamation at the siege of Troy, in the *Iliad* (p. 65), and, more ridiculously, Pyrrhus' employment (as related by Polybius) of the "exceeding terrible" sound of a hidden elephant's cry—which "loud proclamation" he expected would terrify the Romans (pp. 66–67). To point up the ludicrousness of Burgoyne's imputed imitation of these classical models, he is compared to "the great Don-Quixotte[, who] made himself still more great, by a constant and careful perusal of green, black & grey-coloured knights, and by a magnanimous and steady resolution to emulate their warlike glory and atchievements" (p. 66). Thus Burgoyne's "roar" at Ticonderoga, and "second roar" at Lake George, while "audible at a great distance," were ineffectual; his intention to "roar on to Albany" was met with the nonroaring but really courageous resistance of the Virginian Major-General Horatio Gates, who led an American army to a stunning victory over Burgoyne. "His proclamatory voice"—which even in England earned him the epithets "vaporing Burgoyne," "Pomposo," and "Hurlothrombo"[53]—"shall not be heard any more," Brackenridge exults, "in the woods of North-America" (p. 67).

Burgoyne's vaporing was actually full of pious sentiment: he claimed to be acting "in consciousness of Christianity."[54] Brack-

53. Robert Middlekauff, *The Glorious Cause: The American Revolution, 1763–1789* (New York: Oxford Univ. Press, 1982), p. 373.
54. Qtd. in Middlekauff, *The Glorious Cause*, p. 372.

enridge's purpose was to destroy that claim, reserve the badge of Christian righteousness for the American cause, and tar Burgoyne with the brush of pagan classicism. And when he adduced Cervantes to reinforce this set of equations, he drew a connection that would later inform his novel, *Modern Chivalry:*

> [Burgoyne] had made himself acquainted with the great killing times, at several periods, on the border of the Greek and Roman empires, so that if the hero of Cervantes had it in his power to boast a superior knowledge in the laws of chivalry and knighthood, yet the British general was considerably before him in the skill of Caesar-hood and Alexander-ship. (p. 68)

Brackenridge's later novelistic satire on the imaginary identification of revolutionary Americans with Greek and Roman precursors would repeat this subversive comparison of such fantasmatic American classicism to the foolish knight's similar identification with the antiquated codes of romantic chivalry. *Modern Chivalry* would brilliantly reduce this comparison to a paradox: the "modern" chivalry of Captain Farrago is precisely his deluded immersion in classical republican models, an anachronistic attempt to collapse the difference between classical antiquity and eighteenth-century America. And Farrago's tendency to bombast is given a new appearance when its precedent in Brackenridge's portrait of Burgoyne's vaporing is recalled.

Brackenridge goes on to cite "another species of writing not less familiar to the general, and that is the French and English tragedy" (p. 69). This, added to his alleged acquaintance with Homeric poetry and ancient history, accounts for his ability to "get upon his buskins, and talk—rotundo ore—with a swelling mouth" (p. 70). One wonders how Brackenridge's audience of soldiers responded to this fanciful satire on Burgoyne's literary education—it is hard to imagine it inspiring them to military valor. Fight against Burgoyne because he reads too much? Perhaps Brackenridge believed he could tap into the soldiers' resentment of literate elitism, but in any case, having disposed of Burgoyne's claim to "speaking great things," he goes on to Burgoyne's "blasphemies," and here, he says, is where "I mean to be serious" (p. 70). For it is the impious subtext of Burgoyne's bragging that will offend Americans who are intolerant of calumnies and defamations of their God. Here Brackenridge's patient close reading of Burgoyne's proclamation reveals that while it may "[seem] to hold forth something rational, and pious" — the conjunction of the two adjectives is noteworthy — "you will find that it is not so much an acknowledgement of the superintendency of God, as an oath that verily in spite of all opposition, he will do what he proposed" (p. 71). "The best we can say of it, is, that when he meant to pray, he naturally fell into the idiom of an oath. Such is the force of habit, on the human mind, and so hard is it to speak in a language different from that to which we have been long accustomed" (p. 72). In contrast, "we may easily account for the ignominious exit of Burgoyne. It is to be resolved not so much into our skill and bravery, as into the providence of God, which he had slighted and despised" (p. 73). The Americans rightly trusted not to their own "skill, resolution, or diligence," but to "the great disposer of events" (p. 74). Unlike the military commander who insisted that "fortune had no share" in his success, and thereby invited God to arrange for him to enjoy martial success no longer, Americans gained their victory precisely by virtue of God's intercession, and would continue to enjoy its benefits as long as they continued to rely on it. And it is this faith, Brackenridge avers — in a remarkably creative conceptual innovation — that will remove America from the cyclical course of events to which history has consigned Burgoyne and his ilk — a course marked by "reverse of fortune," where after every success the resultant pride entails that "the wheel returns" and failure ensues (p. 75).

> It is for this reason that I look upon the present to be the most critical point of time, that has yet revolved to America. We set out very weak, and we were sure of the providence of God, because we were sure that we needed it. We were beaten very low, and we despaired not, because there were many instances of those who had emerged from the deepest situation of trouble and distress.

We have emerged according to our hope, and have struck off a main limb from the body of the tyrant. We may again be overcome. It is an easy thing for the providence which rules the world to lay us lower than he hath yet raised us, and to make our present eminence serving to a fall more terrible.

If we would be still victorious, let us be *still humble*. Was I to see in these united states, a departure, in any instance, from that spirit of sobriety, with which at first we set out, I should fear that it presaged us a great reverse of fortune. I never thought it possible that a people who had virtuously rejected every luxury, and every vain amusement, could be overcome in so just a cause. I never could believe it in the course of providence, that a people could be conquered, whose practice it had now become to go to the house of prayer, instead of to a horserace, and to church instead of a ball-room. Should this practice be reversed, we should have just ground to apprehend that our fortune also should be reversed with it. (pp. 75–76)

Brackenridge tacks back and forth between "fortune" and "providence," seeming at first glance to use them indistinguishably. Yet the logic of his exposition has it that the cyclical dynamic of "fortune" — of revolving, rise and fall, reverse and reverse again — can be displaced by the permanent linearity of the "course of providence" if only Americans will permanently trust in it. The cycle is not necessary; it will operate only if God allows for it to do so, and he will do so only when Americans cease to rely on him.

The implication, struggling to emerge here from the confused rendering of a combined cyclical-providential historical scheme, is made explicit in the next (the sixth) sermon. Here (to abbreviate matters), Brackenridge takes off from the "*crisis* to America" described at the end of the previous sermon, the "situation where a reverse of fortune doth usually take place," that is, after a remarkable success (p. 77). Exhorting his listeners to stand fast, he interprets the renewed wrath of George III as a sign that "he knoweth that he hath but a short time" (p. 79). Like "the devil, who, in the late age of the world, and just before the *millennium*, is about to act with redoubled fury, knowing, that in a short time, he shall be shut up in the dark abode of hell," the British tyrant can be expected to "act, next campaign, with a still more dispairing vengeance" (pp. 79, 86). Finally, a strict equation is proposed:

> The reign of the tyrant is the reign of satan. I trust that a short space of time shall fix the limit to them both. War and fierce debate shall shew themselves no more. Tranquillity and days of happiness shall again be ours. The husbandman now destitute of habitation, shall return to his dwelling-house. The tear shall be wiped from the eye of the fair virgin, driven from the city, where she had been delicately bred. The prisoner shall be lifted from the jail, and have his name placed with those who have suffered for their country. The soldier shall retire from the danger of the camp, and the wooden leg and the grey hairs of valour shall be honourable. (p. 87)

This recalls Brackenridge's typological exegesis in the fourth sermon (the first of his three sermons expounding verses from Revelation), where he flatly suggested, "It is possible Saint John may have had his eye, upon a later period. The present time and the George of England may be that which is pointed out in this place of scripture" (p. 50). That sermon, titled "The Agency of Heaven, in the Cause of Liberty," inaugurated the explicitly millennial argument that culminates here with a glowing description of God's new order of things ordained for America:

> Be cheared, O my country, for thy garden-bower, and thy walls shall be built again. Thy meads shall be decked with grass, and the grain shall be heavy on thy fields. The villages shall rise from their rubbish and their smoke, and new towns shall smile along thy streams.
>
> Commerce shall extend her wings, and come from every shore. It will be pleasant to see a new *Exchange* in every fair metropolis upon our coast. . . .

Science shall be planted in our country, and many
seminaries shall again shew their heads. Like fair lights,
and pyramids of fire, they shall shoot up in every state.
The muses every where shall strew the land with flow-
ers; and slumbering bards shall yet awake, to sing of
nature, and the praise of men.

Religion shall again come down and live upon the
earth. Free exercise of conscience shall be allowed everywhere. Bigotry—vile bigotry that springs from ignorance, shall fly away. Truth, pure truth shall dispel
the fog and vapour of the mind. The light of knowledge, like the light of day shall kindle heat in the pious
soul. Days, happy days are yet before us. (pp. 87–88)

VI. Chronotopic Equation

The apostrophe to the millennial future that the Revolution
promised to call into existence with which Brackenridge ended his
sixth sermon to the soldiers, effects an ideological transformation
that is familiar to us from Max Weber and others. It is perhaps
most blatantly represented by one feature: "It will be pleasant to
see a new *Exchange* in every fair metropolis upon our coast"
(p. 87). Free enterprise enlists the forward-looking historical figuration of time prepared by millennial discourse. Much recent
scholarship on the American Revolution has depicted its motiva-
ting ideology as strongly committed to precapitalist modes of production and social relations. Recently this scholarly consensus has
been challenged, in the interest of depicting the Revolution once
again as a liberal bourgeois movement, and of qualifying the characterization of eighteenth-century American political ideology
as "commercial republicanism" rather than a revolt against
modernity.[55]

55. Drew R. McCoy, *The Elusive Republic: Political Economy in Jeffersonian
America* (Chapel Hill: Univ. of North Carolina Press, 1980); Joyce Appleby,
"Commercial Farming and the 'Agrarian Myth' in the Early Republic," *Journal of
American History* 68 (1981–82): 833–49, and *Capitalism and a New Social Order:
The Republican Vision of the 1790s* (New York: New York Univ. Press, 1984); Ralph
Lerner, "Commerce and Character: The Anglo-American as New-Model Man,"
William and Mary Quarterly 3d ser., 36 (1979): 3–26; Joseph J. Ellis, "Culture and

What Brackenridge's sermons — and, later, his novel — help us to recall is the historical solidarity between emergent free enterprise and Protestantism. What he trusted would make soldiers fight was not an unbalanced constitution or the specter of commercial corruption, but rather a vision of progressive freedom, commercial growth, and rampant prosperity. These sermons, and the later novel that further elaborated the patterns of thought introduced there, help us to see that the marriage of convenience between classical republicanism and apocalyptic Protestantism at the moment of Revolution was not a marriage made in heaven: the fundamental incompatibilities in the conceptual underpinnings of the two discursive formations may have been temporarily obscured by the surface congruities of the two systems, but during and after the Revolution those contradictions reasserted themselves. Republicanism in its strong anticommercial form came to appear as the anachronism it was, while forward-looking revolutionary millennialism emerged transformed from its association with the secular political theory of civic virtue. In its new form its positive theological content was substantially drained away, and its temporal figuration put in the service of capitalist striving. It is as if, in the crucible of revolutionary rhetorical amalgamation, a chemical reaction had taken place; when the fires died down, the slag of antimodern republicanism was discarded, and the purified component of protomodern, Protestant-inflected liberalism remained.

A liberal market society formed and developed fairly quickly after the Revolution, and this fact effectively consigns the reactionary discourse of classical republicanism to the role of ideology in the strong sense of false consciousness. If republican ideas survived into the nineteenth century, they did so as a mystification of real social processes.[56] This is, of course, the fundamentally Marxian sense of ideology, expounded notably in *The Eighteenth Brumaire of Louis Napoleon,* and aptly described by Althusser as the

Capitalism in Pre-Revolutionary America," *American Quarterly* 31 (1979): 169–86.

56. See Rowland Berthoff, "Independence and Attachment, Virtue and Interest: From Republican Citizen to Free Enterpriser, 1787–1837," in Richard L. Bushman et al. eds., *Uprooted Americans: Essays to Honor Oscar Handlin* (Boston: Little, Brown and Company, 1979), p. 119.

substitution of an imaginary and deceptive representation of social relations for a more truthful representation.[57] In the useful terms articulated by Raymond Williams, the classical republican discourse was "residual," a lingering trace of an older social formation, while the millennial discourse, while not newly invented by any means, corresponded to an "emergent" social formation.[58] And, as Williams has said, it is one of the chief uses of such residual discourses to disguise change and innovation as stability and restoration. Republican rhetoric enabled the creation of a liberal market society to masquerade nostalgically as a reversion to an older order of things. Such a description of the social function of American revolutionary rhetoric would not surprise Brackenridge, who in *Modern Chivalry* dramatized some of the many ways in which "imagination governs the world" (p. 65). The factitiousness of republican traditionalism in America is what its historians have ignored: it is what Eric Hobsbawm has called a "constructed" or "invented" tradition.[59]

One of *Modern Chivalry*'s great virtues is its unmystified depiction of this factitiousness and anachronism. Strangely, critics who have commented on Brackenridge's use of Cervantes have insisted that the affiliation is a tenuous one and that Brackenridge's purposes are essentially different from those of his literary precursor.[60] On the contrary, I think Brackenridge modeled his narrative closely on Cervantes, and that the elusiveness of his purposes—

57. Louis Althusser, "Ideology and Ideological State Apparatuses (Notes Towards an Investigation)," in *Lenin and Philosophy and Other Essays,* trans. Ben Brewster (New York: Monthly Review Press, 1971), pp. 127–86. An inestimably valuable critique of Althusser's conception of ideology is in Stuart Hall, "Signification, Representation, Ideology: Althusser and the Post-Structuralist Debates," *Critical Studies in Mass Communication* 2 (1985): 91–114.

58. Raymond Williams, "Base and Superstructure in Marxist Cultural Theory," in *Problems in Materialism and Culture* (London: Verso, 1980), pp. 31–49.

59. Eric Hobsbawm, "Introduction: Inventing Traditions," in Eric Hobsbawm and Terence Ranger, eds., *The Invention of Tradition* (New York: Cambridge Univ. Press, 1983), pp. 1–14.

60. Joseph H. Harkey, "The *Don Quixote* of the Frontier: Brackenridge's *Modern Chivalry,*" *Early American Literature* 8 (1973): 193–203; William L. Nance, "Satiric Elements in Brackenridge's *Modern Chivalry,*" *Texas Studies in Literature and Language* 9 (1967): 381–89. Nance claims, quite implausibly, that Brackenridge's satirical intentions are fundamentally different from those of Cervantes (p. 383), and that Captain Farrago "is not a caricature," but rather is "the representative of reason" and "equivalent to Brackenridge himself" (p. 385). On the contrary, Farrago *is* a caricature, a caricature *of reason.*

their endless ironic displacement—is fundamentally true to Cervantes. Brackenridge's exposure of Captain Farrago's deluded, wishful, nostalgic devotion to republican ideals that are out of place in a modern nation is analogous to Cervantes' exposure of his knight's foolish revival of the codes of romantic chivalry. The title's reference to anachronism, *Modern Chivalry*, says as much. It is hard, then, to understand one critic's not unusual claim that with respect to Cervantes's "contrast between the knight and his squire," "the allegory is somewhat reversed in *Modern Chivalry*. Teague represents the unenlightened, impetuous majority, the Captain, the rational minority."[61] Rather, to put it simply, the Captain represents an outmoded pretense of rationality and a reactionary attachment to a deferential social protocol, while Teague represents emergent democracy. To say this isn't to deny that Brackenridge has misgivings about the emergent egalitarian social order; he obviously does. It is only to say that his irony cuts both ways, and that if the final effect of the satire of *Modern Chivalry* is to cut one way more vigorously than the other, it cuts against the Captain's nostalgia more violently than it does against Teague's optimistic, disorderly hopes for social change. Brackenridge discovers much comedy, of course, in the dialogic encounter of residual and emergent political and social forms, but it is evident that, in the manner of the novelistic heteroglossia so sympathetically traced by Bakhtin (a tradition in which *Modern Chivalry*, of all early American texts, most belongs),[62] the writer's deepest investment is in the subversive, transgressive, energizing agency of the rogue, the knave, and the fool.[63]

Although officially committed by its narrative voice to the authority of traditional republican ideals, it is not the case that that voice can be unproblematically assimilated to Brackenridge. *Modern Chivalry* performs some fairly complex narrative feats: the Cap-

---

61. Harkey, "The *Don Quixote* of the Frontier," pp. 193, 194.

62. Without citing Bakhtin, William R. Hoffa, in "The Language of Rogues and Fools in Brackenridge's *Modern Chivalry*," *Studies in the Novel* 12 (1980): 289–300, has placed the work in the tradition of Erasmus, Rabelais, Butler, Burton, Cervantes, Sterne and Swift.

63. Wendy Martin, "The Rogue and the Rational Man: Hugh Henry Brackenridge's Study of a Con Man in *Modern Chivalry*," *Early American Literature* 8 (1973): 179–92.

tain's dramatized voice has a certain tentative authority on many occasions, as does that of the omniscient narrator. But there is also an implied author who is identical to neither of those two voices, and that implied author cannot be simply identified with Brackenridge, whose varied career as schoolmaster, preacher, lawyer, journalist, and judge is not in all respects smoothly continuous with his career as fiction writer. Like the commitment to normative literary style with which the narration begins, but which the actual written performance regularly betrays, the narrative voice's authority is regularly put in question precisely by its resemblance to the ridiculous Captain Farrago's. As Farrago's weak grasp of reality is constantly pointed up by the events that confound him, so the narrator's observations on those events seem more and more feeble. The novel is finally, for better or worse, committed to the triumph of Teague O'Regan and all that he represents: Teague has all the fun, his subversive energy is what propels the narrative (and the narrator's pained, cramped animadversions on Teague's trangressions are what block it), and — what is often not noted — Teague eventually overcomes Captain Farrago's resistance to his ambitious striving. John Farrago is at first Teague's master; then he is Teague's patron; and finally he is a cranky but admiring witness to Teague's successes. William Spengemann has expressed it well:

> Because Brackenridge's ideal program can gain nothing but negative support from the experiences of Farrago and Teague, he is temperamentally disinclined to view their adventures as having any intrinsic educative merit. Like all domestic novelists, he sees all action as the result of some unwelcome deviation from ideal normality and all events as inherently unfortunate. If the world had been what he wanted it to be, no action — and hence no novel — would have been necessary. Because he was a novelist as well as a polemicist, however . . . his work betrays the novelist's usual tendency to like his characters more than his extrinsic purposes might warrant.[64]

64. William Spengemann, *The Adventurous Muse: The Poetics of American Fiction, 1789–1900* (New Haven: Yale Univ. Press, 1977), pp. 95–96.

As Spengemann says, it is part of the program of the picaresque novel that, despite its best intentions, it ends up being "seduced" by the "bizarre behavior and especially [the] vernacular, earthy speech" of its vulgar protagonist.[65] In this basic affection for the vitality of Teague, Brackenridge sacrifices much of his investment in the pompous sentiments of Captain Farrago and the judicious commentary of the narrator. It is true that both Farrago and the narrator are exponents of civic virtue, natural aristocracy, and other elements of eighteenth-century oppositional ideology, as Michael Gilmore has carefully noted.[66] It is also true that that ideology is anachronistically irrelevant in Teague's world, and that *Modern Chivalry* is, in its largest terms, carefully posed to deconstruct that ideology.

This deconstruction can easily be described in the terms Bakhtin provides. As I have said, the narrative chapters belong to Teague; he, (not Farrago, as Wendy Martin claims)[67] is the novel's protagonist. He instigates and Farrago merely reacts. The discursive chapters of "observations" mostly endorse the Captain's pretensions, and, as any reader knows, those chapters are flat, repetitive, and boring. That the course of the novel is marked, as I have shown, by the gradual displacement of those chapters of "observations" by chapters of narrative, is one measure of the slow discreditation of the narrative point of view and its alignment with Captain Farrago's ideology. But this shift operates also to effect a displacement of one of what (following Bakhtin) I will call "chronotopes" by another.[68] The essay chapters and the narrative chapters respectively correspond to different temporal and spatial schemes, and those chronotopic schemes can be roughly articulated with real conditions of social existence in postrevolutionary America. One of the most impressive accomplishments of *Modern*

65. Ibid., p. 96. Cathy N. Davidson likewise finds that "the picaresque . . . countered [the] official attempt to homogenize the *polis* with a rambunctious heterogeneity." See Davidson, *Revolution and the Word*, p. 153.

66. Michael T. Gilmore, "Eighteenth-Century Oppositional Ideology and Hugh Henry Brackenridge's *Modern Chivalry*," *Early American Literature* 13 (1978): 181–92.

67. Wendy Martin, "On the Road with the Philosopher and the Profiteer: A Study of Hugh Henry Brackenridge's *Modern Chivalry*," *Eighteenth-Century Studies* 4 (1971): 241.

68. Mikhail Bakhtin, "Forms of Time and of the Chronotope in the Novel: Notes Toward a Historical Poetics," in *The Dialogic Imagination*, pp. 84–258.

Chivalry is its massive but subtle articulation of literary forms with contemporary social formations, and its implicit tracking of a tectonic drift in those social formations. Simply stated, the narrative chapters embody a linear temporal scheme and a horizontal diagram of egalitarian social relations; conversely, the essay chapters embody a static (or cyclical) temporal scheme and a vertical diagram of hierarchical social relations. In the narrative chapters, time operates: minutes and hours and days pass, Teague has adventures, and the social mobility to which egalitarian democracy is committed is comically dramatized. On the contrary, the essay chapters respond to this social motion by asserting a synchronic conceptual system meant to control and limit such social mobility: they repeat endlessly the formulas of an ideology of static, closed, hierarchical social relations, and do so from a point of view that holds, as Spengemann noted, all change to be necessarily unfortunate. Change is thematized, in the manner of classical thought, as corruption; and amelioration, when it is admitted, is figured as a reversion to a prior state of affairs.

These two chronotopic schemes are first explicitly presented in Chapter III of the first Volume, where the Captain has his first encounter with mass democracy. To his dismay, he discovers that the vulgar multitudes are on the verge of electing a mere unlearned weaver to the state legislature, rather than the "man of education" who is his opponent (p. 13). The latter candidate addresses the crowd as Farrago rides up: he modestly praises his own talents and derides those of his competitor, the "illiterate handicraftsman" who would, he says, do better to remain "in the sphere where God and nature has placed him" (p. 13). The Captain, whose equestrian elevation is a constant figure of what he believes to be his disinterested attachment to the public weal, speaks to the crowd in support of the educated candidate. He urges that "to rise from the cellar to the senate house, would be an unnatural hoist," "a reversion of the order of things" (p. 14). While gassing on to this effect, he does not notice that, beneath his gaze, class resentment is fueling the radical democratic imagination, and that Teague, "hearing so much about elections, and serving the government, took it into his head, that he could be a legislator himself" (p. 15). With the support of his fellow Irishmen, "the fluctuation of the popular mind, and a disposition to what is new and ignoble" make it more than likely that he will win elected office. When the Captain notices what is going on, he is put quite out of countenance, and unwisely betrays his contempt for the crowd by his undiplomatic expostulations:

This is making the matter still worse, gentlemen: this servant of mine is but a bog-trotter; who can scarcely speak the dialect in which your laws ought to be written; but certainly has never read a single treatise on any political subject; for the truth is, he cannot read at all. The young people of the lower class, in Ireland, have seldom the advantage of a good education; especially the descendants of the ancient Irish, who have most of them a great assurance of countenance, but little information, or literature. This young man, whose family name is Oregan, has been my servant for several years. And, except a too great fondness for women, which now and then brings him into scrapes, he has demeaned himself in a manner tolerable enough. But he is totally ignorant of the great principles of legislation; and more especially, the particular interests of the government. A free government is a noble possession to a people: and this freedom consists in an equal right to make laws, and to have the benefit of the laws when made. Though doubtless, in such a government, the lowest citizen may become chief magistrate; yet it is sufficient to possess the right; not absolutely necessary to exercise it. Or even if you should think proper, now and then, to shew your privilege, and exert, in a signal manner, the democratic prerogative, yet is it not descending too low to filch away from me a hireling, which I cannot well spare, to serve your purpose. You are surely carrying the matter too far, in thinking to make a senator of this hostler; to take him away from an employment to which he has been bred, and put him to another, to which he has served no apprenticeship: to set those hands which have been lately employed in currying my horse, to the draughting bills, and preparing business for the house. (pp. 15–16)

A reasonably attentive reading of a speech such as this shows how far wide of the mark are critics who vaunt Farrago as the mouthpiece of Brackenridge, or as a simple representative of political rationality and moderation. His own words expose him as an apologist for privilege, one who uses the rhetoric of republicanism to preserve his own interests. His understanding of the social world is defined by contrasts between high and low, education and ignorance, master and servant, nobility and vulgarity. His own convenience he values more highly than the public choice. The crowd is not fooled:

> The people were tenacious of their choice, and insisted on giving Teague their suffrages; and by the frown upon their brows, seemed to indicate resentment at what has been said; as indirectly charging them with want of judgment; or calling in question their privilege to do what they thought proper. It is a very strange thing, said one of them, who was a speaker for the rest, that after having conquered Burgoyne and Cornwallis, and got a government of our own, we cannot put in it whom we please. This young man may be your servant, or another man's servant; but if we chuse to make him a delegate, what is that to you. (p. 16)

In this passage the allusion to Burgoyne registers exactly the antielitism Brackenridge had himself sought to provoke against Burgoyne in the sermon discussed above. What is most significant is the next sentence: "He may not be yet skilled in the matter, but there is a good day a-coming" (p. 16). As against Farrago's insistence that every man stay put forever in the social place to which he was "bred," the crowd's appointed speaker asserts that though not "yet" qualified for office, he soon may be, for "there is a good day a-coming." And they understand that it is their Revolution that enabled them to imagine such a good day; it was acting on the expectation of that day that they made their Revolution. This undeformed echo of the rhetoric of millennial expectation that Brackenridge himself uttered in his revolutionary sermons completes the chronotopic equation that the whole novel institutes. Democracy, economic freedom, and social equality borrow the

temporal scheme of millennial progress, while classical republicanism, now exposed as the ideology of economic privilege, adheres
to the model of corruption and restoration.

VII. Ethnic Idioms

Among the kinds of social fractures that interfered with the integration of the new American nation, one of the most charged was
the ethnic diversity of the population. And in Pennsylvania in the
postrevolutionary period, the caricatured "wild Irishman" was the
standard metonym for ethnicity in general. Thus Brackenridge's
creation of the superstitious, unenlightened Teague O'Regan as
the comic foil to Captain Farrago's enlightened republicanism was
an invention that spoke to the prejudices and fears of the time, and
addressed in a striking way the problematic nature of an American
nationality that aimed to ground loyalty in rational assent rather
than ethnic loyalty.

The second essay of *The Federalist*, written by John Jay, offered
a series of reasons why the United States must necessarily be a
single nation. One reason is the geography of the continent: "It
has often given me pleasure to observe, that Independent America
was not composed of detached and distant territories, but that one
connected, fertile, wide spreading country was the portion of our
western sons of liberty."[69] This is a version of what Myra Jehlen
has called the theory of "American incarnation," the continental
landscape itself mystically determining the nature of the social formation.[70] Jay's next reason is analogous:

> With equal pleasure I have as often taken notice, that
> Providence has been pleased to give this one con-
> nected country, to one united people, a people de-
> scended from the same ancestors, speaking the same
> language, professing the same religion, attached to the
> same principles of government, very similar in their

69. *The Federalist*, ed. Jacob E. Cooke (Middletown, Connecticut: Wesleyan
Univ. Press, 1961), p. 9.
70. Myra Jehlen, *American Incarnation: The Individual, the Nation, and the Continent* (Cambridge, Massachusetts: Harvard Univ. Press, 1986).

manners and customs, and who, by their joint counsels, arms and efforts, fighting side by side throughout
a long and bloody war, have nobly established their
general Liberty and Independence.[71]

This amazing counterfactual assertion — disinformation, we might
now call it — is, in its casual erasure of obvious facts, worthy of the
greatest of America's political fantasists. "This country [i.e., the
land] and this people" — both entities essentially integral, in Jay's
presentation — "seem to have been made for each other."[72] The
fact of the matter, of course, was quite otherwise. The continent
was extensive, interrupted by nearly impassable mountain ranges,
wide rivers, swamps and deserts; it was already inhabited by indig-
enous peoples; it was invaded by immigrants who spoke different
languages, adhered to different faiths, followed different customs,
were variously enslaved and free; and only by a vast stretch of
the imagination could be considered to be "descended from the
same ancestors."

It was this last claim that was, perhaps, the most ideologically
charged among Jay's tendentious representations. This was because the new nationality that was being constructed in America
was of a new kind: based on consent rather than descent, as Werner Sollors has aptly put it,[73] it was, in the words of Yehoshua
Arieli, "not a natural fact but an ideological structure."[74] Now it
is, of course, true that nationality is never simply a "natural fact."
It is always a social and historical artifice, a matter of imagined
identity and community. But the derivation of the word *nation*
itself from the root from which *nature* is also derived (*gene-*, to
give birth, beget) is plain evidence of the long historical affiliation
of the concepts of nationality and of genetic origin. The nation,
on this account, is an extension of the family and the tribe, its
unity underwritten by biological connection.

That this is, in any modern nation, a simple myth does not pre-

71. *The Federalist*, p. 9.
72. *The Federalist*, p. 9.
73. Werner Sollors, *Beyond Ethnicity: Consent and Descent in American Culture*
(New York: Oxford Univ. Press, 1986).
74. Qtd. in Dale T. Knobel, *Paddy and the Republic: Ethnicity and Nationality
in Antebellum America* (Middletown, Connecticut: Wesleyan Univ. Press, 1986),
p. 40.

vent it from having strong effects. But in the United States the myth could not be sustained except at the expense of common sense. Ethnic plurality was a conspicuous phenomenon that posed a fundamental threat to the incipient factitious American nationality. Immigrants brought their primordial loyalties to their origins, their kin, and their languages with them, and while devices of hyphenation and melting-pot theories were invented to mitigate this threat, it inconveniently happened that, in a nation where abstract consent was the only guarantee of national unity, ethnic identities of immigrants were often exaggerated both subjectively and in interethnic perceptions. Ethnic diasporas are as often marked by consolidation and intensification of ethnicity as by its lapse.

In Pennsylvania in the late eighteenth century, the Irish became, synecdochically, the representative group posing the ethnic threat. The Germans had been the bogeys in the 1750s, when Franklin asked "why should the *Palatine Boors* be suffered to swarm into our Settlements, and by herding together establish their Language and Manners to the Exclusion of ours?"[75] To Peter Collinson he wrote in 1753 that

> those who come hither are generally of the most igno-
> rant Stupid Sort of their own Nation, and as Igno-
> rance is often attended with Credulity when Knavery
> would mislead it, and with Suspicion when Honesty
> would set it right; and as few of the English under-
> stand the German Language, and so cannot address
> them either from the Press or Pulpit, 'tis almost impos-
> sible to remove any prejudices they once entertain.[76]

This is the model of the ethnic stereotype in republican America: non-Anglo immigrants are superstitious and ignorant peasants, unfitted for citizenship in an enlightened democracy. Germans did assimilate, however: while there were no German members of the Pennsylvania Assembly in 1755 and 1756,[77] in 1775 they comprised 18 percent of the Assembly.[78] Germans comprised 27 per-

75. Franklin, *Writings,* p. 374.
76. Ibid., p. 472.
77. Wayne L. Bockelman and Owen S. Ireland, "The Internal Revolution in Pennsylvania: An Ethnic Religious Interpretation," *Pennsylvania History* 41 (1974): 130.
78. Ibid., p. 129.

cent of the delegates to the Provincial Convention in June, 1776, and 29 percent of the Constitutional Convention in July of the same year.[79] Although anti-German prejudice undoubtedly survived in spite of such evidence of successful participation in public affairs, the focus of anti-ethnic animus had shifted to the Irish.

Something like 4,000 Irish had arrived into Philadelphia every year in the five years preceding the Revolution. While the war itself stemmed the influx of immigrants for nearly ten years, the Treaty of Paris in 1783 saw the flow of immigrants resume, and by 1791 the prewar levels had been reached again. Throughout the 1790s the Irish immigration averaged 3,000 per year.[80] This was unmistakably startling in a city with a population of only 28,522 in 1790. Of Philadelphia's population increase in the 1790s (44.5 percent), most of it was growth by immigration, owing to the yellow fever epidemics that nearly wiped out the natural growth rate; and more than half of the immigrants (56 percent) were Irish. Philadelphia's population growth by Irish immigration between 1790 and 1800 was 19 percent.[81] Many of the Irish immigrants — probably two-thirds — did not settle in Philadelphia, but pushed on westward to western Pennsylvania, or to Ohio or Tennessee; but, when Jefferson was elected president, Irish immigrants were 12 percent of the resident population of the city.[82]

Amid the xenophobia and general political paranoia of the American 1790s, the Irish thus were an obvious target for stigmatization. Harrison Gray Otis gave an excitable speech in Congress on July 1, 1798, defending the proposed Naturalization Act against those Jeffersonians who saw its twenty-dollar tax on naturalization certificates as an attempt to withhold suffrage from immigrants who were, by and large, tending to support Jeffersonian political candidates. The act, according to Otis, would exclude "the mass of vicious and disorganizing characters who can not live peaceably at home, and who, after unfurling the standard of rebellion in their own countries, may come hither to revolutionize

79. Ibid., p. 143.
80. Edward C. Carter II, "A 'Wild Irishman' Under Every Federalist's Bed: Naturalization in Philadelphia, 1789–1806," *Pennsylvania Magazine of History and Biography* 94 (1970): 332–33.
81. Ibid., p. 342.
82. Ibid., pp. 343, 342.

ours." Otis especially did "not wish to invite hoards of wild Irishmen, nor the turbulent and disorderly of all parts of the world, to come here with a view to disturb our tranquility, after having succeeded in the overthrow of their own governments."[83] Like Jay's misrepresentations in *The Federalist,* discussed above, Otis's invocation of "tranquility" in the 1790s was deluded if not dishonest, but his reversion to the notion of revolution indicates that his real interest lay in establishing a nonrevolutionary politics in a postrevolutionary society.

The majority of the Irish immigrants were so-called Scotch-Irish, Ulster Presbyterians; gradually more and more Catholics, both from Ulster and from the southern counties of Ireland, joined the exodus, in flight from civil and religious strife. William Cobbett published his *Detection of a Conspiracy formed by the United Irishmen, with the Evident Intention of Aiding the Tyrants of France in Subverting the Government of the United States* in 1798, combining nativist hysteria with the traditional American rhetoric of the paranoid style to stimulate anti-Irish sentiment. Although Brackenridge's initial creation of Teague O'Regan preceded the full flowering of this anti-Irish propaganda, it was for that reason able to attract, as such prejudice grew, a readership prepared to enjoy its caricature. Brackenridge had, in fact, first experimented with the bog-Irish stereotype in 1770, in the novel he wrote in collaboration with Philip Freneau, *Father Bombo's Pilgrimage to Mecca.* Picaresque in form, as *Modern Chivalry* would be, this tale traced an American counterpilgrimage, reversing the direction of the westward migrations that populated America with Europeans; its destination in the holiest city of Islam, the birthplace of Mohammed, further subverted the master teleology of American mythic history. This comic inversion utterly undermined the ideology so patriotically represented in Brackenridge's other collaboration with Freneau, *A Poem on the Rising Glory of America* (1772), composed for the commencement exercises of their Princeton class of 1771 and elaborating upon the received theory of westward civilizational progress. In Book 3d, Chapter 1st of *Father Bombo's Pilgrimage,* Bombo affects an Irish brogue in order to secure protec-

83. Qtd. in ibid., p. 334.

tion from the Irish captain and crew of the privateer that takes over his own ship. This chapter, which was one of Brackenridge's contributions to the collaboration, offers a full realization of the standard literary stage Irishman.[84] The prototype of this stereotype was the servant Teague in Robert Howard's *The Committee* (1665), and a dense succession of Teagues followed in English-language literature in the seventeenth and eighteenth centuries.[85] In *Modern Chivalry,* Brackenridge discussed his choice of this comic stereotype:

> It has been asked, why, in writing this memoir; have I taken my clown, *from the Irish nation?* . . . The American has in fact, yet, no character; neither the clown, nor the gentleman. So that I could not take one from our own country; which I would much rather have done, as the scene lay here. But the midland states of America, and the western parts in general, being half Ireland, the character of the Irish clown, will not be wholly misunderstood. (p. 405)

Recognizing that "on the Irish stage, it is a standing character," and a familiar type in Great Britain too, Brackenridge apologizes for having "not been able to do it justice, being but half an Irishman, myself, and not so well acquainted with the reversions, and idiom, of the genuine Thady" (p. 405).

The "idiom," of course, is the feature of the stereotype that functions significantly in the prose of *Modern Chivalry,* but it is the "reversions" (of which the idiom may be considered in part as an instance) that are especially important from a historical and ideological point of view. The word *reversions,* after its primary signification in the law of estates (the reversion of property under certain conditions to its donor), has another less specific meaning, which is the act of returning or reverting to a primitive or ancestral condition, practice, or belief. Bombo's Irish masquerade gave Brackenridge ample opportunity to exercise his skill in presenting

---

84. Hugh Henry Brackenridge and Philip Freneau, *Father Bombo's Pilgrimage to Mecca,* ed. Michael Davitt Bell (Princeton, New Jersey: Princeton Univ. Library, 1975), pp. 73–79.

85. N. F. Blake, *Non-Standard Language in English Literature* (London: Andre Deutsch, 1981), pp. 104–107.

the Irish as superstitious, ignorant, priest-ridden, and credulous: a reversion to premodern, unenlightened modes of consciousness.

The essential characteristic of the stereotypical bog Irishman, as the anthropologist Mary Douglas has written, is his tenacious and unthinking adherence to archaic beliefs, customs, practices, rituals, and allegiances.[86] As immigrants into modernity, they nevertheless remain loyal to premodern modes of thought and expression. Douglas finds Basil Bernstein's distinction, which I earlier referred to with respect to Franklin in chapter 2, between elaborated and restricted codes, useful in describing the bog-Irish type: he remains immured within his restricted code—a style of verbal expression that assumes a small-scale, local social context, in which a variety of understandings and references can be taken for granted and thus need not be explicitly articulated. The bog Irishman speaks and thinks as though he and his interlocutors were situated in the closed and simple environment of the old-country village, and he is unable to think and speak as if he were capable of making lexical and syntactic choices that did not always have such a narrow deictic reference.

What is curious and incisive about Brackenridge's use of Teague and the cultural stereotype he exemplifies is that, if anything, it is Teague O'Regan who is most able to maneuver socially between contexts, to imagine himself crossing boundaries and transgressing hierarchies, and to express himself intelligibly in social contexts for which his upbringing and education did not fit him. And it is Captain Farrago, paradoxically, who seems entrenched in a code that restricts him to an outmoded social order. The argument has been made by a historian that, contrary to the usual scholarly representation, there was a "fundamental affinity" between the "peasant-smallholder or artisan-proprietor outlook of most European immigrants to America" and the "classical republican ideals with which the American Revolution endowed the United States."[87] Identifying, as I have done, and as Brackenridge did in the *Six Political Discourses Founded on Scripture,* "the half-

86. Mary Douglas, *Natural Symbols: Explorations in Cosmology* (New York: Pantheon, 1982), pp. 37–53.

87. Rowland Berthoff, "Peasants and Artisans, Puritans and Republicans: Personal Liberty and Communal Equality in American History," *Journal of American History* 69 (1982): 579.

static, half-progressive American conflation of republican virtue
with millennial striving," and aligning with these temporal models
a social ideal that promoted, simultaneously, the value of individual personal liberty *and* that of communal equality, Berthoff finds
that the worldviews of European peasant immigrants were surprisingly quite compatible with the different American social context into which they entered. Citing recent studies of premodern
European peasant social experience that reject our quaint inherited picture of unchanging routines and profound traditionalism
in favor of a surprising degree of social mobility and a remarkable
degree of protomodern, self-interested, individualistic, market-
oriented social belief and behavior, he speculates that peasant immigrants of this kind were only too ready to become bourgeois
Americans.

> Not only . . . did almost all kinds of people of Euro-
> pean origin share a common pattern of modern practi-
> cal experience: headlong economic change, unsettling
> of traditional primary institutions, disordering of the
> social order, and reactionary, often self-defeating,
> spasms of reform. They also shared an ideology, for all
> that it was an often unstable mixture of static peasant-
> Puritan-republican nostalgia and dynamic secular-
> millennial progressivism.[88]

Teague O'Regan and his author would seem to support this view,
for this bog Irishman is only too ready to forget his ascriptive
social origins and write his own ticket to acquisitive success.
Teague manages to do so in spite of the thick brogue that marks
him in the text of the novel as aberrant.

VIII. Phonology and Politics

The circumstances of political groundlessness — the sensation of a
nation constituted out of speech acts, resting on no ancient authority, arbitrarily located on a geography to which it had no immemorial attachment, composed of conflicting languages and

88. Ibid., p. 598.

multiple ethnic, religious, and racial fractions — resulted in the
1790s in what appeared to some observers to be a general legitimation crisis. In the words of a recent historian of the period, the
1790s were "characterized by the deepening and broadening of
the country's political and sectional divisions," and by the institu-
tionalization of those divisions in the formation of contesting political parties.[89] The large problem of legitimation-by-words had
been present to Brackenridge constantly while writing *Modern
Chivalry,* and had been thematized in a variety of ways, as I have
shown: both in the action of the story and in the content of the
editorial commentary, but also in the very form of the text, which
exhibited its fractures and sought ways to overcome its divisions
by linguistic and textual means. These concerns reached a particular climax in Volume IV (1797), published in one of the years of
most discouraging national crisis, and reflecting in its plot Brackenridge's recent involvement in one of the most violent episodes
of the national legitimation crisis, the Whiskey Rebellion of
1794.[90]

The previous installment of *Modern Chivalry,* Book III (1793),
had opened with a restatement of Brackenridge's initial linguistic
program: "Proceeding with my object; the giving an example of a
perfect stile in writing, I come now to the third volume of the
work" (p. 161). This reaffirmation of the ideological project of
language normalization coincides, not surprisingly, with the historical moment of Constitutional ratification, and seems to align
Brackenridge's ambitious literary/linguistic project quite closely

89. James Roger Sharp, *American Politics in the Early Republic: The New Nation
in Crisis* (New Haven: Yale Univ. Press, 1993), p. 11. Cathy N. Davidson discusses
the ways in which the picaresque novel — of which *Modern Chivalry* is her chief
example — "mobilizes disharmonious ideologies . . . [producing] a raw (if ener-
getic) republic, a diverse and divided society in which the inherent contradictions
of republican discourse have not been totalized." Davidson, *Revolution and the
Word,* p. 165.

90. Thomas P. Slaughter, *The Whiskey Rebellion: Frontier Epilogue to the American
Revolution* (New York: Oxford Univ. Press, 1986). Summary accounts of the Whiskey Rebellion can be found in Sharp, *American Politics in the Early Republic,* pp.
92ff., and Stanley Elkins and Eric McKitrick, *The Age of Federalism: The Early American Republic, 1788–1800* (New York: Oxford Univ. Press, 1993), pp. 461ff. Brackenridge's role is described in Claude Milton Newlin, *The Life and Writings of Hugh
Henry Brackenridge* (1932; repr. Mamaroneck, New York: Paul P. Appel, 1971),
pp. 134ff. Brackenridge himself wrote *Incidents of the Insurrection in the Western
Parts of Pennsylvania, in the Year 1794* (Philadelphia: M'Culloch, 1795).

with the elation of national consolidation. The Constitution was ratified by the necessary nine-state minimum in 1788, and George Washington took office a year later; the national capital was moved from New York to Philadelphia in 1790, and in 1791 the Bill of Rights was ratified by the states, thus easing some of the anti-Federalist misgivings about the Constitution and presumably solidifying a national consensus. The "Conclusion of the Third Volume" contained the summons referred to earlier in this chapter, Brackenridge's imaginarily oral/aural address to his silent and unresponsive readers: "I wish I could get this work to make a little more noise," he wrote. "Will no body speak? What? Ho! are ye all asleep in the hold there down at Philadelphia?" (p. 250). This outburst plainly betrays a certain nervousness about the literary public sphere, a sense that the arena of communication is not perfectly operative; but it also registers a continuing hope that communicational solidarity will not lapse, and that the print medium can retain the charisma of voice.

Volume IV, published four years later, begins with the self-conscious textual suture also mentioned earlier: "A Chapter to Be Referred to the Third Volume at the Conclusion" (p. 253). Although George Washington had in 1797 just retired from the Presidency, this chapter retrospectively situates its events during the first national administration, describing Teague's appointment by President Washington to the post of excise officer (p. 254). Teague will soon enough discover, when he attempts to perform his duties as a tax collector in western Pennsylvania, that the authority of the federal government invested in him is not universally respected by the populace; but for the moment he is elevated from personal servant to public servant, and Captain Farrago hires in his place a new bog-trotter, a rigid Presbyterian immigrant from Scotland named Duncan Ferguson. This "raw Scotchman" (p. 257), unlike Teague, has no ambition to elevate himself either socially or politically. On the contrary, he is a rigid adherent of conservative principles in religion and politics: mortally horrified when another traveler's valet expresses unorthodox religious opinions (possibly derived from "Thomas Paine's Age of Reason, which had been published about this time," thus placing the action around 1794/95 [p. 260]), he also deplores the general mediocrity of economic and social status in America, recalling nostalgically the status distinctions in his native Scotland: "It is settled wi' a better stock o' people; and we hae dukes and lairds amang us; no as it is here, where ye may gae a day's journey, and no hear of a piper at a great house, or see a castle; but a' the folks, and their habitiations, luking just for a' the warld like our cotters in Scotland" (p. 265). Duncan repeatedly protests against the lack of social hierarchy and the inversions of social hierarchy he observes in America. "Every thing seems to be *orsa versa* here; the wrang side uppermost" (p. 267). "I see they hae every thing tail foremost in this kintra, to what they hae in Scotland: a gauger a gentleman; and weavers in the legislature" (p. 282). Duncan is thus scandalized when he and Captain Farrago meet Teague on the road, for he judges the office of taxman to be "next to a hangman in our kintra," hence entitled to no respect (p. 268); Brackenridge here seems to be indicating economically that an ancient prejudice against tax-collectors, part of an ethnically marked peasant world view, was part of the explanation for this particular resistance to the encroachment of federal authority. And of course, as a Protestant, Duncan finds Teague's Irish Catholicism to be a vile primitive superstition (p. 269). Teague and Duncan are on the verge of a violent altercation when Captain Farrago soothes them, ineffectually urging "that we cultivate peace, and have no difference" (p. 269).

Farrago's pacification of these sectarian and political opponents is only intermittently effective, for Teague in turn is scandalized to have his former master stoop so low as to employ as a servant "dat teef-luking son o'd a whore, dat has no more manners, dan a shape stealer in Ireland . . . de son of a whore, to spake to your honor wid a brogue upon his tongue, in such words as dese" (p. 271).[91] The narrator explains: "By the brogue, Teague meant the Scottish dialect, which Duncan used" (p. 271). Teague's blissful unawareness of his *own* brogue would seem to be a simple piece of dramatic irony to which we, as readers, are invited to be alert: they both have brogues, but neither one can hear his own, despite being alert to the other's, while we readers are able to detect both. The question arises, however, whether perhaps we too are oblivi-

---

91. Notice that Teague's vulgarism, "son o'd a whore," is corrected to the normal "son of a whore" a moment later; whether this is Brackenridge's inconsistency

ous of our own speech irregularities. Thus the relativization here of brogue or dialect effectively prevents the reader (who, after all, in the silent act of reading is imaginarily performing *both* brogues) from exempting himself from the taint of nonstandard speech. What if we, like Teague or Duncan, are stupidly unconscious of our own defective pronunciations too?

The collapse of the spoken norm performed here by Brackenridge, or performed by the reader at Brackenridge's instigation, leaves us to try to imagine what normative linguistic medium might be a creditable alternative to this *mise-en-abyme* of self-consuming oral norms, or, more properly, this echo chamber of competing and relational pronunciational norms that cancel out each other's claims to normality. And since Brackenridge, in asking his readers to produce silently the aural referents of the words on the page, is also asking them to confront the social, religious, and political differences embodied here phonologically, the mere linguistic problem on the page and in the reader's ear stands in for the attendant political problems of the 1790s.

Captain Farrago, weary of Teague's and Duncan's incessant bickering, in order to separate the combatants urges Teague to go on ahead of them to "open up an office in the district," while he and Duncan "remain a day at the public house where he then was, in order to give the revenue officer the advantage of the start" (p. 275). The day's interval Farrago concocts for the sake of peace between the Scotchman and the Irishman opens up as well a gap in the narrative discourse for Brackenridge to fill. And here it is as if a casual comic moment a few pages earlier, in which Teague's inability to read his wristwatch is exploited for Farrago's amusement, will suggest a line of inquiry and speculation having to do with the potential virtues of nonphonetic language(s).

> But Teague, said the Captain, how can you distinguish
> the figures of your watch, so as to tell the hours of the
> day; you that do not understand figures?
> By my shoul, said Teague, and I never tought of dat.

---

or Teague's self-correction is unclear. It is, of course, consistent with the Irishman's aspersions on the Scotchman's vocal irregularity that he should strive to mimic the norm himself.

Will not de figures spake for demselves, when I look
at dem. I am sure, I saw the son of a whore dat I got
her from, look at her, and tell the hour o' de day, like
a pracher at his books. (p. 270)

Teague's innumeracy (rather a disqualification for a revenue officer, one might think) as well as his illiteracy (he is so innocent of
letters that a preacher he has observed reading is imagined to have
been somehow *hearing* the pages speak)[92] are funny enough, but
Brackenridge has a sly purpose here. The fantasy of a semiotic system that would be immediately legible without training, a language that would operate naturally not conventionally, is here represented as the odd wish of a simple fool, but of course it was also
the cherished dream of countless intellectuals in this period. In
particular, many of the universal language schemes took as their
utopian model that of a nonalphabetic, nonphonetic language
(sometimes imagined as being as nonarbitrary as numbers were
held to be). Thus Teague's trust that numerical figures could
"spake for demselves, when I look at dem," unconsciously parod-
ies the fantasies of, among others, certain members of the American Philosophical Society.

Brackenridge drops the topic quickly but returns to it in the
next chapter when concocting an adventure for Captain Farrago
and Duncan to occupy them while Teague goes forward speedily
to his destination. The Captain takes the opportunity of an unoc-
cupied day to visit a cave in the area of which he had heard and
"which was thought to be a great curiosity" (p. 275). Brackenridge had at least once before let his imagination dwell in a cave:
his second work of prose fiction, a story called "The Cave Of
Vanhest," which appeared serially in the *United States Magazine*
from January to July 1779, had concerned a cultivated hermit who

92. Cf. Olaudah Equiano, *The Life of Olaudah Equiano, or Gustavus Vassa the Af-
rican. Written by Himself* (1837; New York: Negro Universities Press, 1969). First
published in 1789, one of the most famous passages in Equiano's narrative describes how after often seeing his master reading, he "had a great curiosity to talk
to the books" as he thought his master did: "For that purpose I have often taken
up a book, and have talked to it, and then put my ears to it, when alone, in hopes
it would answer me; and I have been very much concerned when I found it remained silent" (p. 62). Just possibly Brackenridge was inspired by Equiano's com-

sought refuge from the disorders of revolution in a New Jersey
cavern. Described as "a kind of gothic building in the bosom of
the mountain,"[93] the seemingly primitive and natural dwelling-
place is in fact furnished with all the accouterments of ancient civilization—china, silver, vases, chintz, rich carpets, and so forth.
This oxymoronic association of a *cave* with ancient *civilization,*
with the dense elaboration of long-preserved cultural forms, sub-
tends Brackenridge's cave episode in *Modern Chivalry* too. The
cave's mouth opened onto the bank of a small river, and near the
opening there were "certain rude sculptures, observable on a flat
rock" and "others on a perpendicular one that composed a part of
the bank" (p. 275). Captain Farrago is led to wonder whether
these sculptures—"the figure of the tarapin, the bear, the turkey,
&c."—were man-made or not. These figures, he conjectures,
might have been "made by the animals themselves, while the rock
had been in plastic state, and before it had hardened from clay
into stone" (p. 275)—that is, they might be signs that predate
human cultural agency, signs produced, so to speak, by nature itself. Or, on another conjecture, they might be "the work of the
savages, before the Europeans had possession of the country"
(p. 275). "He lamented that he had not a philosopher at hand, to
determine this. On the bank above, and toward the mouth of the
cave, were a number of petrifactions to be found; the water that
ran here, appearing hence to have a petrifying quality" (p. 275).
This guess that the water flowing out of the cave had petrifying
properties is confirmed when they enter the cave, and discover
that the water oozing there gradually forms stalactites, but also
petrifies the skeletons, bows and arrows, hatchets and other tools
deposited therein; the water *writes,* that is to say: in its flow from
the cave it composes the hieroglyphic text Captain Farrago reads
on the rock surface. The question of this text's authorship seems
undecidable: maybe nature wrote the signs, or maybe the "savages" did. In a sense it doesn't matter whether or not Indians

edy, and tried subliminally to heighten the effect of Teague's primitivism by allying
it with that of an illiterate African-American slave.

93. Hugh Henry Brackenridge, "The Cave of Vanhest," in *A Hugh Henry Brackenridge Reader, 1770–1815,* ed. Daniel Marder (Pittsburgh: Univ. of Pittsburgh
Press, 1970), p. 79.

made the pictographs, however, because, as the narrator says shortly after, what makes it likely that aborigines produced them is the fact that "there is no alphabetic mark of any language" near them (p. 280). That is, native American languages are strictly pictographic, not phonetic, and thus are as "natural" as if flowing water or the animals themselves had made them.

The oozing water in the cave turns out to be capable not only of gradual petrification of human remains and implements, but also of *instant* petrification of human bodies themselves. In another part of the cave they find

> trees in their natural position, with wasps nests on them, all petrified; and buffaloes standing under, in their proper form, but as hard as adament. A bleak wind, with a petrifying dew, had arrested them in life, and fixed them to the spot; while the mountain in a series of ages, had grown over them. That which struck the Captain most, was an Indian man reduced to stone, with a bundle of peltry on his back. If the virtuosi of Italy, could have access to this vault, there would be danger of them robbing it of some of these figures, in order to compare with the statues that have been made by hands. (p. 277)

Brackenridge was an ardent longtime proponent of Indian extermination, so it is not hard to see that this fantasy of instant Indian petrification — their immediate conversion into inert pseudoantiquities — expresses, at the very least, a genocidal wish. Here the natives are happily extinguished by natural processes, not by European invaders; and they are converted *for* European settlers into artworks that endow America with a handy, immemorial past, one that rivals in its aura of ancient civilization even the remote past signified by the neo-Roman sculptural art of the invoked Italian virtuosi. Brackenridge's cave fantasy answers exactly the need of the new nation for an ancient past deeply rooted in the landscape, and an attendant nonphonetic linguistic system that would obviate the altercating voices of the politically divisive present.

Following this eerie chapter, the narrator predictably produces a chapter "Containing Observations," signaling the relative anomaly, at this late stage of the novel, of such rational-discursive chapters by addressing his readers: "It may be observed, that as I advance in my book, I make fewer chapters, by way of commentary, and occupy myself chiefly with the narrative" (p. 278). Thus drawing attention (as he calls a halt) to his narrative of escalating social fractiousness, his nonnarrative chapter then proceeds to dwell in the cave, as it were, comparing these pictographs with others he has seen, speculating on their origins, lamenting the disappearance of the "savages of taste" (p. 280) or "more improved race" (p. 281) who made them (and who were destroyed by less civilized natives — "barbarians of the north" [p. 261] — who invaded and occupied the territory). Thus displacing responsibility for the destruction of these superior native tribes onto other, more primitive Indians, the universal pictographic language that is now their only trace is left in the possession of the succeeding white settlers, whose "connoisseurs" are urged "to apply to the legislature of the state" to preserve the cave and its contents for Euro-American posterity (p. 277).

The utility of this conservation is indicated elliptically when the narrator compliments himself on possessing "the distinguishing characteristic of a man, a taste for the fine arts" that enables him to appreciate these sculptures (p. 281). In what looks at first like an odd mental wandering or irrelevant outburst of political pique, the narrator observes that such artistic taste is "too little valued in America, where a system of finance, has introduced the love of unequal wealth; destroyed the spirit of common industry; and planted that of lottery in the human heart; making the mass of the people gamblers; and under the idea of speculation, shrouded engrossing and monopoly every where" (p. 281). The suddenness of this editorial intrusion seems to measure Brackenridge's growing opposition to Hamiltonian economic policy and its emphasis on paper wealth. The basic Jeffersonian argument against Hamilton's Treasury is fully implied here: money has no intrinsic value when it is hostage to financial markets and when wage labor replaces household and agricultural labor. "Taste" here means not just art appreciation but the republican taste for rootedness in the soil, for a universal language that would be without referential ambiguity, and for the impulse to "cultivate peace and have no difference" that is condensed in the wish for a nonalphabetic, nonphonological, silent language given to men as the gift of nature.

CHAPTER FIVE

Coda: The Voice of Patrick Henry

> *It is all speaking, speaking, speaking.*
> *William Wirt to Judge Dabney Carr, August 20,*
> *1815.*

THE VOICE OF PATRICK HENRY gave to the American Revolution its "impulse," William Wirt wrote in 1818. This "revolutionary impulse,"[1] proceeding from the voice of Henry, was the necessary force that produced all subsequent revolutionary action: "It was he alone, who, by his single power moved the mighty mass of stagnant waters, and changed the silent lake into a roaring torrent" (p. 433). In fact, "there can be no room for a candid doubt that, but for the bold spirit and overpowering eloquence of Patrick Henry, the people would have followed the pacific counsels" of more moderate leaders and submitted to British impositions rather than armed themselves for independence (p. 434).

Wirt's biography of Henry places the "supernatural voice" (p. 142) of his subject at the center of American history: it is the motive force—the "pure source," to recall James Wilson's phrase of 1793 (see chapter 1 above)—of the Revolution. It is, however, a strangely absent force or source, since Wirt admitted both that he himself had never heard Henry's voice, and therefore could not describe it from personal knowledge, and that he had been hard pressed to find what he called "a single authentic trace" of that

---

1. William Wirt, *Sketches of the Life and Character of Patrick Henry,* 9th ed. (Philadelphia: De Silver, Thomas & Co., 1836), p. 432. Further page references will be given parenthetically in the text.

voice (p. 82 n). Patrick Henry's celebrated speeches were never written down, hence did not survive in manuscript or in print; and even if they had survived, the written text would be a necessarily inadequate representation of the sublime effects that Henry's voice had by all accounts produced in his listeners' ears. So what Wirt had to do—all that he *could* do—was gather the recollections of those who *had* heard Henry speak and could give a firsthand description of those effects, and ask them to consult their memories as carefully as possible. Such descriptive accounts, however, even when combined with reconstructed written texts of Henry's words, could at best only vaguely approximate the phenomenological force of the vocal and auditory event.

Much of Wirt's research for his biography of the Virginian orator therefore consisted of a painstaking but hopeless effort to gather textual traces—as nearly authentic as possible—of Henry's voice. He first designed to write the biography in the summer of 1805, and immediately began to gather sources. He wrote to survivors of the founding era, all those who he believed might provide personal knowledge of the subject (p. v). The project took on the character of a determined attempt, at a moment when the revolutionary generation was aging and dying, and its memory was receding, to recover the origin of the Revolution and, indeed, of the new nation. Wirt's claim was that that origin could be located in the voice of Patrick Henry. His book was therefore governed by the trope of revolutionary vocalization that had precedents in earlier reflections on the Revolution and, indeed, in the texts of the Revolution itself.

William Wirt was one of the more peculiar public figures of the postrevolutionary era. Born in 1772, making him by one year the junior of Charles Brockden Brown, he began his practice of law in Virginia in the post-Constitutional year of 1792. He first came to public notice as a defense counsel to James Callender (later a notorious calumniator of Jefferson, purveyor of the scandalous rumor that the president had fathered children by his alleged slave mistress Sally Hemings), when Callender was prosecuted under the Alien and Sedition Acts. Wirt was thus allied, despite Callender's later anti-Jeffersonianism, with the nascent political-ideological formation of Jeffersonian Republicanism, formed in part in opposition to the notorious Federalist laws against sedition which found in Callender's pamphleteering a target for prosecution. Wirt would again be publicly allied with Jeffersonianism in 1806 as a prosecutor of Aaron Burr for treason, when Burr's plot to form a new republic in the west was discovered. Even as Wirt ascended to legal eminence, he coveted literary fame, and so he published several series of essays — *The Letters of the British Spy* (1803), *The Rainbow* (1804), *The Old Bachelor* (1810–13) — that achieved considerable contemporary popularity if not long-term critical esteem. Wirt eventually placed his hopes for permanent literary eminence on the success of his arduously researched biography of Patrick Henry, which he published finally in 1817. This work culminated a theme that had been present in his earlier writings, and that was a guiding motive in his public career: the theme of a general political declension from the heroic time of the Revolution, and the importance of oratory — of leadership *viva voce* — in the recovery of lost political greatness.

The biography of Henry met with a mixed critical reception. It was quite unabashedly laudatory, even hagiographic, and in its manner ornate and apologetic — thus earning from Jefferson, who assisted Wirt in his research and vetted the manuscript, a harsh and dismissive private judgment, delivered in 1824 to a visiting Daniel Webster, who made a record of Jefferson's words during his visit to Monticello:

> [Wirt] sent the sheets of his work to me, as they were printed, & at the end asked for my opinion. I told him it would be a question hereafter, whether his work should be placed on the shelf of *history,* or of *panegyric.* It is a poor book, written in bad taste, & gives so imperfect an idea of Patrick Henry, that it seems intended to show off the *writer,* more than the subject of the work.[2]

Such privately held opinions had no effect on Wirt's public rise: just as the book appeared in 1817, he was named attorney general of the United States by President James Monroe, a post he held

2. Daniel Webster, *The Papers of Daniel Webster, Correspondence,* ed. Charles M. Wiltse (Hanover, New Hampshire: Univ. Press of New England, 1974), 1: 373.

for twelve consecutive years, continuing through the administration of John Quincy Adams. With Andrew Jackson's election in 1829, Wirt returned to private life and to his own legal practice, in Baltimore now. Somewhat reluctantly he accepted the dubious honor of serving as the presidential candidate of the Anti-Masonic Party in 1831; he actually supported the candidacy of Henry Clay, the likely Whig candidate, but, knowing that the Anti-Masonic Party wouldn't ever support Clay, he consented to receive the Anti-Masonic nomination in an effort to try to unify the Whigs and Anti-Masonics against Jackson. The Whigs stayed with Clay, however, unconvinced that such a coalition could defeat Jackson, and although Wirt then wished to withdraw, he felt he couldn't desert those who had put him forward. Needless to say, he was not elected. His final years were spent in a fruitless attempt to establish a German immigrant colony on land he owned in Florida. Wirt died in 1834, and his chief achievements, despite his preference for literary glory, were his tenure as attorney general and his systematization of that office's practices (he began the cumulation and preservation of the office's opinions, to establish a body of precedent for his successors).

Wirt's career was consistently marked by an intense concern for the condition of the political public sphere, the quality of national leadership, and the important role of speech and language in political practice. The biography of Patrick Henry was the project in which he was most strenuously invested: it was an attempt to recapture the vocal origin of the United States, the originary utterance of America, or whatever traces of it were still recoverable. In the records of Wirt's laborious, painstaking, and endlessly frustrating research, we may find traces of the era's belief in such an originary utterance, and evidence of the period's sense of that utterance as a fading and nearly inaudible memory.

When Wirt undertook to write a biography of Patrick Henry, he didn't know the crucial literary and historiographical problems he would encounter, problems that would lead him to call this work of writing "the most oppressive literary enterprise that ever I embarked in."[3] Patrick Henry's voice was the central fact of the

3. John P. Kennedy, *Memoirs of the Life of William Wirt, Attorney General of the United States,* 2 vols. (Philadelphia: Lea and Blanchard, 1849), 1: 387.

statesman-orator's life, as Wirt saw it, but that voice was now faint and irrecoverable. Wirt complained, while doing his research, that "the incidents of Mr. Henry's life are extremely monotonous. It is all speaking, speaking, speaking. 'Tis true he could talk: — 'Gods! how he *could* talk!' but there is no acting 'the while.' . . . And then, to make the matter worse, from 1763 to 1789, covering all the bloom and pride of his life, not one of his speeches lives in print, writing or memory."[4] Despite this initial readiness to conceive of speaking and acting as necessarily different phenomena, Wirt soon realized that for Henry and other founders, the distinction could not be sustained: to speak *was* to act.

Wirt's biography was criticized for having unfairly privileged Patrick Henry's voice as the unmoved mover of revolutionary action. Wirt had been concerned, as were others, to isolate the beginning of the Revolution — to name its origin, its first cause. There was, not surprisingly, some rivalry between Massachusetts and Virginia for the honor of inciting the rebellion, and Wirt, a Virginian himself, predictably chose to assign the honor to his home state. He also somewhat less predictably assigned the incendiary honor of revolutionary instigation to the upper classes of Virginia, and claimed, somewhat preposterously (since Henry was known as an uncouth and ill-educated person) that Patrick Henry was their leader: "The American revolution is universally admitted to have begun in the upper circles of society. . . . Since, then, the upper circle of society did not take its impulse from the people, the only remaining inquiry is, who gave the revolutionary impulse to that circle itself? It was unquestionably Patrick Henry" (p. 432). Henry, in this account, not only imparted to the upper classes the revolutionary impulse they then transmitted to the people at large, he did it more than once. Quoting Jefferson's claim "that 'Mr. Henry certainly gave the first impulse to the ball of the revolution,'" Wirt cited 1764 — the year of the Stamp Act — as "memorable for the origination of that great question which led finally to the independence of the United States" (p. 59). Henry came into a legislative body filled with other powerful voices — Edmund Pendleton "had that silver voice* of which Cic-

    4. Kennedy, 1: 388–89.

ero makes such frequent and honourable mention [*Vox argen-
tea. See the Brutus, *passim.*]" (p. 65), while Richard Henry Lee
had "the canorous voice* of Cicero [*Vox canora. See the Brutus,
passim.]" (p. 68) — and he had the temerity to introduce in his
"voice of thunder" (p. 83), and employing what Jefferson (who
heard him on the spot) called "torrents of sublime eloquence" (p.
78), his celebrated resolutions in opposition to the Stamp Act. On
May 30, 1765, newly elected to the Virginia House of Burgesses,
a virtual political unknown, Henry, by virtue of sublime vocal
prowess, immediately made himself "the first statesman and orator
in Virginia," "the idol of the people of Virginia" (p. 84). "The
impulse thus given by Virginia, was caught by the other colonies"
soon after (pp. 84–85). Wirt does not give his readers the speech
with which Henry imparted this impulse; in fact, he condemns
another historian's "skeleton of Mr. Henry's speech" as "apocry-
phal," insisting that the only "authentic trace" of the speech is an
"anecdote" (p. 82 n) concerning, ironically, a *pause* in the speech:

> It was in the midst of this magnificent debate, while
> he [Henry] was descanting on the tyranny of the ob-
> noxious act, that he exclaimed in a voice of thunder,
> and with the look of a god: "Cesar had his Brutus —
> Charles the First, his Cromwell — and George the
> Third — ('Treason!' cried the speaker — 'Treason, trea-
> son!' echoed from every part of the house. It was one
> of those trying moments which is decisive of character.
> Henry faltered not for an instant; but rising to a loftier
> attitude, and fixing on the speaker an eye of the most
> determined fire, he finished his sentence with the
> firmest emphasis) — *may profit by their example.* If *this* be
> treason, make the most if it."*

---

*I had frequently heard the above anecdote of the cry
of treason, but with such variations of the concluding
words, that I began to doubt whether the whole might
not be fiction. With a view to ascertain the truth, therefore, I submitted it to Mr. Jefferson, as it had been
given to me by Judge Tyler, and this is his answer: —

"I well remember the cry of treason, the pause of Mr.
Henry at the name of George III., and the presence of
mind with which he closed his sentence, and baffled
the charge vociferated." The incident, therefore, becomes authentic history. (pp. 83–84)

Wirt's biographical text may be said to be about how a voice and
an act of speech become "authentic history," understanding "history" here in both its usual senses, as *histoire* and *recit* — the event
and its written record. It is about how the voice of Patrick Henry
could "create the destinies of nations" (p. 137) and how its traces
could be the stuff of historical narrative.

Henry, according to Wirt, gave the Revolution *another* start ten
years later, in 1775, both when he "excited the people, . . . put
them into motion" by leading an armed band to secure a muni-
tions magazine (p. 434), and then again when he urged Virginia
to arm itself for defense against the British in his celebrated "Liberty or Death" speech. In the case of this latter speech, unlike the
one of 1765, Wirt risked ridicule when he chose to reconstruct its
text, to try to represent its sublimity in writing. The speech he put
together, and published first in the *Portfolio* magazine in December
1816 in advance of the book's appearance, was thereafter much
reprinted and recited, and has occasioned much critical commentary and dispute over the question of authenticity. The history of
this critical quarreling has been amply detailed;[5] what is of interest
here is not whether Wirt's version of Henry's speech is authentic
(whatever that may mean), but the fact that the speech and the
question of its authenticity have been the site of such patriotic
historical investment. If one took the reasonable view that a revolution doesn't have an assignable beginning, but rather is a complicated processual phenomenon resulting from numerous causes
that are finally inscrutable, one would not care so much about the
authenticity of Henry's speech. It is because it *is* assigned as *the*
(or at least *an*) origin of the Revolution that its authenticity or
purity — its integrity as a beginning — matters.

5. David A. McCants, "The Authenticity of William Wirt's Version of Patrick
Henry's 'Liberty or Death' Speech," *Virginia Magazine of History and Biography* 87
(1979): 387–402.

* * *

The American Revolution thus had several beginnings, but all of them were located by Wirt in the powerful vocalization of Patrick Henry. To specify such an origin was, some critics contended, biased, reductive, inaccurate, even fictive; such was the criticism offered by John Adams, for one, who wrote breathlessly to Wirt in 1818, right after publication, arguing that "the resistance to the British system for subjugating the colonies, began in 1760, and in 1761, in the month of February, when James Otis electrified the town of Boston, the Province of Massachusetts Bay and the whole continent, more than Patrick Henry ever did in the whole course of his life."[6] Wirt, in his reply to Adams, willingly conceded that he had given Henry and Virginia too much credit, and that to invest in an oratorical moment such causal influence was to specify the inception of the Revolution too particularly.[7] When Wirt, now attorney general of the United States, delivered a eulogy for both Adams and Jefferson before the House of Representatives, recognizing the extraordinary coincidence of their simultaneous deaths on July 4, 1826 — fifty years to the day after the Declaration of Independence — he made some amends (possibly remembering Adams's resentment) for his earlier elevation of Patrick Henry's and Virginia's originary role by distributing the privilege of revolutionary instigation more widely, and he effected this redistribution in a way that elaborated the conceit of a vocal origin: the "almost superhuman eloquence of Henry" inspired Jefferson, Wirt averred, while the equally transcendent eloquence of James Otis did the same for Adams, and "whether Otis or Henry first breathed into this nation the breath of life, (a question merely for curious and friendly speculation,) it is very certain that they breathed into their hearers that breath which has made them both immortal."[8] This was some heavy breathing indeed, for it definitively located the Revolution's origin in the nearly immaterial motion of an evanescent breath of air.

6. Kennedy, *Memoirs,* 2: 45.
7. Ibid., 2: 46–48.
8. Wirt, "Wirt's Eulogy on Jefferson," *The Writings of Thomas Jefferson,* 20 vols., ed. Andrew A. Lipscomb and Albert Ellerg Bergh (Washington, D.C.: The Thomas Jefferson Memorial Association, 1905), 13: xv, xvi.

The records of Wirt's researches on Patrick Henry show him searching obsessively for adequate written means faithfully to represent Henry's eloquence. "I never heard nor saw Mr. Henry," he wrote to Jefferson in 1810, "and am, therefore, anxious to have a distinct view of the peculiarities of his character as a man, a politician, and an orator; and particularly of the grounds and points of his excellence in the latter aspect."[9] He appealed to St. George Tucker for first-hand testimony:

> Sketch, as minutely as you could, even to the color of his eyes, a portrait of his person, attitudes, gestures, manners; a description of his voice, its tone, energy, and modulations; his delivery, whether slow, grave and solemn, or rapid, sprightly, and animated; his pronunciation, whether studiously plain, homely, and sometimes vulgar, or accurate, courtly and ornate, — with an analysis of his mind, the variety, order and predominance of its powers; his information as a lawyer, a politician, a scholar; the peculiar character of his eloquence, &c.[10]

To Dabney Carr he wrote,

> I have sometimes a notion of trying the plan of [Carlo Giuseppe Guglielmo] Botta, who has written an account of the American war [*Storia della guerra Americana,* Paris, 1809], and made speeches himself for his prominent characters, imitating, in this, the historians of Greece and Rome; but I think with Polybius, that this is making too free with the sanctity of history. Besides, Henry's eloquence was all so completely *sui generis* as to be inimitable by any other: and to make *my* chance of imitating him still worse, I never saw or heard him.[11]

Wirt asked Richard Morris for criticism, submitting to Morris the manuscript of the biography, and when Morris returned it with-

---

9. Kennedy, *Memoirs,* 1: 279.
10. Ibid., 1: 129.
11. Ibid., 1: 389.

out any criticism, Wirt wrote back chiding Morris, and providing some "hypothetic strictures . . . the very remarks to which I fear my book is liable": "your book abounds with many striking specimens of the false sublime. . . . The speeches that you give as his, contradict your own pompous descriptions of his eloquence."[12] Wirt had allowed himself, he recognized, to risk an attempt to recover the irrecoverable, to simulate in writing the vocal sublime: he had reconstructed, as well as he could, Henry's famous "Liberty or Death" speech, only to find his anxious forebodings justified. The authenticity of the speech was disputed then, and is challenged to this day.[13]

Wirt's narrative account of Henry's first public speech — an argument before the bar in Hanover county — is a classic paean to the vocal sublime, and it shows him characteristically falling back on the trope of inexpressibility to convey the excessively powerful effects of Henry's oratorical delivery:

> For now were those wonderful faculties which he possessed, for the first time, developed; and now was first witnessed that mysterious and almost supernatural transformation of appearance, which the fire of his own eloquence never failed to work in him. . . . His action became graceful, bold, and commanding; and in the tones of his voice, but more especially in his emphasis, there was a peculiar charm, a magic, of which any one who ever heard him will speak as soon as he is named, but of which no one can give any adequate description. They can only say that it struck upon the ear and upon the heart, *in a manner which language cannot tell.* (pp. 43–44)

"I have tried much to procure a sketch of this celebrated speech," Wirt wrote. "But those of Mr. Henry's hearers who survive, seem to have been bereft of their senses" (p. 46). These contemporary auditors could tell how they *felt* while they listened, but could not recall what they had heard. Jefferson, for instance, confessed to

12. Kennedy, 1: 367.
13. See n. 5, above. The speech is in Wirt, *Sketches,* pp. 137–42.

Daniel Webster, when Webster visited him in 1824, that he had sometimes been rendered insensible by the influence of Henry's voice:

> His eloquence was peculiar; if indeed it should be called eloquence, for it was impressive & sublime beyond what can be imagined. Although it was difficult when he had spoken, to tell what he had said, yet while he was speaking, it always seemed directly to the point. When he had spoken in opposition to *my* opinion, had produced a great effect, & I myself been highly delighted & moved, I have asked myself when he ceased, "What the Devil has he said," & could never answer the enquiry.[14]

The result of Wirt's obsessive search for Patrick Henry's voice was a series of prose descriptions in the biography that tried to represent the charisma of that voice. One of the more charming of these descriptions comes near the end of the *Sketches,* where Wirt is summoning all his literary powers to convey what he has repeatedly said is unconveyable, the phenomenologically exquisite effects of Henry speaking:

> His voice was not remarkable for its sweetness; but it was firm, of full volume, and rather melodious than otherwise. Its charms consisted in the mellowness and fulness of its note, the ease and variety of its inflections, the distinctness of its articulation, the fine effect of its emphasis, the felicity with which it attuned itself to every emotion, and the vast compass which enabled it to range through the whole empire of human passion, from the deep and tragic half whisper of horror, to the wildest exclamation of overwhelming rage. In mild persuasion, it was as soft and gentle as the zephyr of spring; while in rousing his countrymen to arms, the winter storm that roars along the troubled Baltic, was not more awfully sublime. It was at all times per-

14. Webster, 1: 372.

fectly under his command; or rather, indeed, it seemed to command itself and to modulate its notes, most happily to the sentiment he was uttering. It never exceeded, or fell short of the occasion. There was none of that long-continued and deafening vociferation, which always takes place when an ardent speaker has lost possession of himself— no monotonous clangour, no discordant shriek. Without being strained, it had that body and enunciation which filled the most distant ear, without distressing those which were nearest him: hence it never became cracked or hoarse, even in his longest speeches, but retained to the last all its clearness and fulness of intonation, all the delicacy of its inflection, all the charms of its emphasis, and enchanting variety of its cadence. (pp. 428–29)

This "irresistibly captivating" voice (p. 56), and the originary words it utters, both so intensely fetishized in postrevolutionary American culture, represented, as I began this book by saying, an insecure— historically and culturally ungrounded— nation's wish for a foundation of political and social unity, and at the same time it represented a myth of unconstrained, intentional, national self-invention. In the phenomenological integrity of the speaking voice, its imaginary conjunction of intention and expression— in Wirt's words describing Henry, its "clearness and fulness," its lack of discord, its seeming autonomy ("it seemed to command itself") — a divided and contentious nation found its preferred image of its origins. If it is true that the identity of the Western nation has been imaginarily embodied in a myth of "a unanimous people assembled in the self-presence of its speech,"[15] this myth encountered unique interferences in the United States. As Marc Shell has recently reminded us, while taking to task many of the studies of the politics of language in America and American language-planning for assuming an unproblematical anglophone monoglottism in the face of the manifest fact of American polyglottism, "If ever there were a polyglot place on the globe— other

15. Jacques Derrida, *Of Grammatology*, trans. Gayatri Chakravorty Spivak (Baltimore: Johns Hopkins Univ. Press, 1976), p. 134.

than Babel's spire—this [the United States in the early national period] was it."[16] Thus the image of a polis in unison (as Brackenridge showed) was defective in a polyglot nation. And James Wilson's figure of a "complete body of free persons united together," the concordant group of "natural persons . . . who spoke [the United States] into existence,"[17] similarly failed to address the manifest polyglottism of the United States, its manifestly discordant set of voices. Wirt's reduction of this discordant vocal mass to a single charismatic originary voice tries to erase these contentious sounds. Wirt's devoted description of this indescribable vocal phenomenon fairly vibrates with a yearning for the distant sound of the voice of Patrick Henry, a voice in the sonorous encompassment of which a vague and fractious nation could hear the wished-for tones of its original presence.

16. Marc Shell, "Babel in America: or, The Politics of Language Diversity in the United States," *Critical Inquiry* 20 (1993): 105.
17. See above, chapter 1.

INDEX

Adams, John, 18, 22, 24–25, 30–32, 33, 43, 57, 58, 59, 60, 188, 189, 209, 173; *Defence of the Constitutions of Government of the United States of America*, 31–32
Adams, John Quincy, 32, 269
Addison, Joseph, 117, 118–19n, 136
Adorno, Theodor, 186–87
Albanese, Catherine L., 225n
Alien and Sedition Acts, 267
Althusser, Louis, 241–42
American Philosophical Society, 261
American Revolution, 6, 14–15, 17, 21, 24, 30–33, 40–42, 44–45, 50, 55–57, 59, 66, 94, 99–101, 124–32, 137, 144, 147, 150, 157, 172–74, 188, 200, 240–41, 255, 266–67, 270, 272–73; antipatriarchal rhetoric of, 102, 132; dramatic quality of, 24–25; relationship to French Revolution, 45–50. See also *Autobiography of Benjamin Franklin;* Brackenridge, Hugh Henry; Henry, Patrick; *Wieland*
Anderson, Benedict, *Imagined Communities*, 5–6, 8
Andresen, Julie Tetel, 15n

Anti-Masonic Party, 269
Appleby, Joyce, 55n, 240n
Arendt, Hannah, 50–51
Arieli, Yehoshua, 250
Aristotle, 22
Articles of Confederation, 232
Augustine, Saint, 108
Austin, J. L., 163
Autobiography of Benjamin Franklin (Franklin), 99–144; American Revolution in, 101–2, 124–32, 144; conciliation in, 100, 111, 138–44; drama of filial autonomy in, 100, 102–18, 144; initiation into language in, 112–18, 159; textualized selfhood in, 110, 123n, 131–38; verbal imposture in, 118–24

Babel, 95, 278
Bailyn, Bernard, 70n, 225n, 226, 227
Bakhtin, Mikhail, 9, 28, 203–4, 205, 243, 245
Ball, Terence, 41
Bancroft, George, 229n
Baron, Dennis, 15n
Barthes, Roland, 123
Bastille, 61
Begriffsgeschichte, 40, 54n
Bell, Michael Davitt, 148n

Benveniste, Émile, 17, 26, 112–13n, 120, 170

Bercovitch, Sacvan, 8, 109, 225n, 226, 229n

Bernstein, Basil, 136–37, 255

Berthoff, Rowland, 241n, 255–56

Berthoff, Warner, 49n

Bible, 17, 18, 142–43n; Psalm 18, 119–20; source of American Revolutionary rhetoric, 224–29, 248

Bildungsroman, 206

Bill of Rights, 258

Bloch, Ruth, 225n, 227

Bonaparte, Napoleon, 58, 195–96

book topos, 108

Boon, James, 14

Boston, 69, 273

Botta, Carlo Giuseppe Guglielmo, 274

Brackenridge, Hugh Henry, 9, 28, 203–65, 278; in Pittsburgh, 207; in Whiskey Rebellion, 257; Scottish birth of, 221; service in American Revolution, 229–40. Works: "The Cave of Vanhest," 261–62; *Gazette Publications*, 230; *Incidents of the Insurrection*, 257n; *The Modern Chevalier*, 208; *Modern Chivalry*, 7, 8, 203–65; "Observations on the Country at the Head of the Ohio River," 21n; *Six Political Discourses Founded on Scripture*, 231–40, 255

Braddock, Edward, 76–77

Bradford, Andrew, 140

Breitwieser, Mitchell, 7, 109n, 209

broadside, by "Tradesman," 33–34, 96–98

Brown, Charles Brockden, 9, 28, 145–202, 267; anti-Jeffersonianism of, 194–202; as lawyer, 146, 180–81, 188;

childhood of, 179; political pamphleteering of, 193–202; Quakerism of family, 179–80. Works: *An Address to the Congress*, 195, 200–202; *An Address to the Government*, 194, 195–97, 198; *Alcuin*, 178, 194; *The British Treaty*, 195, 198–200; *Memoirs of Stephen Calvert*, 187; *Monroe's Embassy*, 194–95, 197–98; "New French Political Nomenclature," 49; "On the Scheme of an American Language," 49–50; "Series of Original Letters," 181–85; "Statements of destruction produced by the French Revolution," 49; *Wieland*, 5, 7, 8, 74n, 145–202

Brown, William Hill, *The Power of Sympathy*, 176–77n

Burgoyne, John, 233–37

Burke, Edmund, 40, 55, 60, 61, 62, 163

Burr, Aaron, 84, 268

Burton, Sir Richard, 243n

Bushman, Richard L., 141n

Butler, Samuel, 208, 243n

Bynack, V. P., 15n

Callender, James, 267

Camissards, 152

Carr, Dabney, 274

Carter, Edward C., II, 252n

Castoriadis, Cornelius, *The Imaginary Institution of Society*, 1

Cervantes, Miguel de, 236, 242–43, 243n

charisma, 4, 42, 44, 88, 278

Chaucer, Geoffrey, *Canterbury Tales*, 104

Chesapeake-Leonard Affair, 84

Cheyfitz, Eric, 204n

Chisholm v. Georgia, 19–21

Cicero, 22, 158–65, 270–71; *Pro Cluentio*, 161–65, 177

Cmiel, Kenneth, 10
Clay, Henry, 269
Cobbett, William, 253
Colbourn, H. Trevor, 74n
Cole, Charles, 194
Collins, John, 116
Collinson, Peter, 251
Committee of Correspondence
  (Massachusetts), 69, 99
conciliation, Franklin's style of,
  100, 111
consent, 157, 164, 232–33, 250
Constitution: of the United
  States, 19–21, 28, 40, 42, 44–
  45, 85, 188–89, 194, 215, 252,
  257–58; of France, 60
Cooper, Thomas, 84–85
Cotton, John, 108, 108–9n,
  113n
Cotton, Roland, 108n
Cowie, Alexander, 145n
Cox, James M., 101–2n
Crèvecoeur, J. Hector St. John de,
  Letters from an American Farmer,
  175–79
Cushing, Thomas, 69–70, 77

Dartmouth, William Legge, 2d
  Earl of, 69–70
Davidson, Cathy N., 10, 206n,
  245n, 257n
Davis, David Brion, 176
Davis, Elizabeth, 110n
Dawson, Hugh J., 105n
Declaration of Independence, 3,
  4n, 21–23, 44, 65, 188, 273
deferral, 99–100, 123, 125, 133,
  135, 137, 144, 153, 156, 165,
  215
de la Chappelle, 173
Deleuze, Gilles, 132n
Demosthenes, 230
Denham, Thomas, 121–22
Derrida, Jacques, 25, 277; "Decla-
  rations of Independence," 3n,

22–23; "Double Session,"
  134n; *Of Grammatology,* 277n;
  Speech and Phenomena, 137,
  167–69
Destutt de Tracy, comte, 58
Dickinson, John, *Letters from a
  Farmer in Pennsylvania,* 188
dictionary, 52, 63
Dillard, J. L., 223n
Diodati, Charles, 46
Douglas, Mary, 255
Dupont de Nemours, Pierre Sam-
  uel, 85, 86

Edwards, Jonathan, 120n
Egnal, Marc, 134n
Elliott, Emory, 10, 148n, 225n,
  227
Ellis, Joseph J., 240–41n
eloquence, 21, 32, 116, 274
Enlightenment, 160
Equiano, Olaudah, 261n
Erasmus, Desiderius, 243n
ethnicity, 10. See also *Modern
  Chivalry*

Federalist, 249, 253
Federalist party, 57, 81, 85–86,
  160, 164, 268
Ferguson, Robert A., 10, 148n,
  161, 180
Fielding, Joseph, 211
Fisher, Mary, 103n
Fishman, Joshua, 15n, 204n,
  217n
Fliegelman, Jay: *Declaring Independence,* 4n, 10, 44n; *Prodigals and
  Pilgrims,* 10, 102, 132n, 148n,
  178–79, 190
Folger, Peter, 107, 110–11
form, literary, 6–9, 99, 127; of *Autobiography of Benjamin Franklin,*
  126–30, 133–34; of *Modern
  Chivalry,* 203, 206, 246; of *Wieland,* 146

Fortescue, Sir John, *De Laudibus Legum Angliae,* 104, 155, 156

Franklin, Abiah, 105, 107

Franklin, Benjamin, 2, 9, 23–24, 28, 33, 62, 87, 88, 99–144, 175, 208, 218, 251, 255; Albany Plan of, 77, 125, 126n; ancestry of, 103–12; and Hutchinson letters, 67–71; as colonial diplomat, 67–78; as postmaster, 76–77, 128; as printer, 116, 118–19n, 121; as "Silence Dogood," 114–15, 133; Cockpit, encounter in, 76; family name of, 104–5, 112–13; first published writing, 114–15; imitates *Spectator,* 116–18; Junto of, 119, 141; phonetic alphabet, design of, 101n; Senecan prose style of, 133; Socratic method of, 138–40; stammering of, 135–37. Works: *Autobiography,* 7, 8, 99–144, 151, 178; "Edict by the King of Prussia," 72–76, 157–58, 220; "A Parable on Brotherly Love," 143n; "Silence Dogood," 114, 133

Franklin, Uncle Benjamin, 104, 106, 110, 112–13, 134

Franklin, James, 103, 114–15, 133, 142–43

Franklin, John, 103

Franklin, Josiah, 105, 115–18, 140–44

Franklin, Thomas, 106

Franklin, William, 72, 103, 128, 128n

Franklin, William Temple, 104

French Revolution, 23, 40, 42, 44–46, 54–57, 66; relationship to American Revolution, 45–50

Freneau, Philip: *Father Bombo's Pilgrimage to Mecca* (with Brackenridge), 253; *A Poem on the Rising Glory of America* (with Brackenridge), 253

Furtwangler, Albert, 10

Fussell, Edwin, 148n

Gates, Horatio, 235

Gemeinschaft, 183

George III, King, 43, 74, 94–95, 232, 233, 238, 239, 271–72

Giddens, Anthony, 8–9

Gilmore, Michael, 10, 245

Godwin, William, 194

Gramsci, Antonio, 15–16

Great Awakening, 172

Greenblatt, Steven, 204n

Greene, Jack P., 103

Greven, Philip, 132n

Gustafson, Thomas, 10–11, 15n, 30n

Guattari, Felix, 132n

Habermas, Jürgen, 80, 186

Hall, Stuart, 242n

Halliday, M. A. K., 205

Hamilton, Alexander, 264

Hamilton, Andrew, 109n

Harkey, Joseph H., 242n

Harris, William F., II, 28

Hatch, Nathan O., 224

Hawthorne, Nathaniel, 13

Hemings, Sally, 267

Henry, Patrick, 4n, 5, 22, 172, 266–78; "Liberty or Death" speech, 8, 272, 275

Hesford, Walter, 148n

Hillsborough, Wills Hill, 1st Earl and 2d Viscount of, 102

history, 54, 92, 145; and language, 54–66

Hobbes, Thomas, 198

Hobsbawm, Eric, 242

Hoffa, William R., 243n

Homer, 48; *Iliad,* 235

Horkheimer, Max, 132n

Howard, Robert, *The Committee,* 254

Howe, General, 175

Humphreys, David, 59–60

Hunt, Lynn, 23n, 42
Husserl, Edmund, 186–87
Hutchinson, Thomas, 67–71,
    76–78
Hutchinson letters, controversy
    over, 67–78

ideology, 58
interpellation, 60
Irish, literary stereotype of, 249,
    251–56
Irving, Washington: *History of
    New York,* 2, 81–82, 88–93;
    "Rip Van Winkle," 43, 93–96;
    Salmagundi, 2, 8, 78–84, 149
Irving, William, 78n

Jackson, Andrew, 269
James, Abel, 129–30, 131, 134,
    218
James, Henry, 211; *Nathaniel
    Hawthorne,* 13; "The Question
    of Our Speech," 13–14
Jay, John, 59, 249–50, 253
Jefferson, Thomas, 2, 17, 18–19,
    21–22, 25, 45–49, 50, 51, 52–
    53, 56, 57, 58, 60, 66, 86–87,
    88, 146, 163–64, 193, 194,
    197, 209, 227, 252, 264, 268,
    270, 273, 275–76; Embargo
    policy of, 83, 200–201; in
    Irving, *History of New York,*
    81–82, 88–90; in Irving, *Sal-
    magundi,* 83–86, 88. Works:
    Autobiography, 23, 87; *Notes on
    the State of Virginia,* 104; *A Sum-
    mary View of the Rights of British
    America,* 155–56
Jehlen, Myra, 249
John, Saint, 239
Johnson, Samuel, 38, 39, 40, 216
Jones, Howard Mumford, 217
Jordan, Cynthia S., 11

Kammen, Michael, *A Season of
    Youth,* 42n

Keimer, Samuel, 139–40
Keith, Sir William, 121–23, 130,
    142
Kramer, Michael P., 11, 15n
Kramnick, Isaac, 224n, 225n
Kreyling, Michael, 148n

Lacan, Jacques, 1n, 106–7n,
    113–14
Lafayette, marquis de, 56
language, 1; and subjectivity,
    112–18, 120; English, Henry
    James on, 13–14; standardiza-
    tion, 15–16, 33, 171, 204–5,
    216–17; universal, 261
law, 148–49, 172, 174, 180–92
Lawrence, D. H., 135
Lee, Richard Henry, 271
Lefort, Claude, 80
legitimacy, 4, 146–47, 164;
    foundationlessness of in Uni-
    ted States, 6, 146, 157, 256–
    57
legitimation, discursive, 15, 44,
    80, 174, 257
Lemay, J. A. Leo, 107n, 109–10n,
    128n
Lerner, Ralph, 240
letters, 67–78
Levinas, Emmanuel, 78
Lévi-Strauss, Claude, 113n
liberal ideology, 183–86, 241
Lienesch, Michael, 228
Lindberg, Gary, 141n
Lipset, Seymour Martin, 3n
Locke, John, 22, 32, 153, 190,
    191
logocracy, 2, 8, 79–85
logos, 18–19
London Chronicle, 72, 73
Longfellow, Henry Wadsworth,
    18
Lynen, John, 119–20n

Macherey, Pierre, 206n
Madison, James, 164, 188, 209

Mansfield, William Murray, Baron, 72
Martin, Terence, 11
Martin, Wendy, 243n, 245
Marx, Karl, *Eighteenth Brumaire*, 25, 241
Massachusetts, 69, 270, 273
Mather, Cotton, *Magnalia Christi Americana*, 107–10
McCoy, Drew R., 240n
McKeon, Michael, 205–6
Mecom, Jane, 144
Melville, Herman, 211
Merleau-Ponty, Maurice, 27, 168
Michelet, Jules, 54–55
Middlekauff, Robert, 235
mimicry, 150–51
Modern Chivalry (Hugh Henry Brackenridge), 203–65; chronotopic schemes in, 240–49; ethnic dialects in, 219–23, 249–56; formal structure of, 206–16; hybrid rhetoric in, 224–40; phonology and politics in, 256–65; professional jargons in, 223; purpose as linguistic model, 216–24, 257
Moffatt, Thomas, 68
Monroe, James, 268
Montesquieu, Charles-Louis de Secondat, 78n
Monthly Magazine, 49
Moravians, 152
Moretti, Franco, 206
Morgan, Edmund S., 226
Morris, Richard, 274–75
Mueller, Janel, 218n
muteness, 6

Nance, William L., 242n
nation, 1–2, 250–51; imaginary status of, 1, 5–6; linguistic constitution of, 100
neology, 2, 45–53, 66

New England Courant, 114, 133
New York, 258
Nietzsche, Friedrich, 56, 160
Norton, Anne, 28

oaths, 38–39
oedipal conflict, Franklin's, 102, 114n, 115, 132n, 144
Oliver, Andrew, 68, 70, 71
oriental persona, Irving's use of, 78
originary utterance, 16, 21, 28, 150, 256, 278
Osborne, Charles, 119–21, 122, 135
Ossian, 230
Otis, Harrison Gray, 252–53
Otis, James, 172, 273

Paine, Thomas, 45, 47, 60–66; *The Age of Reason,* 258; *Common Sense,* 17, 65; "The Forester," 63–66; *The Rights of Man,* 17, 60, 61, 66
Parliament, 99, 188
Pattee, Fred Lewis, 173n
Patterson, Mark R., 11
Paulding, James Kirk, 78n
Peale, Charles Willson, 16–17n
Pendleton, Edmund, 155–56, 270–71
Pennsylvania, 9, 128, 172, 174, 189, 251–52
Pennsylvania Evening Post, 38–40
Pennsylvania Gazette, 37–38, 134
Pennsylvania Journal, 34–36
Pennsylvania Packet, 16, 27, 29, 63
performative, 3–4, 7, 44, 89, 149–50, 163, 216; Declaration of Independence as, 22–23, 25
Persons, Stow, 228n
Philadelphia, 9–10, 128, 141, 150, 152, 166, 179, 207, 252, 258
Pittsburgh, 207

Pocock, J. G. A., 41, 155, 225n, 226
Poe, Edgar Allan, 67–68
Polybius, 235, 274
polyglottism, 203–4, 277–78
Portelli, Alessandro, 11
Portfolio, 272
Price, Richard, 45
print, 3, 5, 173
promise, 121, 162–63
Propp, V., 166
Proud, Robert, 180
pseudonyms: "Anglus Americanus," 35; "Antoninus," 36; "Anxious By-Stander," 37; "Apologist," 38; "B.," 38; "C.," 49; "C. M. Scævola," 35; "Cassandra," 63; "Cato," 63–65; "Forester" (Thomas Paine), 63, 65; "Moderate Man," 35; "Mustapha Rub-Dub Keli Khan" (Washington Irving), 78–86, 88; "Philadelphian," 37; "Philadelphus," 37; "Reasonable Whiggess," 38; "Sidney," 35–36; "Silence Dogood" (Benjamin Franklin), 114; "Tradesman," 34–35
Public Advertiser, 71, 72
Puritans, 91, 109–10, 160, 227

Quixote, Don, 235

Rabelais, François, 243n
Ralph, James, 114n, 119, 122, 135
Randolph, Thomas Jefferson, 86
rationality, 3–5, 58–59, 249
Read, Allen Walker, 15n
Reign of Terror, 188
Renza, Louis, 123n
Republican party, 57, 81, 85–86, 160, 267
republicanism, 155, 171, 224–29, 241, 248–49, 255

retrodiction, 47, 92
Revolution of 1800, 56
rhetoric, and American Revolution, 25, 224–40
Ridgely, J. V., 148n
Rollins, Richard M., 15n
Roth, Martin, 93
Rousseau, Jean-Jacques, 163
Ruland, Richard, 217
Rush, Benjamin, 21, 24–25, 31, 50, 58, 59, 147, 213
Russo, James, 148n, 191

Sartre, Jean-Paul, 132n
Saussure, Ferdinand de, 41
saxon myth, Franklin's satirical use of, 74–76; Brown's use of in *Wieland,* 151–52, 154–58
Schroyer, Trent, 226n
Schwartz, Barry, 43
Seed, David, 110n
Seltzer, Mark, 148n, 149–50
semantic change, 2, 28–45, 100, 178
Serres, Michel, 71
Seven Years War, 126, 150, 157, 174
Shalhope, Robert, 224–25n
Shays Rebellion, 51
Shea, Daniel, 109
Shell, Marc, 277
Sidney, 22
silence, 85–88, 114, 265
Simpson, David, 11, 15n
Sollors, Werner, 250
Southern Quarterly Review, 18, 27n
sovereignty, 189; voice as source of, 20–21, 173–74
Spectator, 117, 120, 129
speech, 43–44, 147
spelling-pronunciation, 33
Spengemann, William, 244–45, 246
Spenser, Edmund, *Faerie Queen,* 104

stammering, 6, 135
Stamp Act, 68, 270–71
state, 20
Steele, Sir Richard, 117
Stein, Stephen J., 225n
Sterne, Lawrence, 243n
Stewart, Garrett, 220
Stout, Harry S., 172
Strout, Cushing, 225n
Supreme Court, 19, 188
Swift, Jonathan, 216, 243n

Temple, John, 69
Thucydides, 29–30, 31
titles of nobility, 60
Tocqueville, Alexis de, 45, 47, 54
Todorov, Tzvetan, 204n
Tompkins, Jane, 148n, 193
Tönnies, Ferdinand, 183
Treaty of Paris, 87, 180
Trumbull, John, 59
Tucker, St. George, 274
typography, 73–74, 112–13, 220

Unger, Roberto Mangabeira, 189;
  Knowledge and Politics, 185; Law
  in Modern Society, 183–84
United States Magazine, 261

Vaughan, Benjamin, 101, 129–
  30, 131, 134, 218
ventriloquism, 6, 150–51, 159,
  164, 165–74
Vergennes, Charles Gravier, comte
  de, 62
Virginia, 270–71, 273
voice, 3–5, 146, 164, 173–74,
  266–78; see also sovereignty
Volney, Constantin François de
  Chasseboeuf, comte de, 85
Voloshin, Beverly, 148n

Waldo, John, 47, 52
Warfel, Harry, 49n
Warner, Michael, 3–4n, 11, 44n

Warren, Mercy Otis, 175
Washington, George, 16n, 42–43,
  56, 86, 87, 88, 95, 175, 188,
  189, 209, 224, 229, 258
Watts, Steven, 49n
Weber, Donald, 225n
Weber, Max, 240
Webster, Daniel, 268, 276
Webster, Noah, 33, 216, 217
Wedderburn, Solicitor General,
  76
Weekly Magazine, 173, 181
Weinstein, Brian, 15n
Whatley, Thomas, 68, 69
Whatley, William, 69
Whigs, 269
White, James Boyd, 30
Whitefield, George, 172
Wieland, or The Transformation: An
  American Tale (Brown): Ameri-
  can Revolution and, 174–80;
  Ciceronian oratory in, 158–65;
  critical interpretations of, 147–
  48, 193; family genealogy in,
  149–54; law in, 148–49, 172,
  174, 180–92; legal epistemol-
  ogy in, 149, 185, 186–92; liber-
  alism and, 184–86, 189; political import of, 193–202; saxon
  myth in, 151–52, 154–58; ventriloquism in, 150–51, 165–74
Wilcocks, Alexander, 180, 188
Williams, Raymond, 242
Wills, Garry, 224n
Wilson, James, 18, 19–21, 25,
  27n, 155–56, 188, 191–92,
  266, 278
Wirt, William, 8, 22, 266–78; as
  attorney general, 268; as presidential candidate, 269; defends
  James Callender, 267; eulogizes
  Adams and Jefferson, 273; re-
  constructs Patrick Henry's "Liberty or Death" speech, 272,
  275; writes biography of Pat-

rick Henry, 266–78. Works: eulogy for Adams and Jefferson, 273; *The Letters of the British Spy,* 268; *The Old Bachelor,* 268; *The Rainbow,* 268; *Sketches of the Life and Character of Patrick Henry,* 266–67, 275n, 276–77
Wollstonecraft, Mary, 194

Wood, Gordon S., 45, 225n
Woodbridge, John, 108
words, 78–86
writing, 4, 21

Xenophon, *Memorabilia,* 138

Ziff, Larzer, 3n, 11, 44n, 225n